THE HANDBOOK

TO

ENGLISH HERALDRY.

Seal of Sir RICHARD DE BEAUCHAMP, K.G., Fifth Earl of WARWICK:
died A.D. 1439.   No. 448.—See pages 208, 321.

Seal of Sir THOMAS DE BEAUCHAMP, K.G., Third Earl of WARWICK:
died A.D. 1369.   Date of the Seal, 1344.
No. 446 —See No. 447, page 320; also see page 321.

"To describe . . . emblazoned Shields."—MILTON

THE HANDBOOK TO
ENGLISH
HERALDRY

BY

CHARLES BOUTELL, M.A. 1812 – 1877

AUTHOR OF "THE MONUMENTAL BRASSES OF ENGLAND,"
EDITOR AND PART AUTHOR OF "ARMS AND ARMOUR IN ANTIQUITY
AND THE MIDDLE AGES," ETC.

WITH

NEARLY FIVE HUNDRED ILLUSTRATIONS
Drawn and Engraved on Wood by Mr. R. B. UTTING and Others

ELEVENTH EDITION

THOROUGHLY REVISED WITH AN ADDITIONAL CHAPTER BY

A. C. FOX-DAVIES
OF LINCOLN'S INN BARRISTER-AT-LAW

ROYAL ARMS (1340-1405)

LONDON: REEVES & TURNER
1914

Printed by BALLANTYNE, HANSON & Co.
at the Ballantyne Press, Edinburgh

PREFACE

TO THE ELEVENTH EDITION

THIS standard work of reference has been revised throughout, and enlarged by the addition of an extra chapter on Peerage Dignities.

A. C. FOX-DAVIES.

LINCOLN'S INN, *November* 1913.

PREFACE

TO THE TENTH EDITION

IN the revision of this well-known work I have held my hand, rather than the contrary, trying to bear always in mind that it was the hand-book of Mr. Charles Boutell and not a production of my own. My alterations have been concerned chiefly in bringing the volume up to date, a necessity imposed by the creation of new orders of knighthood, and change of Sovereign. I have certainly omitted a few remarks which I have thought might be the cause of leading students of the science astray: I have altered ambiguous wording to emphasise the real, and I have no doubt the originally intended meaning. But in many points which, being deductions, are naturally matters of opinion, I have left herein various expressions of Mr. Boutell's opinion, with which I can hardly say I personally altogether agree or would myself put forward. I hold that it is no part of an editor's duty to air his own opinions under the protection or repute of another's name, and herein I have inserted nothing for which my own opinion is the only authority.

A. C. FOX-DAVIES.

LINCOLN'S INN, *June* 1908.

No. 2.	No. 1.	No. 3.
St. Edward.	St. George.	St Edmund.

AUTHOR'S PREFACE

THIS Volume, specially prepared for the use of students at an early period of their study of English Heraldry, commends itself also to those inquirers who may desire to obtain some general information on the same subject, without having any intention to devote to Heraldry much either of their time or of their serious regard.

The success, no less extraordinary than gratifying, of my larger work on Heraldry, led me to hope that a not less favourable reception might be extended to a simpler and much shorter essay, more decidedly elementary in its aim and character, and yet as far as possible within its limits complete. Such a treatise I have endeavoured to produce in this Volume.

Inseparably associated with the History of our Country, and more particularly when our national History becomes

ix

the Biography of eminent Englishmen, English Heraldry
has the strongest claims upon the attention not only of all
Historians, but also of all who desire to become familiar
with their writings. In like manner, Heraldry may be
studied with no less of advantage than of satisfaction by all
Artists, whether Architects, Sculptors, Painters, or En-
gravers. Nor is it too much to assert that some knowledge
of Heraldry, in consequence of its singular and comprehensive utility, ought to be estimated as a necessary
element of a liberal education. In confirmation of my own
views, I am tempted to quote the following passage from
M. GOURDON DE GENOUILLAC'S introduction to his excellent "Grammaire Héraldique," published at Paris:—
"Le blason," says M. de Genouillac, "est une langue qui
s'est conservée dans sa pureté primitive depuis les siècles,
langue dont la connaissance, est indispensable aux familles
nobles, qui y trouvent un signe d'alliance ou de reconnais-
sance, aux numismates, aux antiquaires, aux archéologues,
enfin à tous les artistes, gens de lettres, &c.; cependant
cette langue est presque inconnue, et la plupart des per-
sonnes qui possedent le droit de porter des armoiries
seraient fort en peine de les expliquer selon les termes
techniques!" Heraldry, indeed, I believe to be a study
worthy to be universally regarded with affectionate respect,
as it certainly is eminently qualified to inspire such a
sentiment in every class of student.

In this spirit I have here treated the elements of the
Heraldry of England, confident that, of those who may

accompany me as far as I shall lead them, very many will not be content to stop where I shall take leave of them. Thus much I promise my companions—I will be to them a faithful guide. They may trust to my accuracy. I have made no statement, have adduced no example, nor have I exhibited any illustration, except upon authority. I myself like and admire what is real and true in Heraldry ; and it is by the attractiveness of truth and reality that I desire to win for Heraldry fresh friends, and to secure for it firm friendships.

It will be understood that from the authority, the practice, and the associations of the early Heraldry of the best and most artistic eras, I seek to derive a Heraldry which we may rightly consider to be our own, and which we may transmit with honour to our successors. I do not suggest the adoption, for present use, of an obsolete system. But, while I earnestly repudiate the acceptance and the maintenance amongst ourselves of a most degenerate substitute for a noble Science, I do aspire to aid in restoring HERALDRY to its becoming rank, and consequently to its early popularity, now in our own times. This is to revive the fine old Heraldry of the past, to give to it a fresh animation, and to apply it under existing conditions to existing uses and requirements : not, to adjust ourselves to the circumstances of its first development, and to reproduce as copyists its original expressions. It is not by any means a necessary condition of a consistent revival of early Heraldry, that our revived Heraldry should admit no devia-

tion from original usage or precedent. So long as we are
thoroughly animated by the spirit of the early Heralds, we
may lead our Heraldry onwards with the advance of time.
It is for us, indeed, to prepare a Heraldry for the future, no
less than to revive true Heraldry in the time now present.
We may rightly modify, therefore, and adapt many things,
in order to establish a true conformity between our Heraldry
and the circumstances of our own era: for example, with
advantage as well as propriety we may, in a great measure,
substitute Badges for Crests; and we shall do well to
adopt a style of drawing which will be perfectly heraldic,
without being positively unnatural.

The greater number of my Illustrations have been engraved only in outline, with the twofold object of my being
thus enabled to increase the number of the examples, and
to adapt the engravings themselves to the reception of
colour. It will be very desirable for students to blazon
the illustrations, or the majority of them, in their proper
tinctures: and those who are thoroughly in earnest will not
fail to form their own collections of additional examples,
which, as a matter of course, they will seek to obtain from
original authorities. With the exception of a few examples,
my Illustrations, considerably over 400, have all been
executed expressly for this work; and they all have been
engraved by Mr. R. B. UTTING. The chief exceptions
are thirteen admirable woodcuts of Scottish Seals, all of
them good illustrations of Heraldry south of the Tweed,
originally engraved for Laing's noble quarto upon "The

Ancient Seals of Scotland," published in Edinburgh. Scottish Heraldry, I must add, as in any particulars of law and practice it may differ from our Heraldry on this side of the Tweed, I have left in the able hands of the Heralds of the North : at the same time, however, the Heraldry of which I have been treating has so much that is equally at home on either side of "the Border," that I have never hesitated to look for my examples and authorities to both the fair realms which now form one Great Britain.

C. B.

CONTENTS

CHAPTER V

CHAPTER VI

CHAPTER VII

CHAPTER VIII

CHAPTER IX

CHAPTER X

CHAPTER XI

CHAPTER XII

CHAPTER XIII

CHAPTER XIV

CHAPTER XV

CHAPTER XVI

CHAPTER XVII

CHAPTER XVIII

b

CHAPTER XIX

CHAPTER XX

CHAPTER XXI

CHAPTER XXII

CHAPTER XXIII

LIST OF ILLUSTRATIONS

NOTE.—*Several illustrations used herewith in connection with the new Orders created of recent date are inserted by arrangement with the Editor of Debrett's "Peerage."*

ENGLISH HERALDRY

CHAPTER I

INTRODUCTORY

Early Popularity of Heraldry in England—Origin of English Heraldry; Definition; Characteristics; Developments; Early Uses; not connected with Earlier Systems—Ancient Heraldry—Past and Present Treatment of the Subject.

"What! Is it possible? not know the figures of Heraldry! Of what could your father be thinking?"—ROB ROY.

No. 4

THE sentiment unquestionably was his own which Sir Walter Scott made delightful Di Vernon express when, with indignant surprise, she asked Frank Osbaldistone of what his father could have been thinking, that he had been permitted to grow up without any knowledge of Heraldry. Sir Walter was right in his estimate of the high value of Heraldry as an element of education: and, in professing herself a votaress of the Herald's "gentle science," it was quite right in Di Vernon to suggest to other ladies that it would be well for them if Heraldry should find favour in their eyes also. The age of Rob Roy, however, was far from being

A

in harmony with heraldic associations : nor was the author
of "Waverley" himself permitted to accomplish more,
than to lead the way to that revival of a popular sympathy
with every expression of early Art, which now forms one
of the most remarkable characteristics of our own era.

In the olden time, in England, the love of Heraldry,
which was prevalent amongst all classes, was based upon an
intelligent appreciation of its worthiness. A part of the
feudal system of the Middle Ages, and at once derived from
the prevailing form of thought and feeling, and imparting
to it a brilliant colouring peculiar to itself, Heraldry exercised a powerful influence upon the manners and habits of
the people amongst whom it was in use. By our early
ancestors, accordingly, as Mr. Montagu has so happily
written, "little given to study of any kind, a knowledge of
Heraldry was considered indispensable : " to them it was the
"outward sign of the spirit of chivalry, the index, also, to a
lengthened chronicle of doughty deeds." And this Heraldry
grew up, spontaneously and naturally, out of the circumstances and requirements of those times. It came into
existence, because it was needed for practical use ; it
was accepted and cherished, because it did much more than
fulfil its avowed purpose. At first, simply useful to distinguish particular individuals, especially in war and at the
tournament, English Heraldry soon became popular ; and
then, with no less rapidity, it rose to high honour and
dignity.

From the circumstance that it first found its special use
in direct connection with military equipments, knightly
exercises, and the *mêlée* of actual battle, mediæval Heraldry
has also been entitled ARMORY. Men wore the ensigns
of Heraldry about their persons, embroidered upon the
garments that partially covered their armour,—and so they
called them *Coats-of-Arms :* they bore these same ensigns
on their shields,—and they called them *Shields-of-Arms :* and

in their Armorial Banners and Pennons they again displayed the very same insignia, floating in the wind high above their heads, from the shafts of their lances.

The Heraldry or Armory of England, an honourable and honoured member of the illustrious family of mediæval European Heraldry, may be defined as a symbolical and pictorial language, in which figures, devices, and colours are employed instead of letters. Each heraldic composition has its own definite and complete significance, conveyed through its direct connection with some particular individual, family, dignity, or office. Every such heraldic composition, also, is a true legal possession, held and maintained by an express right and title: and it is hereditary, like other real property, in accordance with certain laws and precedents of inheritance. But in this respect heraldic insignia are singular and unlike other property, inasmuch as it is a general rule that they cannot be alienated, exchanged, or transferred otherwise than by inheritance or other lawful succession. Exceptions to this rule, when they are observed occasionally to have occurred, show clearly their own exceptional character, and consequently they confirm the true authority of the rule itself. It will be understood, as a necessary quality of its hereditary nature, that the significance of an heraldic composition, while " definite and complete " in itself, admits of augmentation and expansion through its association with successive generations. Thus, the Royal Shield of EDWARD III. is "complete" as the heraldic symbol of that great monarch, and of the realm under his rule: and yet this same shield, equally "complete" (with one simple modification) as the heraldic symbol of each successive Sovereign till the death of ELIZABETH, has its significance infinitely augmented and expanded through its hereditary association with all the Sovereigns of the Houses of Plantagenet and Tudor.

Until the concluding quarter of the twelfth century, the

traces of the existence of Heraldry are faint and few in
number.   Early in the thirteenth century the new science
began to establish itself firmly amongst our ancestors of
that age ; and it is certain that, as soon as its character and
capabilities were in any degree understood aright, it grew
speedily into favour; so that in the reign of HENRY III.
(A.D. 1216–1272) Heraldry in England had confirmed
its own claims to be regarded as a Science, by being
in possession of a system, and a classification of its
own.

The Crusades, those extraordinary confederacies without
a parallel in the history of civilised nations, were themselves
so thoroughly a matter of religious chivalry, that it was
only an inevitable result of their existence that they should
give a powerful impulse to the establishment and development of Heraldry in its early days.

But Heraldry, from the time of its first appearance in
England, was found to be valuable for other uses besides
those which so intimately connected it with both real and
imitative warfare, with the fierce life-and-death conflict of
the battle-field, and with the scarcely less perilous struggle
for honour and renown in the lists.   Very soon after the
Norman Conquest, in consequence of their presence being
required to give validity to every species of legal document,
SEALS became instruments of the greatest importance;
and it was soon obvious that heraldic insignia, with a representation of the knightly shield upon which they were
displayed, were exactly suited to satisfy every requirement
of the seal-engraver.   By such means Heraldry became
interwoven as well with the peaceful concerns of everyday
life, as with the display of martial splendour and the tur-
moil of war.

Many attempts have been made to set aside the opinion
that the Heraldry of the Middle Ages in England was a
fresh creation, a production of indigenous growth : and

great is the ingenuity that has been brought into action to carry back the Heraldry of our own country from the commencement of the thirteenth century through the previous elementary stages of its existence, in order to trace its direct lineal descent from certain decorative and symbolical devices that were in use at much earlier periods. The careful and diligent researches, however, of the most learned Heralds have at present led them almost unanimously to reject all such theories as these, as speculative and uncertain. At the same time, it is an indisputable fact that, in all ages of the world, and amongst all races of men, some form of symbolical expression has been both in use and in favour. And it is equally true that this symbolism, whatever it may have been, has generally been found in some way associated with a military life and with the act of warfare. Soldiers, and particularly those in high command, have always delighted to adorn their shields with devices that sometimes were significant of their own condition or exploits, or sometimes had reference to their country, or even to their families; and, in like manner, it has been a universal custom to display similar devices and figures in military standards of all kinds. At the time of the Conquest, as is shown in the famous Bayeux Tapestry of the Conqueror's Consort, the shields and standards of both Normans and Anglo-Saxons were painted, and perhaps the latter were embroidered, with various figures and devices; but certainly without any heraldic significance or any personal associations being indicated by these figures and devices, which bear a general resemblance to the insignia of the Legions and Cohorts of Imperial Rome. Figures Nos. 5 and 6 give representations of the standards that are introduced into the Bayeux Tapestry. The same species of decoration, consisting chiefly of painted patterns, with discs, stars, crescents, and some other figures, continued in use in our own country until superseded by a true Heraldry; and may also be assumed to have prevailed in England in much earlier times.

In still more remote ages a more decided heraldic system was displayed upon signets, coins, shields, and standards. In this ancient Heraldry, if so it may be termed, occasionally the important and characteristic quality of hereditary association in certain devices is apparent. Thus, Virgil (Æneid, vii. 657) assigns to

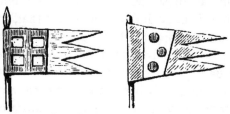

Nos. 5 and 6.   Lance Flags—Bayeux Tapestry.

Aventinus "*insigne paternum*" upon his shield—his hereditary device, derived by him from his father. But these devices generally appear to have their significance in a greater or a less degree restricted, amongst the ancients, to certain particular incidents; consequently in all these examples there is nothing to show that the man who bore one device at one time, did not bear another device at another time.[1] For example, Æschylus, the Greek tragedian (B.C. 600), has recorded that Capaneus, when attacking the

[1] In his "Hand-book of Engraved Gems," Mr. King maintains that "the devices on the signets of the ancients were both hereditary and unalterable, like our armorial bearings;" but, at the same time, he admits that the "armorial bearings," which appear "on the shields of the Grecian heroes in the most ancient pictures extant, the Vase-paintings," "seem to have been assumed at the caprice of the individual, like the knight's *cognisances* at tournaments in the days of chivalry, and not to have been hereditary."—"Hand-book," page 216. Almost immediately, however, Mr. King adds, that traditions exist which represent the mythic heroes bearing "engraved on their signets the same devices that decorated their shields." It would seem that the

city of Thebes, bore on his shield the figure of a warrior carrying a lighted torch, with the motto, "I will fire the city!" But, on another occasion, we have reason to believe that the same Capaneus bore quite a different device, applicable to that other occasion; and this deprives these ancient devices, heraldic as they are in their general character, of that special personal association which true Heraldry requires and, indeed, implies. The beautiful painted vases, the works of Greek artists, that are discovered in such extraordinary numbers and in perfect preservation in some parts of Italy, constantly give most striking representations of the shields of ancient Greek warriors and other personages, with what appear heraldic devices displayed upon them. These shields illustrate, in a remarkable manner, both the appropriate significance of particular devices, and the usage then prevalent for a variety of devices to be borne on different occasions by the same individual. Shields upon vases in the collections in the Museum of the Louvre at Paris, and in the British Museum, where they are easy of access, contain a great variety of devices. The examples, Nos. 7, 8, 9, and 10, are from our own National Collections. No. 7, the shield black, the border and the pegasus red; No. 8, the shield black, and the two dolphins white; No. 9, the shield black, with a border adorned with red discs, the serpent white; No. 10, the shield black, with

argument from such traditions would rather indicate the signet-devices to have been arbitrary, than the shield-devices to have been unalterable. While I readily admit the very interesting devices of antiquity to possess decided heraldic attributes, I cannot consider Mr. King to have shown that, as a general rule, they were held by the ancients themselves to have been either "unalterable" or "hereditary." Possibly, further light may be thrown upon the hereditary quality of ancient Heraldry : but, I certainly do not expect to see any evidence adduced, which would establish a line of descent connecting the Mediæval Heraldry of England with any heraldic system of classic antiquity.

purple border, the three human legs conjoined white.   The
shields, Nos. 9 and 10, are both borne by the goddess
AΘHNH (Minerva); and the remarkable device displayed
on No. 10 is also found on the coins of ancient Sicily.
Other similar shields display lions, horses, dogs, wild boars,
fish, birds, clusters of leaves, chariots and chariot-wheels,

No. 7.   No. 8.

No. 9.   No. 10.

Ancient Shields from Greek Vases.

votive tripods, serpents, scorpions, with many others, including occasional examples of human figures.   In another
collection I have seen an anchor and an Amazon's bow.
A device differing from that in No. 10 only in having the
conjoined limbs in armour, will be found in our own English
Heraldry to be the armorial ensign of the Isle of Man.

This Heraldry of Antiquity is to be regarded as the pre-
decessor, and not as the ancestor of the Heraldry of England.   There may be much that is common to both; but,
there is nothing to show the later system to have been a

lineal descendant from the earlier. It would seem much more likely that Heraldry, when it had been evolved, adopted ready made the emblems of an older civilisation for its own purpose, often appropriating at the same time the symbolism attaching to the emblems. The Heraldry, therefore, that has flourished, declined, and now is in the act of reviving in our own country in almost the full vigour of its best days, I shall treat as an independent science, proceeding from a single source, and from thence flowing onwards with varied fortunes, side by side with the chequered chronicles of England. In the course of its progress from the palmy days of EDWARD III., it has had to encounter, in a degree without precedent or parallel, that most painful and mischievous of trials—the excessive admiration of injudicious friends. Hence, Heraldry was brought into disrepute, and even into contempt, by the very persons who loved it with a genuine but a most unwise love. In process of time, no nonsense appeared too extravagant, and no fable too wild, to be engrafted upon the grave dignity of the Herald's early science. Better times at length have succeeded. Heraldry now has friends and admirers, zealous as of old, whose zeal is guided aright by a sound judgment in alliance with a pure taste. Very much already has been accomplished to sweep away the amazing mass of absurdities and errors which had overwhelmed our English Heraldry, by such men as Nicholas, Nichols, Courthope, Seton, Planché, Walford, Montagu, and Lower: and the good work goes on and prospers, with the most cheering assurances of complete and triumphant success.

CHAPTER II

EARLY HERALDIC AUTHORITIES

Seals: Monumental Effigies, &c.: Rolls of Arms, Official Heraldic Records, &c.—Earliest Heraldic Shields and Banners—Allusive Quality of Early Armory—Attributed Arms.

"Let us begin at the beginning."—PURSUIVANT OF ARMS.

AT the head of the earliest existing authorities in English Heraldry are SEALS. To the fortunate circumstance of the legal importance attached to them we are indebted for the preservation of these equally interesting and valuable relics, in great variety and in very considerable numbers. The heraldic evidence of Seals is necessarily of the highest order. They are original works, possessing contemporaneous authority. Produced with peculiar care and approved by their first possessors, their original authenticity is confirmed by their continued use through successive generations.

Having been in use before the introduction and adoption of Heraldry in England, Seals enable us to compare the devices that preceded true Heraldry with the earliest that are truly heraldic: and thus they show that, in many instances, regular coats-of-arms were derived in their hereditary bearings from similar devices that had been adopted in the same families before the heraldic era. For example: the Seal of John Mundegumri, about A.D. 1175, bears a *single fleur-de-lys*, not placed upon a shield; and, accordingly, here is seen the origin of the *three golden fleurs-de-lys*, borne afterwards upon a blue shield by the descend-

ants of this John, the Montgomeries, Earls of Eglintoun.
Again: the Seal of Walter Innes, A.D. 1431, displays the
shield of arms of his house—*three blue mullets* (stars generally of five rays) on a field of silver, No. 11; and these
mullets may be traced to the *single star*, that appears on

No. 11.—Seal of Walter Innes.   No. 12.—Seal of Wm. Innes.

the Seal of William Innes, or De Ynays, No. 12, appended
to his deed of homage to Edward I., in the year 1295.
I have selected these examples from the "Catalogue of
Scottish Seals," published by Mr. Laing, of Edinburgh,
that I may be enabled here to refer in the highest terms of
admiring commendation to that most excellent work. It
is greatly to be desired that a corresponding publication
should treat, with equal ability, of the Seals of England
which, from the dawn of Heraldry, continue their admirable
examples and illustrations throughout its career.

Monumental Effigies, Sepulchral Memorials, early Buildings, and early Stained Glass, frequently are rich in autho-
ritative examples of "the figures of Heraldry." In addition
to the various forms and combinations of heraldic composition, these works illustrate the early style of drawing
in favour with Heralds during the great eras of mediæval
Art, and they have preserved to us most useful and suggestive representations of various devices in their proper
heraldic aspect. In many instances the Heraldry of early
Monuments and Architecture possesses a peculiar value,
arising from the circumstance of the shields of arms and
other insignia having been sculptured in low relief or
outlined in incised lines, and consequently these devices

and compositions retain their original forms : and, in like manner, the original colouring of the Heraldry of Stained Glass remains safe from restoration or destruction, in consequence of the impossibility of re-painting it.

The early written Literature of English Heraldry is calculated to throw but little light upon either its true character or its history. In addition, however, to the various and numerous official documents of the Heralds' College, several examples of one particular class of heraldic record have been preserved, the value of which cannot be too highly estimated. These are ROLLS OF ARMS—long, narrow strips of parchment, on which are written lists of the names and titles of certain personages, with full descriptions of their armorial insignia. The circumstances under which these Rolls were prepared are obviously not identical and for the most part unknown : but, the exact accuracy of their statements has been established beyond all question by careful and repeated comparison with Seals and other Monuments, and also with Documents which give only an indirect and yet not the less conclusive corroboration to the records of the Rolls of Arms themselves. The earliest of these Rolls at present known date about A.D. 1240 to 1245 ; and since in these earliest Rolls a very decided technical language is uniformly adopted, and the descriptions are all given in palpable accordance with fixed rules which must then have been well understood, we infer that by the end of the first half of the thirteenth century there was in existence a system for the regulation of such matters. Heraldry was perhaps recognised as a Science, with fixed terms and rules for describing heraldic devices and figures, and established laws to direct the granting, the assuming, and the bearing of arms.

The most interesting of these early heraldic Rolls records, in a metrical form, and in Norman-French, the siege and capture of the fortress of Carlaverock, on the Scottish border, by EDWARD I., in the year 1300. In addition to very curious descriptions of the muster of the Royal troops at Carlisle, their march northwards, and the incidents of the siege (which last have a strange resemblance to what Homer has recorded of incidents that took place during the siege of Troy), this Roll gives some graphic personal sketches of the princes, nobles, bannerets, and knights, whose banners and shields of arms are set forth in it with minute exactness. This Roll, as well as several others, has been published, with translations and very valuable notes.

In the Manuscript Collections of the British Museum also, and of other Libraries both public and private, and in the County Histories, and other works of a cognate character, there are many documents which contain various important records and illustrations of early English Heraldry.

In any references to authorities, that it may appear desirable for me to make in the course of this and the following chapters, I must be as concise as possible. A direct reference to Seals, Effigies, &c., will be necessary in each case : 'but, in referring to Rolls of Arms, it will be sufficient to denote the period of the authority in general terms. Accordingly, I shall refer, not to each particular Roll, but collectively to those of each of the following reigns— HENRY III., EDWARD I., EDWARD II., EDWARD III., and RICHARD II. ; and these references will severally be made thus,—(H. 3), (E. 1), (E. 2), (E. 3), and (R. 2).

Amongst the earliest Shields and Banners of Arms, all of them remarkable for their simplicity, many are found to be without any device whatever, their distinction consisting simply in some peculiarity in the colouring. Such examples may be considered to have been derived from pre-heraldic times, and transmitted, without any change or addition, to later periods. The renowned Banner of the Knights Templars, by them called *Beauseant*, No. 13, is black above and white below, which is said to have denoted that, while fierce to their foes, they were gracious to their friends. An ancient Banner of the Earl of Leicester (H. 3) is white and red, the divi-

sion being made by a vertical indented line; No. 14. This design, however, was not the coat of arms of the earl. The Shield of the ducal House of Brittany, closely connected with the Royal Family of England, is simply of the fur ermine; No. 15. The Shield of Waldegrave is silver and red, as in No. 16: and that of Fitz Warine (H. 3), also of silver and red, is treated as in No. 17.

No 13.—Banner of Templars.

No. 14. Banner of Leicester.

No. 15.—Brittany. No. 16.—Waldegrave. No. 17.—Fitz Warine.

Some of the earliest of the simple devices of true Heraldry were evidently adopted from the *structural formation* (or from

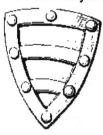

a *structural strengthening*) of the Shields, on which they were displayed. Thus, a raised border, and bands of metal variously disposed in order to impart additional strength to a shield, with distinct colouring, would produce a series of heraldic compositions. A good example occurs in the shield of an early Effigy at Whitworth, Durham, No. 18, in which

No 18.— Shield at Whitworth.

the heads of the rivets or screws employed to fix the border on the shield, appear to have been made to assume

the character of heraldic additions to the simple border
and horizontal bands.   Other primary devices of the same
simple order, which in like manner may have had a structural origin, I shall consider in detail in subsequent
chapters. (See particularly Chapter VI.)

The central boss, at once an appropriate ornament of an
early shield, and an important addition to its defensive
qualities, when extended in the form of decorative metal-
work, would readily suggest a variety of heraldic figures,
and amongst others several beautiful modifications of a
simple cruciform device which it
might be made to assume.   The
figure called an escarbuncle, No.
19, is simply a shield-boss developed into decorative structural
metal-work.   This figure appears
in the Temple Church, London,
upon the shield of an Effigy,
which Mr. J. Gough Nichols has
shown to have been incorrectly
attributed to Geoffrey de Mande-
ville, Earl of Essex.

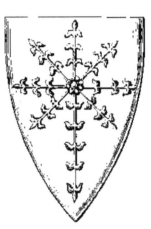

No. 19.—The Escarbuncle.

The greater number of the
earliest devices that appear in
English Heraldry were adopted for the express purpose of
their having some *allusive association*, through a similarity
of sound in their own names or descriptions with the names
and titles or the territories of certain persons, dignities, and
places.   In exact accordance with the principles and aim of
primitive mediæval Heraldry, and in perfect harmony with
the sentiments and requirements of the age in which it grew
up into a science, devices of this kind addressed themselves in very plain and expressive language to the men of
their own era.   In them they saw the kind of symbolical
writing that they could remember, as well as understand.

They also evidently liked the quaint style of suggestiveness that was a characteristic of these allusive devices : and, it is more than probable that there frequently lurked in them a humorous significance, which by no means tended to detract from their popularity.   Devices of this same order have never ceased to be in favour with Heralds and lovers of Heraldry.   They were used in the sixteenth century at least as commonly as in the thirteenth ; but, as would be expected, in the later period they often became complicated, far-fetched, and extravagant.

This allusive quality, distinguished in English Heraldry as "*canting*," has commonly been misunderstood, and therefore incorrectly estimated, by modern writers, who have supposed it to be a fantastic conceit of the Heralds of a degenerate age.   By writers such as these, accordingly, all "*canting arms*" (by French Heralds called "*armes parlantes*") have been absurdly assigned to a separate class, in their estimation having an inferior heraldic grade.

The prevalence of the allusive quality in early arms may be assumed to have been even more general than is now apparent, since so many of the original echoes and allusions have become obscured or altogether lost in the lapse of time, and through the changes that have taken place since the accession of HENRY III. in the French language and in our own also.   The use of the Latin language, again, in the Middle Ages led, at later periods, to translations of names ; French names, too, were translated in the same manner into English equivalents : and, at other times, the sound of a Latin or a French (Anglo-Norman) name was transferred to an English representative having a somewhat similar sound, without the slightest reference to the original signification.   Who, for example, in the name of MONTAGU now recognises instinctively the original allusion to a *mountain* with its *sharply* peaked crests, and so discerns the probable allusive origin of the *sharp* triple points of the devices on the old Montacute shield, No. 20? It is easy to see how much must have been unconsciously done, by such changes in names and their associations, to obliterate what once was clear, significant, and expressive. I must be content here to give, simply by way of explanatory illustration, a very few examples of allusive arms; and, in so doing, it may be well for me to observe that the early Heralds of our country always employed the French

No. 20.
Shield of Montacute.

language as it was spoken in their own times in England as well as in France. In the time of HENRY III., G. de Lucy has for his arms *three lucies*—fish now known as pike: Robert Quency has a *quintefueil*—a flower of five leaves: Thos. Corbett has *two corbeaux*—ravens: A. de Swyne-burne has "*trois testes de senglier*"—three heads of the wild boar, or *swine:* (E. 2), Sir R. de Eschales has *six escallops*—shells: Sir G. de Trompintoun, of Trumpington, near Cambridge, has *two trompes*—trumpets: Sir J. Bordoun has *three bourdons*—pilgrim's staves: Sir G. Rossel has *three roses:* and Sir O. Heron has the same number of *herons.* So also, for the Spanish provinces Castile and Leon, a *castle* and a *lion:* for Falconer, a *falcon:* Butler, *cups:* Forester, *bugle-horns:* Arundel, *hirondelles*—swallows: Wingfield, *wings:* Shelley, *shells:* Pigot, *pick-axes:* Leveson, *leaves:* and Martel, *martels*— hammers. The *Broom-plant* with its seed-

No. 21.—Planta Genista.

pods, in Latin *Planta genista*, No. 21, gave its name to the PLANTAGENET Dynasty. I shall hereafter add several other curious examples of devices of this class, when treating of *Badges, Rebuses,* and *Mottoes.*

There is one class of early arms, which it is important

B

that students of Armory should observe with especial care, lest they be led by them into unexpected errors. These are arms that were invented *after* Heraldry had been established, and then were assigned to personages of historical eminence who had lived and died *before* the true heraldic era. In the days in which every person of prominence bore heraldic arms, and when Heraldry had attained to high renown, it was natural enough to consider that suitable armorial devices and compositions should be assigned to the men of mark in earlier ages, both to distinguish them in accordance with the usage then prevalent, and to treat their memory with becoming honour. Such arms were also in a sense necessary to their descendants for the purposes of quartering. No proof can be shown that the arms said to have been borne by WILLIAM THE CONQUEROR are not of this order—made for him, that is, and attributed to him in after times, but of which he himself had no knowledge.

No. 22.—WILLIAM I.

No. 23.—Saxon Princes.

These arms, No. 22, differ from the true Royal Insignia of England only in there being *two*, instead of *three*, lions displayed upon the shield. The arms of EDWARD THE CONFESSOR, No. 2, were certainly devised long after his death, and they appear to have been suggested to the heralds of HENRY III. by one of the Confessor's coins: the shield is blue, and the cross and five birds (martlets) are gold. In like manner, the arms attributed to the earlier Saxon Sovereigns of England, No. 23, a gold cross upon blue, are really not earlier than the thirteenth century. The arms, No. 2, having been assigned to ST. EDWARD, a patron saint of mediæval England, were long regarded with peculiar reverence. I have placed them, drawn from a fine shield of the thirteenth century in Westminister Abbey, to ake a part in forming a group at the head of my Preface, vith the shields of the two other saintly Patrons of "old England," ST. GEORGE and ST. EDMUND, No. 1 and No. 3 —a red cross on a silver shield, and three golden crowns upon a shield of blue.

CHAPTER III

The English Heraldry that is now in existence—First Debasement of Heraldry—Later Debasement—Revival of English Heraldry—Heraldic Art.

"Sans changer."—MOTTO OF STANLEY.

ENGLISH Heraldry, as it exists amongst us in our own times, is the very same Heraldry that flourished under the kindly influences of the greatest of the Plantagenets, though perhaps modified in some details by changed circumstances. It is not of a new, but of the old, Heraldry of England that I am setting forth the elements. Our Heraldry has had to pass from good days to bad ones : and, having gone through the worst of bad days, the circle at length has revolved, so that we are witnessing the happy change of a vigorous heraldic revival. Heraldry already enjoys a very great popularity ; and, without a doubt, it will become still more popular, in the degree that it is better and more generally understood. For its complete ultimate success, the present revival of true English Heraldry must mainly depend upon the manner in which we apply the lessons that may be learned by us, no less from the warnings of the recent evil days of the science, than from the example of the brilliant ones that preceded them long ago. Nor should we deal faithfully with our revived Heraldry, were we not to form a just estimate of whatever was imperfect in the best era of its early history, in order to apply to present improvement the lessons that thus also may be learned. It must be admitted that the Heralds and Heraldic writers of the 17th century, following the footsteps of some of their immediate predecessors, led the

20

way towards the thorough debasement of their own science. Their example was not without effect upon those who followed them—men quite equal to the perpetration of whatever had not been already done to bring Heraldry into contempt. This was accomplished first, by gravely discoursing, in early heraldic language, upon the imaginary Heraldry of the patriarchal and antediluvian worthies: making a true coat of arms of Joseph's "coat of many colours," giving armorial ensigns to David and Gideon, to Samson and Joshua, to "that worthy gentilman Japheth," to Jubal and Tubal-Cain, and crowning the whole by declaring that our common progenitor, Adam, bore on his own red shield Eve's shield of silver, after the mediæval fashion that would denote his wife to have been an heiress !

Then there set in a flood of allegorical and fantastic absurdities, by which the fair domain of Heraldry was absolutely overwhelmed. Wild and strange speculations, in a truly vain philosophy, interwoven with distorted images of both the myths and the veritable records of classic antiquity, were either deduced from armorial blazonry, or set forth as the sources from whence it was developed. Fables and anecdotes, having reference to less remote eras, were produced in great variety and in copious abundance. The presence in blazon of animated beings of whatsoever kinds, whether real or fabulous, led to rambling disquisitions in the most ludicrously *un*natural of imaginary Natural History. From every variety also of inanimate figure and device, the simplest no less than the more elaborate, after the same fashion some " moral " was sought to be extracted. The technical language, too, of the early Heralds, had its expressive simplicity travestied by a complicated jargon, replete with marvellous assertions, absurd doctrines, covert allusions devoid of consistent significance, quaint and yet trivial conceits, and bombastic rhapsodies. Even the nomenclature of the Tinctures was not exempt from a characteristic

course of " treatment," two distinctive additional sets of titles
for gold, silver, blue, red, &c., having been devised and
substituted for those in general use (see Chapter V.); of these
the one set was derived from the names of the *Planets*, and
employed to emblazon the insignia of Sovereign Princes;
and the other set, derived from the names of *Jewels*, was
applied to the arms of Nobles. In the midst of all the
rubbish, however, which they thus delighted to accumulate,
there may generally be discovered in the works of writers of
this class, here and there, references to earlier usages and
illustrations of original principles which, in the extreme
dearth of genuine early heraldic literature, are both interesting and of real value. Nor are these writings without
their value, estimated from another point of view, as contemporaneous and unconscious commentaries upon the history
of their own times. It must be added that, in more than a
few instances, beneath the surface there lurks a vein of both
political and personal allusion, of which the point and
bearing now are altogether lost, or at the most are only
open to conjecture and surmise. And, again, even in their
most extravagant and frivolous lucubrations, the heraldic
writers of the sixteenth and seventeenth centuries are not
without touches of humour; as when Gerard Legh (A.D.
1562), discoursing of " beastes," remarks of the " Ramme "
that in " aucthoritye he is a Duke, for hee hath the leadyng
of multitudes and flockes of his own kynde ;" and of the ass,
" I could write much of this beaste, but that it might be
thought it were to mine own glorie."

The adoption of additional quarterings for the purpose of display, and the introduction of more complicated
compositions in the time of HENRY VIII., were speedily
followed by the substitution of pictorial representations,
often of a most frivolous and inconsistent character, and
many of them altogether unintelligible without written
explanations, instead of the simple, dignified, and expres-

sive insignia of true Heraldry. For example, in the year 1760, a grant of arms was made to a Lincolnshire family named Tetlow, which, with thirteen other figures, includes the representation of a book duly clasped and orna- mented, having on it a silver penny; while above the book rests a dove, holding in its beak a crow-quill! This was to commemorate one of the family having, with a crow-quill, actually achieved the exploit of writ- ing the Lord's Prayer within the compass of a silver penny. Amongst the most objectionable of the arms of this class are those which were granted to distinguished naval and military officers — arms, that certainly ought to have conferred fresh honour on illustrious names, in- stead of inflicting dishonour upon Heraldry itself. Battles by sea and land, landscapes and sea views and fortified cities, flags of all kinds, with medals and ribbons, all of them intermixed with devices not quite so unheraldic, abound in these extravagant compositions. The arms of Lord Nelson, and still more recently those of General Lord Gough, may be specified as flagrant examples of this degenerate pictorial Heraldry. The Duke of Wellington happily escaped a similar infliction. It would be but too easy to enumerate other equally inconsistent and unheraldic compositions: but, I must be content to refer only to the armorial shield granted to the great astronomer, Sir John Herschel, on which is displayed his forty-foot reflecting telescope, with all its apparatus! These, and all such violations of heraldic truth and consistency, though in some instances they are of very recent date, are now to be assigned to a closed chapter in the history of English Heraldry. But in considering them it must not be for- gotten that this kind of grant was not confined to this country, but flourished to a still greater extent abroad.

In our present revival of English Heraldry, it is essential that we impress upon our minds a correct con-

ception of the twofold character of all Heraldry—that
it is a *Science*, and also that it is an *Art*. We have to
vindicate the reputation of our Heraldry, as well in the
one capacity as in the other. Of very noble heraldic Art
we happily possess original examples in great numbers,
which have been bequeathed to us, as a precious inheritance, from "the brave days of old." The style of Art
that we see exemplified in these early authorities we may
accept almost unreservedly as our own style; and we must
aspire to sympathise heartily with their genuine heraldic
feeling. In our representation, also, of almost all inanimate and natural objects in our own armorial compositions,
as a general rule, we may trust confidently to the same
good guidance. The early method of representation, indeed, must form the basis of our system of treatment;
and, we may faithfully adhere to this rule, and yet occasionally we may find it to be desirable that the form and
the accessories of some devices should be adapted to
modern associations. In truth, it is not by merely copying the works of even the greatest of the early heraldic
artists, that we are to become masters in heraldic Art.
When the copies are good, copying is always valuable,
as a branch of study; but, if it be our highest and only
aim to reproduce the expressions of other men's thoughts,
then copying is worse than worthless. What we have to
do is to express our heraldic Art in the spirit of the early
Heralds, to keep it in harmony with what, in the best of
the early days, they would have accepted as the highest
heraldic Art, and at the same time to show that our heraldic
Art in very truth is our own.

The treatment of animate creatures in Heraldry requires
a certain kind, and also a certain degree, of conventionalism.
Here, as before, in the early Heralds we have excellent
masters; but, here we must follow their teaching with more
of reserve, and with cautious steps. We recognise the happy

consistency of the conventionalism which they displayed in their representation of animate creatures, without any purpose to adopt it in the same degree with them. Had the early Heralds been more familiar with the living presence of the various creatures that they summoned to enter into their service, without a doubt they would have represented them with a much closer conformity to Nature. We must apply our better knowledge, as we may feel confident the early Heralds would have applied a similar knowledge had they been able to have acquired it. Heraldic animals of every kind—lions, eagles, dolphins, and all others—must be so far subjected to a conventional treatment, that they will not exhibit a *strictly* natural appearance : and, on the other hand, being carefully preserved from all exaggerated conventionalisms, they must approach as near to Nature as a definite conventional rendering of natural truth will admit. The lions of the early Heralds, spirited beasts always, generally show a decided disposition to exhibit their heraldic sympathies in excess. They have in them rather too much that is heraldic conventionalism, and not quite enough that is natural lion. And, with the first symptoms of decline in heraldic Art, the treatment of lions showed signs of a tendency to carry conventionalism to the utmost extravagance. The same remarks are applicable to eagles. It must be added, however, that truly admirable examples of heraldic animals occasionally may be found as late even as the commencement of the sixteenth century, as in the chantry of Abbot Ramryge, in the Abbey Church at St. Alban's, and in King's College Chapel at Cambridge. It must be our care to blend together the true attributes of the living lion and eagle, and those also of other living creatures, with the traditional peculiarities of their heraldic representatives. And we must extend the corresponding application of the same principles of treatment to imaginary beings and heraldic monsters, as they occur in our Heraldry.

The shield, No. 24, of Prince JOHN OF ELTHAM, younger brother of EDWARD III., finely sculptured with his effigy in alabaster, in Westminster Abbey (A.D. 1336), and in perfect preservation, gives us characteristic examples of lions of the best heraldic era, their frames, attenuated as they are, being perfect types of fierce elasticity. With this shield may be

No. 24.—Prince JOHN OF ELTHAM, A.D. 1336.

grouped others, having admirably suggestive examples of heraldic lions of a somewhat later date, which are preserved upon the monuments of EDWARD III. and the BLACK PRINCE, severally at Westminster and Canterbury. I shall refer to these fine shields again, and to other admirable examples with them, hereafter (Chapter IX.). The conventionalism in all these examples, however felicitous the manner in which it is treated in them, is very decidedly exaggerated. These examples, and others such as these, are not the less valuable to us because their teaching includes an illustration of the excesses that we must always be careful to avoid. I may here observe, that on the subject of armorial Art I leave my examples (all of them selected from the most characteristic authorities, and engraved with scrupulous fidelity) for the most part to convey their own lessons and suggestions: my own suggestion to students being that, in such living creatures as they may represent in their compositions, while they are careful to preserve heraldic consistency and to express heraldic feeling, they exhibit beauty of form coupled with freedom of action

No. 25. No. 26.

Badge of RICHARD II., Westminster Hall.

and an appropriate expression. "Freedom of action" I intend to imply more than such skilful drawing, as will impart to any particular creature the idea of free movement of frame and limb: it refers also to repeated representations of the same creature, under the same heraldic conditions of motive and attitude. And, here "freedom of action" implies those slight, yet significant, modifications of minor details which, without in the least degree affecting armorial truth, prevent even the semblance of monotonous reiteration. Thus, at Beverley, in the Percy Shrine in the Minster, upon a shield of England the three lions are all heraldically the same; but, there is nothing of sameness in them nevertheless, because in each one there is some little variety in the turn of the head, or in the placing of the paws, or in the sweep of the tail. And again, in Westminster Hall, the favourite badge of Richard II., a white hart, chained, and in an attitude of rest, is repeated as many as eighty-three times; and all are equally consistent with heraldic truth and accuracy, without any one of them being an exact counterpart of any other. In Nos. 25 and 26 two examples are shown from this remarkable series of representations of this beautiful badge, each one different from the other, and yet both really the same.

CHAPTER IV

THE GRAMMAR OF HERALDRY

Section I

The Language of Heraldry—The Nomenclature—Style and Forms of Expression—Blazon—The Shield: its Parts, Points, Divisions, Dividing Lines, Varieties of Form, and Heraldic Treatment.

" The shield hangs down on every breast."—LORD OF THE ISLES.

THE LANGUAGE OF HERALDRY.—The original language of English Heraldry was the Norman-French, which may also be designated Anglo-Norman, habitually spoken at the Court of England in the early heraldic era. After a while, a mixed language succeeded, compounded of English and the original Norman-French ; and this mixed language still continues in use.

NOMENCLATURE.—Like its language, the Nomenclature of English Heraldry is of a mixed character, in part technical and peculiar to itself, and in part the same that is in common use. Thus, many of the figures and devices of Heraldry have their peculiar heraldic names and titles, while still more bear their ordinary designations. Descriptive terms, whether expressed in English or in French (Anglo-Norman), are generally employed with a special heraldic intention and significance. In the earliest Roll of Arms known to be now in existence, which was compiled (as appears from internal evidence) between the years 1240 and 1245, the Nomenclature is the same that is found

in Rolls and other heraldic documents of a later date.
This fact of the existence of a definite Nomenclature
at that time, proves that before the middle of the thirteenth century the Heraldry of England was subject to
a systematic course of treatment, and had become established and recognised as a distinct and independent
Science.

STYLE AND FORMS OF EXPRESSION.—With the Nomenclature, a settled Style and certain fixed technical Forms
of Expression were introduced and accepted in the thirteenth century ; and, since that period, the Style and Forms
of Expression have undergone only such comparatively
slight modifications as tended to render them both more
complete and more consistent. As it was at the first, it
still is the essence of heraldic language to be concise yet
complete, expressive, and also abounding in suggestions
Not a syllable is expressed that is not absolutely necessary ;
not a syllable omitted, the absence of which might possibly
lead to any doubt or uncertainty. In the more matured
style, the repetition of any important word in the same
sentence is scrupulously avoided ; and, where it would be
required, another form of expression is substituted in its
stead. Much meaning also is left to be implied and understood, through inference, either based upon certain accepted
rules and established heraldic usages for the arrangement of
the words and clauses of a sentence, or derived from the
natural qualities and characteristic conditions of certain
figures and devices : but, nothing is ever left to be inferred
when an uncertain inference might possibly be adopted, or
that can be understood clearly and with certainty only by
means of an explicit statement. Superfluous words and
particles of all kinds are altogether omitted. Descriptive
epithets follow the nouns to which they refer : as, a *red cross*
is styled a *cross gules*. The general rules, by which the
arrangement of the words in heraldic descriptive sentences

is determined, will be found in the last subdivision of this chapter. Examples of heraldic Language, Nomenclature, Style and Forms of Expression, will be given in abundance throughout the following chapters and sections of this treatise. With these examples students will do well to familiarise themselves: then, let them prepare additional examples for that "practice," which (as Parker's "Glossary of Heraldry" says, p. 60) "alone will make perfect," by writing down correct descriptions of heraldic compositions from the compositions themselves; after which process they may advantageously reverse the order of their study, and make drawings of these same (or, if they prefer it, of some other) heraldic compositions from their own written descriptions of them.

When any heraldic description of a figure, device, or composition has been completed, a statement is made to signify the person, family, community, or realm whose armorial ensign it may be. This is done by simply writing the appropriate name, after the last word of the description; or, by prefixing the word "for" before the name when it is placed in the same position. Thus, a description of the three lions of England is to be followed by the word— "ENGLAND"; or, by the formula—"for ENGLAND." If preferred, with equal consistency the arrangement may be reversed, and the Name, with or without the prefix "for," may precede the description: thus—"ENGLAND," or "For ENGLAND," three lions, &c. It is to be borne in remembrance, that armorial ensigns are personal inheritances, and—with the exception of Sovereign Princes —by comparison but very rarely relate to *Titles* and *Dignities*.

BLAZON, BLAZONING, BLAZONRY.—When a knight entered the lists at a tournament, his presence was announced by sound of trumpet or horn, after which the officers of arms, the official Heralds, declared his armorial insignia—they "blazoned" his Arms. This term, "to blazon," derived from the German word "*blasen*," signifying "to blow a blast on a horn" (or, as one eminent German Herald prefers, from the old German word "*blaze*" or "*blasse*," "a mark" or "sign"), in Heraldry really denotes either to *describe* any armorial figure, device, or composition in correct heraldic language; or to *represent* such figure, device, or composition accurately in form, position, arrangement, and colouring. But, as a matter of practical usage, pictorial representation is usually allied to the word "emblazon." The word "blazon" also, as a noun, may be employed with a general and comprehensive signification to denote "Heraldry."

THE SHIELD :—ITS PARTS, POINTS, AND DIVISIONS.—Their Shield, which the knights of the Middle Ages derived from the military usage of antiquity, and which contributed in so important a degree to their own defensive equipment, was considered by those armour-clad warriors to be peculiarly qualified to display their heraldic blazonry. . And, in later times, when armour had ceased to be worn, and when shields no longer were actually used, a Shield continued to be regarded as the most appropriate vehicle for the same display. The Shield, then, which with its armorial devices constitutes a *Shield of Arms*, always is considered to display its blazonry upon its face or external surface. This blazoned surface of his shield the bearer, when holding it before his person, presents (or would present, were he so to hold it) towards those who confront him. The right and the left sides of the person of the bearer of a Shield, consequently, are *covered* by the right and left (in heraldic language, the *dexter* and *sinister*) sides of his shield: and so, from this it follows that the dexter and sinister sides of a Shield of Arms are severally *opposite* to the left and the right hands of all observers. The Parts and Points of an heraldic Shield, which is also entitled an "*Escutcheon*," are thus distinguished :—

No. 27. A, *The chief*: B, *The Base*:
C, *The Dexter Side*: D, *The Sinister Side*:
E, *The Dexter Chief*: F, *The Sinister Chief*:
G, *The Middle Chief*: H, *The Dexter Base*:
I, *The Sinister Base*: K, *The Middle Base*:[1]
L, *The Honour Point*: M, *The Fesse Point*.

No. 27.

In blazoning the Divisions of a Shield, the term "*Per*," signifying "in the direction of," is employed sometimes alone, and sometimes (having the same signification) preceded by the word "parted" or "party." The primary Divisions of a Shield are indicated in the following diagrams, Nos. 28–35 :—

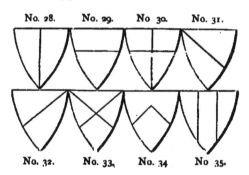

No. 28.   No. 29.   No 30.   No. 31.

No. 32.   No. 33.   No. 34   No 35.

No. 28. *Per Pale*, or *Parted per Pale*, or *Party per Pale*.
No. 29. *Per Fesse*, or *Parted per Fesse*.
No. 30. (Nos. 28 and 29 together) *Per Cross*, or *Quarterly* (the latter is the more usual term).

[1] This term is very seldom if ever used.

C

No. 31. *Per Bend.*　No. 32. *Per Bend Sinister.*
No. 33. (Nos. 31 and 32 together) *Per Saltire.*
No. 34. *Per Chevron.*
No. 35. Tierced in pale (divided into three equal divisions
　　　　by two vertical lines), a form seldom met with
　　　　in English Heraldry.　Technically this in Eng-
　　　　lish Heraldry is simply the representation of
　　　　a pale.　(See Fig. 87.)

To these divisions should strictly be added the further
division *gyronny* (Fig. 147); but neither the term *per* nor
parted per is ever employed in this connection.　As will be
seen, it is a combination of the forms shown in Figs.
30 and 33.

A Shield may be further divided and subdivided, thus :—

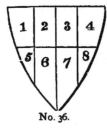

No. 36.

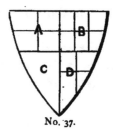

No. 37.

It may be divided into any number of *Quarterings* by lines
drawn *per pale* and *per fesse*, cutting each other, as in No.
36, which Shield is *quarterly of eight :* in like manner the
Quarterings of any Shield, whatever their number (which
need not be an even number), are blazoned as, *quarterly
of twelve, &c.*　This, to whatever extent the dividing of
the Shield may be carried, is *simple Quartering.*　Again: a
quartered Shield may have one or more of its primary
quarters, or every one of them, *quartered :* this, which is
the subdivision of a part, *the quartering of quarters,* is *compound Quartering :* for example, in No. 37, the Shield is first
divided into the *four primary quarters,* severally marked
A, B, C, D; then, so far as the quarters A, B, D are con-

cerned, the "simple quartering" is subjected to the process of "compound quartering," and quarters A, D are *quarters quarterly*, and B is *a quarter quarterly of six*, while C remains unaffected by the secondary process.   The terms "*quarterly quartering*" and "*quarterly quartered*" are used to signify such secondary quartering as is exemplified in A, B, D of No. 37.   The four primary quarters (A, B, C, D of No. 37) are distinguished as *Grand Quarters:* consequently, the quarter B of this example is the *second grand quarter, quarterly of six.*   This term "Grand Quarter" may be employed to distinguish any primary quarter when any quarter in the Shield is "quarterly quartered."

DIVIDING and BORDER LINES, in addition to simple right lines and curves, assume the forms that are represented in the next diagram, No. 38 :—

No. 38. A. *Indented* ....
B. *Dancetté* ....
C. *Wavy* or *Undée* (2 varieties).........
D. *Engrailed*.............
E. *Invected* or *Invecked*
F. *Embattled*............
G. *Raguly* ....
H. *Nebuly* (2 varieties).......
I. *Dovetailed* ....

Two others, less frequently met with, however, are *rayonné* and *flory-counter-flory.*

THE SHIELD : ITS VARIETIES OF FORM.—The front face of an heraldic Shield is generally flat ; but sometimes the curved edges are made to appear as if they had been slightly rounded off.   Some early Shields are represented

as *bowed*—hollowed, that is, in order to cover more closely
the person of the bearer, and consequently having a convex

external contour, as in No. 39. In early examples
of bowed Shields the whole of the armorial
blazonry is sometimes displayed on the face of that
portion of the Shield which is shown. A *ridge*,
dividing them in pale, but not necessarily in any

No. 39.

way acting as an heraldic dividing line, appears in
many Shields, and particularly in those of the fifteenth and
sixteenth centuries. The large elongated Shields that have
been entitled "kite-shaped," and which were in use in the
days of RICHARD I. and amongst the Barons of Magna
Charta, were superseded by the smaller "heater-shaped"

No 40.   No. 42.   No. 41.

Shield as early as the reign of HENRY III. The most
beautiful forms of this Shield are represented in Nos. 40,
41, and 42 : of these, No. 40 has its curves described about
the sides of an inverted equilateral triangle, and then they
are prolonged by vertical lines towards the chief: in Nos.
41, 42, the sides curve from the chief to the base. The
forms of Shields admit of various slight modifications, to
adjust them to varying conditions. Towards the close of
the fourteenth century the form of the Shield is found to
undergo some singular changes: and, at later periods,
changes in form of this kind became generally prevalent.
Nos. 43, 44, exemplify such changes as these: they also
show the curved notch that was cut in the dexter chief
of the Shields of the same periods, to permit the lance

to pass through it as the Shield hung down on the breast: a Shield so pierced is said to be *à bouche*. The Surface of the Shield, No. 43, which is in the Episcopal palace at

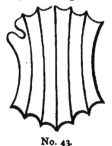 

No. 43. No 44.

Exeter, is wrought into a series of shallow hollows, which curve gracefully from the central ridge, some to the dexter, and others to the sinister. Such a Shield as this may be consistently used in our own Heraldry: but, since now we do not associate lances laid in rest with our heraldic Shields, it appears desirable that we should not draw our Shields *à bouche*. In recent Heraldry the Shield has commonly been made to appear such an unsightly and un-heraldic deformity as is represented in No. 45. Instead of a true heraldic Shield also, a rounded oval with a convex surface, called a *cartouche*, or *cartouche shield*, No. 46, is occasionally used for the display of armorial blazonry; or a circle is substituted for such

No. 45.

an oval. These cartouches probably owe their origin to the usage of placing a Garter of the Order about a Shield (prevalent in the fifteenth century), and to a subsequent period, when we find the omission of the exact outline of the actual Shield. But their frequent appearance in Ecclesiastical Heraldry suggests that perhaps they were deliberately pre-

No. 46 No 47.

ferred to the purely military shield. A *Lozenge*, No. 47, takes the place of a Shield to bear the arms of Ladies, with

the exception of the Sovereign; this very inconvenient substitute for the heraldic Shield was introduced early in the
fourteenth century.

THE SHIELD: ITS HERALDIC TREATMENT.—When a
Shield is represented as standing erect, it is not necessary
to specify that fact, since such a position may be assumed
for a Shield unless another be set forth in blazoning.
Shields are sometimes made to appear suspended by the
guige, or shield-belt (which was worn by Knights to sustain
and secure their Shields to their persons); in some Seals
and generally in architectural compositions, Shields-of-Arms
appear suspended, erect, from their guiges; at Westminster
some of the earliest Shields are thus suspended, with a

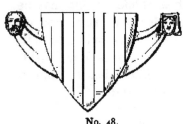

No. 48.
Arms of Provence, Westminster Abbey.

No. 49.
Shield Couché.

very happy effect, from two points of suspension, the guige
passing over sculptured heads, as in No. 48, the Arms of
Provence, borne by ALIANORE of Provence, Queen of
HENRY III.—the *shield* is *gold*, and on it are blazoned
four red pallets. In Seals, the suspended Shield is generally
represented hanging by the sinister-chief angle, as in No.
49; and it hangs thus diagonally from below the helm.
A Shield thus placed is said to be "*couché*." This arrangement is also frequently adopted, when a Shield or an
Achievement of arms is not placed upon a Seal; but in
any case the position has no importance except as a matter
of artistic treatment.

The entire surface of every Shield is termed the "*Field*."

The same term is also applied to *every plain surface*. A Shield is said to be "borne" by the personage to whom it belongs: and in its turn, the Shield "bears" whatever figures and devices may be displayed upon it; whence, all these figures and devices are entitled "*Bearings*" or "*Armorial Bearings*." All figures and devices are also styled "*Charges*"; and they are said to be "*charged*" upon a Shield, Banner, or Surcoat, or upon one another. In blazoning, the field of the Shield is always first noticed and described: next follow the charges that rest upon the field of the Shield itself: then descriptions are given of the secondary bearings that are charged upon others of greater importance. As a general rule, of several charges which all alike rest immediately upon the field of the Shield, the most important is the first to be blazoned; so that the arrangement of blazoning is determined by the comparative dignity of the bearings, as well as by the degree in which charges are nearer to the field and further from beholders. In some cases, however, a bearing charged upon the field of a Shield and many times repeated on a small scale, is blazoned (for the sake of simplicity and clearness of expression) next to the field of the Shield itself:—thus, if a lion be charged on the field of a Shield, and a considerable number of crosses surround the lion, and, like him, are placed on the field of the Shield also—the field of the Shield is blazoned first, the crosses second, and the lion third; and, if a crescent (or other bearing) be charged upon the lion's shoulder, it is the last in the blazon. In quartered Shields the blazoning commences afresh with each quartering. In blazoning armorial banners and horse-trappings, the latter often gorgeously enriched with heraldic blazonry, the dexter side of a flag is always next to the staff, and the head of a horse is supposed always to be looking towards the dexter.

CHAPTER V

THE GRAMMAR OF HERALDRY

SECTION II

*The Tinctures: Metals—Colours — Furs — Varied Fields — Law of
Tinctures — Counterchanging — Diaper — Disposition— Blazoning
in Tinctures.*

> " All the devices blazoned on the Shield
> In their own tinct."—ELAINE.

IN English Heraldry the TINCTURES comprise *Two Metals,
Five Colours*, and *Eight Furs*. They are symbolised or indicated by dots and lines—a very convenient system, said to
have been introduced, about the year 1630, by an Italian
named Silvestre de Petrasancta. Some such symbolisation,
however, may occasionally be found in anticipation of Petrasancta. The system now in use was not generally adopted
till the commencement of the eighteenth century. This
system is never officially employed in a matter of record,
and is now being discarded by many artists. The Metals,
Colours, and Furs are named, their names are abbreviated,
and they are severally indicated, as follows :—

No. 50.　No. 51.　No. 52.　No. 53

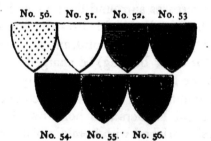

No. 54.　No. 55.　No. 56.

TWO METALS.

TITLES.	ABBREVIATIONS.	SYMBOLISATION.
1. Gold.......... *Or*............	Or............	No. 50.
2. Silver......... *Argent*	Arg.	No. 51.

FIVE COLOURS

	TITLES.	ABBREVIATIONS.	SYMBOLISATION.
1. Blue..........	*Azure*........	*Az*...........	No. 52.
2. Red..........	*Gules*..........	*Gu*...........	No. 53.
3. Black........	*Sable*..........	*Sa.*..........	No. 54.
4. Green........	*Vert*...........	*Vert*.........	No. 55.
5. Purple.......	*Purpure*......	*Purp.*........	No. 56.

(In French Heraldry, *Green* is *Sinople*.)

No. 57. No. 58. No 59

No. 60. No. 61. No. 62.

No. 63. No. 64. No. 65.

EIGHT FURS (not abbreviated).

TITLES.

1. *Ermine,*—black spots on white ....No. 57.
2. *Ermines,*—white spots on black.................No. 58.
3. *Erminois,*—black spots on gold.................No. 59
4. *Pean,*—gold spots on black.........................No. 60.
5. *Vair,*—alternate divisions of blue and white, Nos. 61, 62.
6. *Counter Vair* (note difference of arrangement) No. 63.
7. *Potent*) note different shape of divisions) ....No. 64.
8. *Counter Potent*..No. 65.

Two other Colours, or tints of Colour, are sometimes heard of—*Tenne,* a tawny or orange colour, indicated by vertical lines crossing those of *Purpure:* and *Murrey* or

No. 57A.

Sanguine, a dark crimson red, indicated by diagonal lines from both dexter and sinister, crossing each other. These two are sometimes termed stains, but their real usage was in liveries. The Furs, Nos. 58, 59, 60, 63, 64, and 65, are of comparatively rare occurrence, and do not appear in the best ages of Heraldry. *Vair* and *Ermine* are common. A good early form of *Vair* is shown in No. 62: and in No. 57A, I give a fine example of the treatment of *Ermine,* from the monument of EDWARD III.

In order to avoid repeating or referring to the word "*Or,*" the word "*Gold*" is sometimes used. The Furs, Nos. 61, 62, 63, 64, and 65, are always *argent* and *azure,* unless some other metal and colour be named in the blazoning. Animated beings and all objects, that in Heraldry are represented in their natural aspect and colouring, are blazoned "*proper,*" abbreviated *ppr.* Heraldic charges and compositions, when sketched in outline with pen and ink or with pencil, and with the colours *written* thereon, are said to be "*tricked,*" or "*in trick.*"

VARIED FIELDS.—It is not necessary that the Field of a Shield, or of any Bearing, should be of any one uniform tincture: but varied surfaces are usually tinctured of some one metal and some one colour alternating; and the patterns or devices thus produced are generally derived (the Furs, Nos. 61–65, which are good examples of varied surfaces, being the exceptions) from the forms of the original simple charges that are distinguished as *Ordinaries* and *Subordinaries.* And these varied surfaces or fields are always *flat;* the whole of their devices or patterns are *level,* their metal and colour lying in the same plane. It is evident that, in representing any examples of this class, no shading is to be introduced to denote relief.

Should the field of any charge be divided into a single row of small squares, alternately, *e.g.* of a metal and a colour, as No. 66, it is *Componée* or *Compony* (sometimes written

No. 66.

No. 67.

gobony): if into two such rows, as in No. 67, it is *Counter-Compony:* but, if the field of a Shield, or the surface of any charge be divided into three, or more than three, such rows, it is *Chequée* or *Checky;* thus, the Arms of the Earl de WARENNE are *Chequée or and az.*, No. 68 (H. 3 and E. 2).

THE LAW OF TINCTURES.—Every charge is supposed to rest upon the field of a Shield, or on the surface of some charge. It is a strict rule, that a charge of a metal must rest upon a field that is of a colour or fur ; or, contrariwise, that a charge of a colour must rest on a field that is of a metal or fur,—that is, that *metal be not on metal, nor colour on colour.* This rule is modified in the case of *varied fields,* upon which may be charged a bearing of either a metal or a colour: also, a partial relaxation of the rule is conceded when one bearing is charged upon another, should the conditions of any particular case require such a concession. This rule does not apply to bordures, nor very stringently to augmentations or crests, and it is not so rigidly enforced in Foreign as in British Heraldry. There are, of course, a few exceptions, but they are not numerous, the one usually instanced as an intentional violation being the *silver* armorial Shield of the CRUSADER KINGS of JERUSALEM, No. 69, upon which *five golden crosses* are charged ; the motive in this remarkable exception to an established rule being said to be to cause this Shield to be unlike that of any other potentate. What may be termed the accessories of a charge are not included in this law of tinctures: thus, a silver lion having a red tongue may be charged on a blue shield, and the red tongue may rest on the blue field of the Shield.

COUNTERCHANGING is dividing the field of a Shield in such a manner that it is, *e.g.* in part of a metal and in part of a colour, and then arranging the charges in such a manner that they shall be reciprocally of the same colour and metal:

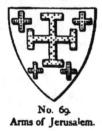

No. 69.
Arms of Jerusalem.

No. 70.
Arms of Fenwick.

thus, the shield of John Fenwick, No. 70 (R. 2) is,—*per-fesse gu. and arg., six martlets, three, two, one, counterchanged ;* that is, the field is red in chief and silver in base, and the birds or parts of the birds on the red field are silver, and those on the silver field are red.

DIAPERING.—This term denotes a system of decorating plain surfaces in various ways, which was in great favour with the early heraldic artists. In the use of Diaper, which is often desirable when artistic reasons suggest its suitability, care must be taken that the decorative designs and patterns do not in any way admit of their being mistaken for charges. This diaper may be executed in low relief, subordinated to the relief of the charges; and it is not required to yield any obedience to the law of tinctures. In the Shield, No 68 (the original, a very noble shield, is at Castle Acre Priory, Norfolk), which is simply *chequée*, the Diapering may be alternately azure and or on the squares that are alternately or and azure; or the Diaper may be dark blue, or sable, or argent on the azure squares, and on the golden ones whatever the artist might consider would be most effective; but the Diaper, in this and in all other examples, must always be subordinate to the area and tincture of the field. The finest known early example of heraldic Diaper in enamel, is the Shield of WILLIAM DE

No. 68.
Shield of Arms of Earl de Warrenne, Castle Acre Priory, Norfolk.

VALENCE, Earl of PEMBROKE, in Westminster Abbey, A.D. 1296. Very beautiful early examples of Diapering have been preserved in relics of heraldic stained glass.

DISPOSITION: BLAZONING.—By *Disposition* is understood the placing and arranging of charges. A single important charge, which has not a fixed position of its own, is placed in the centre of any composition : and minor charges are arranged in their most natural and consistent order and positions, any deviation from which must be specified. A single charge, many times repeated, and small in size, whether with or without any special orderly disposition, is said to be *Semée*—strewn, that is, or scattered over the field, as seed is sown by the hand; or, if the charges are very small or very numerous, the term *poudrée* or *powdered* has sometimes been used. The expression—"*three, two, one,*" signifies that a charge is repeated six times, the Disposition being three in a horizontal row towards the chief of the Shield, then two in a similar row in the centre, and one in base. In the same manner, the expressions—"*four, four, one,*" "*four, three, two, one,*" "*three and one,*" &c.; are used as occasion may require. For other dispositions of charges other appropriate terms will present themselves to our notice, growing out of our subject as it advances.

Should a *Tincture* or a *Number* occur a second time in blazoning a single composition, it must be indicated, not by repeating the word already used, but by reference to it. Thus, if the tincture of the field should occur a second time, reference is made to it in the formula—"*of the field :*" or, perhaps more frequently—"*of the first ;*" or, if the tincture that is named second in order in the blazoning be repeated, it is indicated by the expression—"*of the second ;*" and so on. Again : should there be three fleurs de lys and also three crescents in one and the same composition, having specified the "three fleurs de lys," the number of the crescents would be set forth in the words—"*as many* crescents :" providing nothing else has in the wording of the blazon intervened in such a way as to cause uncertainty by the use of the term ; and so, in like manner, with any other numbers of these or of any other charges.

In descriptive Blazoning, Epithets, which follow their own Nouns, precede the Tinctures that are associated with those nouns: thus, a black rampant lion having golden claws is blazoned,—*a lion rampt. sa., armed or.* In written and printed blazoning, the arrangement of the words and the placing the stops are alike matters of supreme importance. The sentences are to be short. A comma is to mark the end of each complete minor clause or division of a sentence : a colon, each more important clause. A point or period is to follow every abbreviated word, to mark the fact of the abbreviation, but without affecting the additional presence of a comma (as in the blazoning, "*a lion rampant sa.,*") or of a colon, as the case may be; but a second period is unnecessary. It is a very common error to overload heraldic blazoning with commas which, instead of aiding to simplify the sentences, obscure the meaning and perplex the reader. It is always correct to write—"*three lion's heads,*" "*six pilgrim's staves,*" &c.: and always incorrect to write—"*three lions' heads,*" "*six pilgrims' staves,*" &c.; but it is a point printers have an apparently invincible objection to accept.

EMBLAZONING IN TINCTURES.—On this head I must be content to offer to students only a few brief practical observations. The metal *Gold* may be rendered with gold prepared in small saucers, or (most advantageously) in minute slabs; this preparation is applied, like a common watercolour, by moistening the gold with water; and it is desirable previously to have washed the paper, card (or vellum) with diluted white of egg. Gold leaf may also be used, but the process is tedious, and requires both skill and experience to ensure complete success. Yellow paint, again, may be used to represent the metal, the best colours being *cadmium yellow*, or "*aureolin*" (Winsor and Newton) mixed with *Chinese white*. For shading, *carmine*, or *crimson lake*, mixed with gum. For *Silver*, *aluminium* may be used with excellent effect; or *Chinese white;* or the paper may be left white: for shading, *grey* (*blue* and *Indian ink* mixed) and gum. The Aluminium is prepared, like the gold, in minute slabs: it may be obtained, of great excellence, from Messrs. Winsor & Newton, by whom also a very pure preparation of gold is sold; but both the gold and the aluminium slabs are sold by all good artists' colourmen. These Metals may be diapered, as well as burnished, with an agate-burnisher.

For *Azure:*—*French blue*, freely mixed with *Chinese white* and a very little gum, the colour to be laid on thick:

shade with *Prussian blue* mixed with a larger proportion of gum. For *Gules:—Orange vermilion* either pure, or mixed with a very little *cadmium yellow* or *Chinese white*, and still less gum: (never use a brilliant but most treacherous preparation known as "pure scarlet:") shade with *carmine* or *crimson lake*, and gum. For *Vert:—emerald green*, with *Chinese white* and a little gum: shade with dark green, made from mixing *aureolin* (or *gamboge*) with *Prussian blue* and gum. For *Purpure:—*mix *carmine* and *French blue*, with a little gum: shade with a darker tint of the same. For *Sable:—*Very dark *grey*, made by mixing a little *Chinese white* and gum with black: shade with black and more gum.

When the Metals are rendered by gold and aluminium, it is desirable that these tinctures should be applied, and that the diapering and burnishing of the Metals should also be completed with the burnisher, before the adjoining colours are laid on. The burnishing may be executed in two or three hours after the Metals have been applied to the paper; and the paper should be placed upon a piece of glass during the processes of burnishing and diapering.

CHAPTER VI

THE GRAMMAR OF HERALDRY

Section III

The Ordinaries:—The Chief; Fesse; Bar; Pale; Cross, its heraldic varieties; Bend; Saltire; Chevron; and Pile.

"Marks of Hereditary Honour, given or authorised by some supreme Power."—Science of Heraldry.

The Ordinaries.—The simple Charges of early Heraldry, which always have been held in the highest esteem and which are most familiar, are:—The *Chief*, the *Fesse*, the *Bar*, the *Pale*, the *Cross*, the *Bend*, the *Saltire*, the *Chevron*, and the *Pile*. They may be considered to have been derived from various means that were adopted to strengthen Shields for use in combat, the *Cross* always being in great favour from having a definite symbolism of its own. These Ordinaries may be formed by any of the Border Lines, No. 38. Occasionally they are borne alone; but more generally they are associated with other bearings, or they have various figures and devices charged upon themselves. In some cases, presently to be specified, more than one Ordinary may appear in a single composition. The *Bar*, the *Pale*, the *Bend*, and the *Chevron* have *Diminutives*. The *Cross* has many *Varieties*.

The Chief (H. 3), bounded by a horizontal line, contains the uppermost third (or, in practice, somewhat less than the third, of the field of a Shield, as in No. 71. The Shield of Le Botiler, No. 72, is—*Or, a chief indented az.* (H. 3). A Chief may be borne with any other Ordinary except the

Fesse; it may also be charged with any other figures or devices:—thus, for Sire BERNARD DE BRUS, No. 73,—*Az.*, *a chief and a saltire or:* for Sire JOHAN DE CLINTONE, No.

No. 71.

No. 72.—Le Botiler.

74,—*Arg., on a chief az. two fleurs de lys or:* and for Sir JOHAN DE CLINTONE de Madestoke, No. 75,—*Arg., on chief az. two mullets or* (all E. 2). When any charge is s•

No. 73.—De Brus.

No. 74.

No. 75.—De Clintone.

in the uppermost third of a Shield, or when several charges are disposed in a horizontal row across the uppermost part of a Shield, they all are said to be "*in Chief.*"

No. 76.—De Clifford.

No. 77.—De Pateshulle.

No. 78.—Le Vavasour.

The FESSE (H. 3), which crosses the centre of a Shield horizontally, when charged occupies about one-third (or rather less than one-third) of the field; but when without charges, it is usually drawn somewhat narrower. The

Shield of Lord CLIFFORD is,—*Chequée or and az., a fesse gu.*, No. 76. For ROBT. LE FITZ-WATER,—*Or, a fesse between two chevrons gu.*: for JOHN DE PATESHULLE, No. 77,—*Arg., a fesse sa., between three crescents gu.* (all H. 3): for WILLIAM LE VAVASOUR, No. 78,—*Or, a fesse dancette sa.*: for DE HEMENHALE, No, 79,—*Or, on a fesse between*

No. 79.—De Hemenhale.　　　　No. 80.—De Dageworthe.

two chevrons gu., three escallops arg.: and for DE DAGE-WORTHE, No. 80,—*Erm., a fesse gu. bezantée* (all E. 2). When they are disposed in a horizontal row across the centre of a Shield, Charges are "*in fesse.*"

The BAR (H. 3), which may be placed horizontally in any part of the field except in fesse or at the chief of the Shield, is about one-fifth of the field (or sometimes less) in

No. 81.—De Harecourt.　　　　No. 82.—Wake.

depth. A single bar very rarely occurs in blazon. Examples :—*Or, two bars gu.*,—for DE HARECOURT, No. 81 : *Az., two bars dancettée or*,—for DE RIVERES : *Or, two bars gu., in chief three torteaux*,—for WAKE, No. 82. The Diminutive of the Bar is the *Barrulet*, one-half of its width. When they are disposed in couples, Barrulets are *Bars Gemelles*, these not being so deep as the barrulet : thus,

No. 83,—for DE HUNTERCUMBE,—*Erm., two bars gemelles gu.* (H. 3). A Fesse or Bar, when placed between two similar figures narrower than barrulets, is said to be *cotised* by them; or, to be " doubly cotised," when placed between two bars gemelles: thus, for DE LA MERE, No. 84,—*Or, a fesse doubly*

No. 83.—De Huntercumbe.   No. 84.—De la Mere.

cotised (or, *between two bars gemelles*) *az.* (E. 2). An *even* number of bars alternately of a metal (or a fur) and a colour form the varied field which is to be blazoned " *barry*," the number of the bars in every case to be specified—as, " *barry of six*," " *barry of eight*," &c. If the number of bars exceeds *eight* (some writers say *ten*), it is " *barrulée*" or " *barruly*"; and in this case it is not necessary that the number of the bars should be specified, the word *barrulée* being used alone, or the expression " *barrulée sans nombre*," to denote a considerable number, but not a fixed number of bars—the number, however, always to be *even*. But this is a modern refinement of blazon to which little if any attention was paid in early days. It is to be observed that while the bars, whatever their number, if they are blazoned as bars, are to be treated as if they were executed in relief upon the field of a Shield, a Shield that is barry or barrulée has its field formed by bars which are all in the same plane. Examples:—*Barry of six or and gu.*, for FITZ ALAN of Bedale, No. 85 : *Barry of six arg. and az.*, for DE GREY : *Barry of eight or and az.*,—for DE PEN-BRUGGE (all H. 3): *Barrulée arg. and az., an orle of martlets gu.*,—for DE VALENCE, Earl of PEMBROKE, No. 86; in this example *ten* bars are represented, but in the noble enamelled shield of the first De Valence (A.D. 1296) preserved in Westminster Abbey, the bars are *twenty-eight* in number. Charges, not "in fesse" or "in chief," that are disposed horizontally across the field are "*bar-wise.*"

No. 85 —Fitzalan of Bedale.

No. 86.—De Valence.

The PALE. — Like the Fesse, this Ordinary occupies rather less than a central third of the field, but it is *vertical* in its position instead of horizontal. No. 87, for ERSKINE, is—*Arg., a pale sa.* Its Diminutives, the *Pallet* and the *Endorse*, severally one-half and one-fourth of its width,

No. 87 —Erskine.

No. 88.—Grandison.

may be placed vertically in any part of the field. A Pale between two Endorses is "*endorsed,*" but the term *cotised* is also employed with this meaning. An *even* number of Pallets of a metal (or a fur) and a colour set alternately, form the varied field to be blazoned "*paly,*" the number of the Pallets (which lie all in the same plane) always to be specified: thus—*Paly of six arg. and az., on a bend gu.*

three eaglets displayed or, for GRANDISON, No. 88 (H. 3).
Charges that are disposed one above another in a vertical
row are "in pale." This is the arrangement of the three
golden lions of England.

The CROSS (H. 3), formed from a combination of a Fesse
with a Pale, in its simplest form is set erect in the centre of
the field, and it extends to the border-lines of the Shield.
If at any time it may be necessary or apparently desirable
specially to set forth in the blazoning of a Shield, that a
Cross charged upon it does thus extend to the border-lines,
such a Cross is blazoned as a "*Cross throughout.*" No. 1,
Arg., a Cross gu., the armorial ensign of ST. GEORGE, the
special Patron Saint of England, may be blazoned as "*A
Cross of St. George.*" Of this Cross, the great symbol
of the Christian Faith, Spenser says—

> "And on his brest a bloodie Cross he bore,
>   The deare remembrance of his dying Lord . . . .
>   Upon his Shield the like was also scored."
>
>   *Faërie Queen*, I. 1. 2.

A Cross having a narrow border lying in the same plane

No. 89—Cross fimbriated.

No 90.—Cross pointed.

with itself, is "fimbriated," such a border being a "*fimbriation*": thus, No. 89, *Az., a cross gu., fimbriated arg.*, represents the Cross of St. George in our National "Union Jack."
A Cross having its four extremities cut off square, so that it
does not extend in any direction to the border-lines of the
shield, is "*couped*" or "*humettée.*" If the extremities of a
Cross are cut off to points, it is "*pointed,*" as in No. 90.

If its central area is entirely removed, so that but little more than its outlines remain, it is "*voided*," or (H. 3) "*a false Cross*" ("faux croix"): when its four limbs are *equal* in length, it is a "*Greek Cross*," as No. 91 : when the limbs are *unequal*, the lower limb or shaft being longer than the other three, as in No. 92, it is a "*Latin Cross*" or a "long cross": but neither of these two last terms are used regarding the plain cross throughout, not-

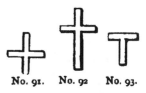

No. 91.   No. 92   No. 93.

withstanding that differences in the shape of the shield may materially alter the proportion of the limbs. If a cross be formed of a shaft and two horizontal limbs only (like the letter T), as in No. 93, it is a "*Tau Cross*," or "*Cross Tau*": if it is pierced at the intersection of the limbs, and the entire central area be voided, it is said to be "*pierced quarterly*." A Latin Cross on steps, is "*on Degrees*," and it is distinguished as a "Calvary Cross." Charges having a cruciform arrangement are "*in Cross*."

The CROSS:—its HERALDIC VARIETIES. The Cross-symbol appears in English Heraldry under very many varieties and modifications of form and condition, some of them

No. 94.
Quadrate.

No 95.
Patriarchal.

No. 96
Fourchée.

of great beauty. The following engraved representations of the various examples are so explicit, that descriptions of them are unnecessary. The Cross *Quadrate*, No. 94. The Cross *Patriarchal*, No. 95. The Cross *Fourchée*, No. 96. The Cross *Moline*, represented charged upon the Shield attributed to the SAXON KINGS OF ENGLAND, No. 23: this

same shield—*Az., a Cross moline or*, is borne by DE
MOLINES or MOLYNEUX, No. 97. The Cross *Cercelée* or
Recercelée (H. 3),—*Gu., a Cross recercelée erm.*, No. 98, for
ANTHONY BEC, Bishop of DURHAM. The Cross *Patonce*
(H. 3),—*Gu., a Cross patonce arg.*, No. 99, from the Seal of

No. 97.—Cross Moline :   No. 98.—Cross Recercelée ;   No 99.—Cross Patonce :
Arms of De Molines.   Arms of Bishop Anthony Bec.   Arms of William de Vesci.

WM. DE VESCI, A.D. 1220. The Cross *Fleury*, No. 100,
should be compared carefully with Nos. 97 and 99, the
Crosses *Moline* and *Patonce*. The Cross *Fleurettée*, No.
101. The Cross *Pommée*, No. 102. The Cross *Botonée*
or *Treflée*, No. 103. The Cross *Crosslet*, or *Crosslet
crossed*, No. 104. The term "*Crosslet*" is strictly applicable

No 100.   No. 101.   No. 102
Fleurie.   Fleurettée.   Pommée.

to any Cross on a very small scale : but it is usually applied
to denote a Cross that is crossed as in No. 104. Small
Crosses Botonée are occasionally used as these "Crosses-
Crosslets,"—as at Warwick in the arms of the BEAUCHAMPS,
the Earls of WARWICK. Crosslets are frequently blazoned
semée over the field of a Shield, in which case the special
term *crusilly* is often used ; and, in smaller numbers, they

also are favourite Charges.   No. 105 is the Cross *Clechée*
or *Urdée*.

The Cross *Patée* or *Formée* is represented in No. 106.
No. 107 is the " *Cross of eight Points*," or the *Maltese* Cross :

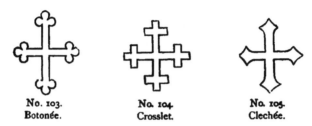

No. 103.   No. 104.   No. 105.
Botonée.   Crosslet.   Clechée.

this example is drawn from the portrait of PHILLIPPE DE
VILLIERS DE L'ISLE-ADAM, elected forty-third Grand Master
of the Knights of St. John of Jerusalem, A.D. 1521 ; this
picture is in the possession of the Earl of Clarendon, K.G.

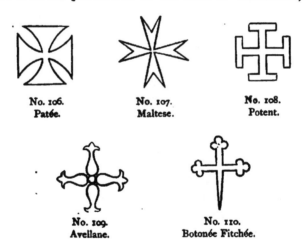

No. 106.   No. 107.   No. 108.
Patée.   Maltese.   Potent.

No. 109.   No. 110.
Avellane.   Botonée Fitchée.

The Cross *Potent*, No. 108.   The Cross *Avellane*, No. 109.
The *Crossed-Crosslet*, and the Crosses *Patée*, *Botonée*, and
Potent, are also drawn having their shaft elongated and
pointed at the base : in this form they are severally blazoned
as a " *Crossed-Crosslet Fitchée* " (or *fitched*), a " *Cross Patée*

Fitchée," &c.,—a Cross, that is, "*fixable*" in the ground: No. 110 is an example of a Cross *Botonée Fitchée.* Several of these varieties of the heraldic Cross occur but rarely; and there are other somewhat fanciful varieties so little in use, as to render any description of them unnecessary. The student of mediæval monumental antiquities will not fail to observe a certain degree of resemblance between some of the Crosses of Heraldry, and those that are incised and sculptured on sepulchral slabs.

The BEND (H. 3) resembles both the Fesse and the Pale in every condition, except that it crosses the field *diagonally* from the dexter chief to the sinister base. No. 111, the Shield of SCROPE, is—*Az., a bend or.* A celebrated contest for the right to bear this simple Shield took place, A.D. 1385–1390, between Sir RICHARD LE SCROPE and Sir ROBERT GROSVENOR, which was decided in favour of the former. No. 112, for RADCLYFFE, is—*Arg., a bend engrailed*

No. 111.— Le Scrope.   No. 112.—De Radclyffe.   No 113.— Le Boteler.

sa. Two uncharged Bends may appear in one composition: thus, for LE BOTELER—*Arg., two bends az.,* No. 113; and for FRERE—*Gu., two bends or* (both H. 3). The Diminutives of the Bend are the *Bendlet* and the *Cotise,* the one containing one-half and the other one-fourth of its area. A Cotise is sometimes borne singly, when it is a *Riband.* A bendlet *couped* is a baton. A Bend between two Cotises is *cotised:* thus, No. 114, for DE BOHUN,—*Az., a Bend arg., cotised or, between six lioncels rampt. gold;* this Shield is engraved from the Seal of HUMPHREY DE BOHUN, fourth

Earl of HEREFORD (A.D. 1298–1322); in it the cotised Bend is very narrow, evidently to give more space for the lioncels. Charges displayed on a Bend *slope with it*— that is, they would be erect, were the Bend to be set vertically and to become a Pale: thus, another DE BOHUN, Sir Gilbert (H. 3), distinguishes his Shield by tincturing

No. 114.
Humphrey de Bohun, 4th Earl of Hereford.

No. 115.
Sir Gilbert de Bohun.

his Bend *or*, and charging upon it *three escallops gules*, as in No. 115. In No. 88, the eaglets also exemplify the disposition of charges upon a Bend. Charges set diagonally on the field of a Shield, in the position in which a bend would occupy, are said to be "*in bend*," and are arranged in the same manner: but it would be quite possible to have three or more charges each disposed bendwise; but yet, nevertheless, when taken together occupying the position of a fesse and therefore described also as in fesse. This distinction between charges bendwise (or bendways) and charges in bend should be carefully noted. A field divided into an *even* number of parts by lines drawn *bendwise*, is "*bendy*," the number of the divisions to be specified: as a matter of course, a field thus

"bendy" becomes a "varied field," in which all the divisions lie in the same plane : thus, No 116, for DE MONTFORD

No. 116.—De Montford.

No. 117.—De Bray.

(H. 3 and E. 2)—*Bendy of ten or and az.* Bendlets are
in relief, as in No. 117, for DE BRAY—*Vairée, three
Bendlets gu.* If a field be divided by lines drawn bendwise,

No. 118.—Paly Bendy.

No. 119.—Barry Bendy.

and also by others drawn either vertically or horizontally,
it is "*paly bendy,*" as No. 118, or "*barry bendy,*" as No.
119. These two forms, which, however, are very rarely

No. 120.—St. Andrew.

No. 122.—De Neville.

No. 121.—De Neville.

met with, should be carefully distinguished from a field
lozengy. A Bend issuing from the sinister chief is a
Bend Sinister.

The SALTIRE (H. 3), a combination of a Bend with a Bend Sinister, may also be regarded as a *Diagonal Cross.* Thus, the Crosses of St. ANDREW of SCOTLAND, and of St. PATRICK of IRELAND are Saltires—the former, No. 120— *Az., a Saltire arg.:* the latter—*Arg., a Saltire gu.* The arms of the great family of NEVILLE reverse those of St. PATRICK, and are—*Gu., a Saltire arg.,* No. 121 : so Drayton has recorded that

> "Upon his surcoat valiant NEVILLE bore
> A silver Saltire upon martial red."
>
> *Barons' War,* i. 22.

Charges set on a Saltire *slope with its limbs* (all, however, pointing to the chief), *the central charge being erect;* and the disposition of charges set *"in saltire"* is the same : a single charge set on a Saltire is blazoned erect on the central point of the Ordinary, as in No. 122, another Shield of NEVILLE, in which the "Silver Saltire" is charged with a *rose gules.* A Saltire may be borne with a Chief, as in No. 73.

The CHEVRON (H. 3), in form and proportions is rather more than the lower half of a Saltire. The Diminutive is a

No. 123.—De Stafford.

No. 124.—Shield of De Clare.

Chevronel, containing half a Chevron, or perhaps less : thus, for DE STAFFORD (E. 2),—*Or, a Chevron gu.,* No. 123 : for the great family of DE CLARE, from whom so many other families derived their Chevrons and Chevronels—*Or, three*

Chevronels gules, No. 124 (H. 3). Two Chevrons may be borne in one composition: or they may appear with a Fesse, as in No. 79: or with a Chief, as (H. 3), for DE

CROMBE—*Erm., a Chevron gu., and on a Chief of the last three escallops or;* for ST. QUINTIN (H. 3)—*Or, three Chevronels gu., a Chief vair.* A field *Chevronée* is of rare occurrence: the three Chevronels of DE CLARE, however, No. 124, appear to have been derived from a field *Chevronée:* certainly, on his seal,

No. 125.
Early Shield of De Clare.

"Strongbow" has the Chevronée Shield, No. 125, about A.D. 1175. Charges set on a Chevron, or disposed "*in Chevron,*" are always placed erect.

The PILE (H. 3), resembling a wedge in form, is borne both single and in small groups. Unless some other disposition on the field be specified, this Ordinary issues from the chief of the Shield. Examples: *Or, a Pile gu., between six and charged with three estoiles* (or *mullets*) *counter-*

No. 126.—De Chandos.   No. 127.—De Brian   No. 128.—De Bassett.

changed,—for ROBERT DE CHANDOS, No. 126: *Or, three Piles az.,* No. 127,—for Sir GUY DE BRIAN; *Or, three Piles gu., a canton erm.,* No. 128,—for DE BASSETT (all H. 3): and (E. 2), *Arg., a Pile engrailed sa.*—for Sir ROB. DE FORNEUS. In early emblazonments three piles appear almost uniformly to be depicted with the points converging.

But a distinction is now made, and when the piles are intended to converge, as in Fig. 128, they are termed "*in point.*"

The probable structural origin of these Ordinaries is sufficiently apparent to render any further comment on that interesting circumstance superfluous.

CHAPTER VII

THE GRAMMAR OF HERALDRY

Section IV

The Subordinaries:—The Canton or Quarter: The Inescutcheon: The Orle: The Tressure: The Bordure: Flanches: The Lozenge, Mascle, and Rustre: The Fusil: The Billet: The Gyron: The Frette—The Roundles.

"The second in a line of stars."—IDYLLS OF THE KING.

THE SUBORDINARIES. This title has been assigned, but without any decisive authority, to another group of devices, second in rank to the Ordinaries. Very few writers agree as to which are ordinaries and which subordinaries; nor does there seem any reason why any distinction between them should exist. Nor, indeed, save that all are exclusively heraldic, why some of them should be regarded as anything more than ordinary charges. These Subordinaries are the *Canton*, the *Quarter*, the *Inescutcheon*, the *Orle*, the *Tressure*, the *Bordure*, *Flanches*, the *Lozenge*, *Mascle* and *Rustre*, the *Fusil*, the *Billet*, the *Gyron*, and the *Frette*. The Canton, by the early Heralds commonly styled the " Quarter," sometimes has been grouped with the Ordinaries. And it must here be observed that the Lozenge, Fusil, Billet, Gyron, and Frette were not used as single charges by the early Heralds; but by them the fields of Shields were divided *lozengy* and *gyronny*, or they were *semée of Billets*, or covered over with *Frette*-work, from which the single charges evidently were afterwards obtained.

The CANTON (H. 3), sometimes blazoned as a QUARTER,

cut off by two lines, the one drawn in pale and the other bar-wise, or in fesse, is either the first quarter of the field of a Shield, or about three-fourths of that quarter, but smaller if not charged. The confusion between the canton and the quarter is due to the fact that ancient arms in which the charge is now, and has been for centuries past, stereotyped as a canton and drawn to occupy one-ninth of the Shield, were uniformly drawn and blazoned in early times with the charge as a quarter. But there is a marked distinction now made between the canton and the quarter. A *Canton ermine* is of frequent occurrence, as in No. 128; but it is generally borne charged, and it always

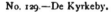

No. 129.—De Kyrkeby.　　　　　No. 130.—Blundell.

overlies the charges of the field of the Shield, as No. 129, for DE KYRKEBY (R. 2)—*Arg., two bars gu.; on a canton of the last a cross moline or;* and, for BLUNDELL (H. 3)— *Az., billettée, on a canton or a raven ppr.,* No. 130.

The INESCUTCHEON (H. 3) is a Shield borne as a charge, and superimposed upon another Shield larger than itself. When one Inescutcheon is borne, it is usually placed on the fesse-point; but several Inescutcheons may appear in one composition. The well-known Shield of the MOR-TIMERS supplies a good example, No. 131 (H. 3)—*Barry of six or and az., an inescutcheon arg.; on a chief gold, gyroned of the second, two pallets of the same:* for DARCY—*Arg., an inescutcheon sa., within an orle of roses gu.,* No. 132 (E. 2):

E

Arg., three inescutcheons gu., for DE WYLLERS (E. 2), No. 133. This is also the well-known Scottish coat of Hay.

No. 132.—Darcy.   No. 131.—De Mortimer.   No. 133.—De Wyllers.

The ORLE (H. 3), blazoned by early Heralds as a "*false escutcheon*" ("*faux escocheon*"), or as an "*inescutcheon voided,*"

No. 134.
De Balliol.

is the border of a Shield or Escutcheon— a Shield, that is, voided of the central area of its field, and, like an Inescutcheon, charged on a Shield. The arms of BALLIOL, No. 134, are—*Gu., an Orle arg.* (H. 3). These arms are blazoned on many Scottish Seals of the greatest interest, and on the Seals of Balliol College, Oxford. Small charges are frequently disposed about the border of a Shield "*in Orle,*" as in Nos. 86 and 132.

The TRESSURE (H. 3) may be regarded as a variety of the Orle; indeed, in its simplest form it is a very narrow Orle, which is generally set round with fleurs de lys. A Tressure thus enriched is represented in No. 135 : in this example all the heads of the fleurs de lys point externally, and all their stalks internally, and this accordingly is blazoned as a "*Tressure flory.*" In No. 136, which, like No. 135, is a single Tressure, the fleurs de lys are so disposed that the heads and stalks of the flowers point alternately in contrary directions : this is blazoned as a "*Tressure flory counterflory.*" From this last example the Tressure that is so well known in the blazonry of the Royal Shield of SCOTLAND differs, in being "*double.*" This, the double

Tressure of Scotland, is a combination of two such single Tressures as No. 136, and it is produced from them in the manner following:—From one such single Tressure, as No. 136, all the alternate heads and stalks of the fleurs de lys that point internally are cut away and removed; then a second similar Tressure, of rather smaller size, is denuded

No. 135.
Single Tressure
Flory.

No. 137.
Double Tressure
flory counterflory.

No. 136.
Single Tressure
flory counterflory.

of all its external adornment, and in that condition it is placed within the former Tressure, leaving a narrow interval between the two. Each component half of this "double Tressure flory counterflory," accordingly, has its own independent series of demi-fleurs de lys, the stalks and heads of the flowers alternating, and the one alternate series pointing externally, while the other points internally. When in combination, these two series of demi-fleurs de lys must be so arranged that the heads of the flowers in one series correspond with their stalks in the other, as in No. 137. I am thus particular in describing the process of producing the Royal Tressure, because it is frequently to be seen incorrectly drawn. No. 138, the Royal Shield of SCOTLAND, now displayed in the second quarter of the Royal Arms

No. 138.—Scotland.

of the UNITED KINGDOM, is thus blazoned—*Or, a lion rampt. within a double Tressure flory counterflory, gu.* It

will be observed that a narrow strip of the golden field of
this Shield intervenes between the two Tressures.   There
are many fine examples of this Shield in Scottish Seals;
in the Garter-plate, also, of JAMES V. of Scotland, K.G.,
at Windsor; and on the Monuments in Westminster Abbey
to MARY Queen of SCOTS (A.D. 1604), and to the Countess
of LENNOX, the mother of Lord DARNLEY (A.D. 1577).
Mr. Seton ("Scottish Heraldry," p. 447) states that the
Tressure may be borne " triple "; and, after specifying the
Scottish families upon whose Shields the same honourable
bearing is blazoned, he adds :—"In the coat of the Marquess of HUNTLY, the Tressure is flowered with fleurs de
lys within, and adorned with *crescents* without; while in
that of the Earl of ABERDEEN it is flowered and counter-
flowered with *thistles*, *roses*, and fleurs de lys alternately."

The BORDURE (H. 3), as its name implies, forms a
border to a Shield : it is borne both plain and charged.

No. 139.—De Waltone.   No. 140.—Richard, Earl of Cornwall.

Thus, for DE WALTONE (E. 2)—*Arg., a cross patée sa.,
within a Bordure indented gu.*, No. 139: for RICHARD, Earl
of CORNWALL, second son of King JOHN (H. 3),—*Arg., a
lion rampt. gu. crowned or, within a Bordure sa. bezantée*,
No. 140.   The Bordure, and its important services in
Heraldry, will be more fully considered hereafter. (See
Chapters XII. and XIII.)

FLANCHES are always borne in pairs; but they are not
of very early date, nor do they often appear in blazon.

Flanches are formed by two curved lines issuing from the chief, one on each side of the Shield: they are shown, shaded for azure, in No. 141; and in No. 142 are their Diminutives, *Flasques* or *Voiders*, shaded for gules. But these diminutives are hardly ever met with. There is a

No. 141.—Flanches.

No. 142.—Flasques.

close resemblance between these charges and a peculiar dress worn by Ladies of rank in the fourteenth and fifteenth centuries; but it is not easy to determine whether the dress suggested the Flanches on the Shield, or was derived from them. One thing, however, is certain—the dress must have possessed very decided good qualities, since it continued

No. 143.—Mascle.

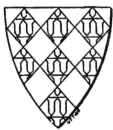

No. 144.—Rustre.

No. 145.—De Burgh, Earl of Kent.

in favour for more than two centuries. It is remarkable that many of the ancient Greek Shields have pierced Flanches.

The Lozenge (E. 2), Mascle (H. 3), and Rustre. The *Lozenge* is a diamond-shaped figure, or a parallelogram set diagonally. The *Mascle* is a *Lozenge voided of the field*, No. 143; and the *Rustre*, No. 144, is a *Lozenge pierced with a circular opening.* In the early days of Heraldry the Lozenge and the Mascle were evidently held to be identical. The Shield of the famous HUBERT DE BURGH, Earl of KENT, in the early Rolls is blazoned as *"masculée"*: but his Seal proves it to have been, as in No. 145, *lozengy vair and gu.* The Lozenge, it will be remembered, is always set erect upon the field of a Shield.

The FUSIL is an *elongated Lozenge.* The Arms of MONT-ACUTE or MONTAGU (see No. 20) are—*Arg., three Fusils conjoined in fesse gu.*, No. 20: the Arms of PERCY are—*Az., five fusils conjoined in fesse or.*

No. 20.— Montacute.   No. 146.—Deincourt.

The BILLET (H. 3) is a small elongated rectangular figure. Thus, for DEINCOURT, No. 146—*Az., billettée, a fesse dancette or.* The early Heralds blazoned a " Fesse Dancette" as simply a "*Dancette*" or "*Danse.*" See also No. 130.

The GYRON, a triangular figure, not known in English blazon as a separate charge (except perhaps in the one

case of the arms of Mortimer), gives its title to the *gyronny field*, which is more commonly found in the Heraldry of the North than of the South. The field gyronny generally, and more particularly in Scotland, is divided into *eight pieces:* but the divisions are sometimes six, ten, twelve, or even sixteen in number. A

No. 147. Campbell.

Roll of the time of HENRY III. has, for WARIN DE

BASINGBORNE—"*Gerony d'or et d'azur.*" The Arms of CAMPBELL are—*Gyronny or and sa.*, No. 147.[1] Here, where there are eight pieces or divisions, it is not necessary to specify the number; but if they were either more or less than eight the blazon would be—*gyronny of six, of ten, &c.*

The FRETTE, in more recent Heraldry, has generally superseded the original *field fretty*. This interlaced design, whether borne as a distinct figure, as No. 148, or repeated

No. 148.—A Frette.

No. 150.—Trellis Clouée.

No. 149.—De Etchingham.

over the field of a Shield, as in No. 149, differs from a field lozengy or gyronny, in being a bearing charged *upon* the field of a Shield, and not a form of varied surface: No. 149, for DE ETCHINGHAM (E. 2), is—*Az., fretty arg.* An early variety or modification of Frette is the *Trellis* or *Treille*, in which the pieces do not interlace, but all those in bend lie over all those in bend sinister, and they are fastened at the crossings with nails—"*clouée,*" as in No. 150. RICHARD DE TRUSSELL or TRESSELL (H. 3) bears—*Arg., a trellis gu., clouée or.*

The ROUNDLES, or ROUNDLETS. These simple figures, in constant use in every age of Heraldry, are divided into two groups, which correspond with the division of the Tinctures into "Metals" and "Colours."

The first group contains the two Roundles of the *Metals*, which are *flat discs*: 1, The *Bezant*, or golden Roundle, No. 151, which has apparently derived its name from

[1] In the illustration the colours are unfortunately reversed.

the Byzantine coins with which the Crusaders, when in the East, would have been familiar. 2, The Silver Roundle, or *Plate*, is from the Spanish "Plata"—*silver*. When Bezants or Plates appear in considerable numbers, the field on which they are charged is said to be "*bezantée*" or "*platée*." See No. 140.

The second group contains the five Roundles of the *Colours*, which are *globular*, and are usually shaded accordingly. The *Torteau*, No. 152, in the plural *Torteaux*, is

No. 151.—Bezant.   No. 152.—Torteau.   No. 153.—Fountain.

gules: the *Hurt* is azure: the *Pellet* or *Ogress* is sable: the *Pomme* is vert: and the *Golpe* is purpure. These distinctive titles, which are more calculated to perplex the student than to simplify his study, are of comparatively recent origin, the early Heralds having used the terms "*Bezant*," "*Plate*," and "*Torteau*," with the general designations "*Roundle*" and "*Pellet*," adding the tinctures for the others. Examples:—*Az., bezantée,* for WM. DE LA ZOUCHE: *Or, on a fesse gu. three plates,* for ROGER DE HUNTINGFIELD: *Arg., ten torteaux, four, three, two, one,* for ALEX. GIFFARD (all H. 3). See also Nos. 80, 82.

A circular figure or Roundle that is *barry wavy arg. and az.,* is blazoned as a "*Fountain*," No. 153. Examples:

—*Arg., three fountains,* for WELLES: *Arg., a Chevron sable between three fountains,* borne by a family named *Sykes,* their name being an ancient term signifying a well or fountain. An *Annulet,* or a plain ring, No. 154, was sometimes blazoned as a "*false Roundle*"—a Roundle, that is, pierced, and having its central area removed.

No. 154. Annulet.

CHAPTER VIII

THE GRAMMAR OF HERALDRY

Section V

Miscellaneous Charges: — Human Beings — Animals — Birds — Fish —Reptiles and Insects—Imaginary Beings—Natural Objects— Various Artificial Figures and Devices—Appropriate Descriptive Epithets.

"The Formes of pure celestiall bodies mixt with grosse terrestrials; earthly animals with watery; sauage beasts with tame; fowles of prey with home-bred; these again with riuer fowles; reptiles with things gressible; aery insecta with earthly; also things naturall with artificiall."
—Guillim's "Display of Heraldry," A.D. 1611.

Thus, in his own quaint fashion, the enthusiastic old Herald of the seventeenth century indicates the number and variety of the Charges, which in process of time had been introduced into Armory even before his era. In earlier days the Charges of Heraldry were much less varied, comparatively few in their numbers, and generally of a simple character. It will readily be understood, however, that fresh figures and devices would continually appear in blazon; and also that these, in their turn, would lead the way for the introduction of further varieties and new modifications.

Human Beings are of very rare occurrence, except as Supporters. Parts of the human frame constantly appear, but they are more generally borne as Crests upon helms than as charges on shields. " Moor's heads " or "Saracen's heads" appear in some coats, with arms, hands and legs: and a human heart is well known as a charge in the coat of

the famous house of DOUGLAS, where it was placed to commemorate the duty entrusted by ROBERT BRUCE to the
"good Sir JAMES DOUGLAS," that he should bear with him
the heart of his Sovereign and friend to the Holy Land,
and bury it there. Sir James fell, fighting with the Moors of
Spain, A.D. 1330. This Shield of Douglas is a characteristic example of the gradual development of armorial composition. About A.D. 1290, the Seal of WILLIAM, Lord
DOUGLAS, displays his Shield, No. 155, bearing—*Arg.,
on a chief az. three mullets of the field.* Next, upon the
field of the Shield of WILLIAM, Lord DOUGLAS, A.D. 1333,
there appears, in addition, *a human heart gules,* as in

No. 155.   No. 156.   No. 157.

Shields of Douglas.

No. 156. And, finally, the heart is ensigned with a
royal crown, as in No. 157, this form appearing as early
as 1387.

The Shield of the ancient kingdom of the ISLE OF MAN,
No. 158, still continues to be the heraldic ensign of that

No. 158.
Isle of Man.

island: it is—*Gu., three human legs in
armour ppr., conjoined in the fesse-point at
the upper part of the thighs, and flexed in
triangle.* This true curiosity of Heraldry
leads Mr. Planché to remark, that "the
arms of MAN are *legs*" ("Pursuivant of
Arms," p. 112). The Shield represented in
No. 158 is drawn from an original ex-
ample of the age of EDWARD I. in the Heralds' College.
At later periods, the armour of the conjoined limbs is repre-

sented in conformity with the usages then prevalent, and golden spurs are added. The ancient symbol of the island of Sicily, in which the limbs are without either armour or clothing, has been represented in No. 10: this device also appears in ancient examples with a human head at the junction of the limbs. Three human arms, united in the same manner, are borne on the shield of the mediæval family of TREMAINE.

Human figures, winged and vested, and designed to represent ANGELS, are occasionally introduced in English

No. 159.—Shield of St. Alban's Abbey (partly restored).

Heraldry, their office generally being to act as "Supporters" to armorial Shields. Fine examples, in admirable preservation, may be seen boldly sculptured in the noble timber-roof of Westminster Hall; also in panels over the principal entrance to the Hall, and in various parts of the Abbey of Westminster. In the grand Abbey Church of St. Alban at St. Alban's, numerous other examples of great excellence yet remain, the works of Abbot John de Wheathamstede, about A.D. 1440. In No. 159 I give a representation of the Shield of Arms of the Abbey of ST. ALBAN—*Az.*, *a saltire or*, supported by Angels, and the Shield ensigned by the Mitre of Abbot Thomas De la Mere, as it is represented in his noble Brass in the Abbey Church. The Shield and the Angel Figures are the work of Abbot John. The Heads of the Figures, which are destroyed in the original, are restored from stained glass of the same period in the Abbey Church. Figures of Angels holding Shields of Arms—each figure having a shield in front of its breast, are frequently sculptured as corbels in Gothic churches.

In the earliest Rolls of Arms, the Lion is the only animal that is found in blazon, with the sole addition of Boar's heads. Deer, dogs, bulls, calves, rams, and a few other animals subsequently appear to share heraldic service and honours with the king of beasts. In modern Armory, however, almost every living creature has been required to discharge such duties as Heralds have been pleased to assign to them. The Lion of Heraldry I leave to be considered, with the Eagle, in the next Chapter. In comparatively early blazon, the *Bear* is borne by FITZ URSE : the *Calf,* by CALVELEY and DE VELE : the *Ram*, by RAMSEY and RAMRYGE : the *Lamb*, by LAMBERT and LAMBTON : the *Otter (loutre*, in French), by LUTTREL : the *Hedgehog* (Fr., *herrison*), by DE HERIZ, afterwards HARRIS : and so also, in like manner, some other animals appear as *armes parlantes* (see p. 15).

With the lordly Eagle a few other Birds are associated in early Heraldry : and, after a while, others join them, including the Falcon, Ostrich, Swan, Peacock or Pawne, and the Pelican borne both as a symbol of sacred significance, and also by the PELHAMS from being allusive to their name. Cocks, with the same allusive motive, were borne by COCKAYNE : Parrots, blazoned as " *Popinjays*," appear as early as HENRY III. : and in a Roll of EDWARD II., the Sire MOUNPYNZON has a Lion charged on the shoulder with a Chaffinch—in French a *Pinson.* The favourite bird, however, of the early Heralds is the Martlet, the heraldic Martin, a near relative of the Swallow or *Hirondelle.* The Martlet is practically always represented in profile, at rest, and with its wings closed. . The few exceptions are modern. In some early examples the feet are shown, as in No. 160 : but, in the Shield of Earl WM. DE VALENCE in Westminster Abbey. A.D. 1296, the Martlet appears feetless, as in No.

No. 160.—Early Martlet.

No. 161.—Martlet.

161 ; and at a later period this mode of representation was generally adopted. French Heralds deprive their Martlets of beak as well as feet.

"As the symbol of a name," writes Mr. Moule, "almost all Fish have been used in Heraldry ; and in many instances Fish have been assumed in Arms in reference to the produce of the estate, giving to the quaint device a twofold interest " (" Heraldry of Fish," p. 13). The earliest examples are the Barbel, the Dolphin, the Luce (or Pike), the Herring, and the Roach. In conjunction with fish we may perhaps consider the Escallop which, as a charge, belongs to the earliest period of Heraldry. The Barbel, so named from the barbs attached to its mouth to assist it in its search

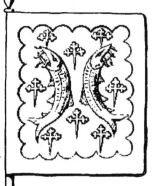

No. 162.
Banner of De Barre.

for food, was introduced into English Heraldry by JOHN, Count DE BARRE, whose elder brother married ALIANORE, eldest daughter of EDWARD I. At Carlaverock he displayed, as the chronicler has recorded, "*a blue banner, crusilly, with two Barbels of gold, and a red border en-*

·*grailed,*" No. 162. The Dolphin, borne by GILES DE FISH-
BOURNE (H. 3), and afterwards introduced into several
English Shields, is best known as the armorial ensign
of the DAUPHIN, the eldest son and heir apparent of the
Kings of France, who bore, marshalled with the arms of
FRANCE—*Or, a Dolphin az.* This title of "Dauphin"
was first assumed by CHARLES V., who succeeded to the
Crown of France in 1364. In No. 8 I have shown
after what manner the Dolphin was represented by an
ancient Greek Artist: in the Middle Ages the heraldic
Dolphin appeared as in No. 163. GEFFREY DE LUCY

No. 163.—Dolphin. No. 165.—Escallop.

No. 164.—De Lucy.

(H. 3) bears—*Gu., three Lucies or.* On his marriage with the
heiress of ANTHONY, Lord LUCY, in 1369, HENRY, fourth
Lord PERCY of Alnwick, quartered these three fish, with his
own lion (blue on a golden field) and his fusils (gold on a
blue field), upon the well-known Shield of the Earls of
NORTHUMBERLAND (Chapter XI.).

Another Carlaverock Banneret, ROBERT DE SCALES,
whom the chronicler declares to have been both "hand-
some and amiable" as well as gallant in action, had "*six
escallops of silver on a red banner.*" This beautiful charge
of the escallop, happy in its association with the pilgrims
of the olden time, and always held in high esteem by
Heralds, is generally drawn as in No. 165.

Reptiles and Insects occur but rarely in English Heraldry. Bees, Flies, Butterflies, and Snails are sometimes found, but they have no place in the earliest Rolls of Arms. Bees, as might be expected, appear in the Arms of *Beeston*. *Azure, three Butterflies*, are the Arms of MUSCHAMP, and they are carved twice in the vaulting of the cloisters at Canterbury. Upon a monumental brass in the Church of Wheathampstead, in Hertfordshire, the Shield of HUGO BOSTOCK (about A.D. 1435) bears,—*Arg., three Bats, their wings displayed, sa.*

Imaginary and Fabulous Beings, some of them the creations of heraldic fancy when in a strangely eccentric mood, frequently appear as Supporters ; and, in some cases, they take a part in the blazonry of Shields, or they are borne independently as Badges. A very brief description (all that is necessary) of the greater number of these monsters of *un*natural history will be given in the "Glossary of heraldic terms," in Chapter X. ; consequently, it is enough here merely to refer to them as having a place in blazon. The Griffin or Gryphon, the most worthy of the group, is comparatively common. The Dragon and the Wivern or Wyvern, both of them winged monsters, differ in this respect, that the former has four legs, while the latter has two only. In early blazon this distinction was not always observed. The Cockatrice, always having two legs, is a Wyvern with a cock's head.

Natural Objects of all kinds are blazoned as Charges of Heraldry, and they will be found described and illustrated in their proper places in Chapter X. They include the *Sun*, the *Moon*, the *Stars ;* also such terrestrial objects as *Trees, Flowers, Fruits, Sheaves and Ears of Corn, Leaves, Chaplets, &c.* And with these Charges I may group the always beautiful Fleur de Lys, and the Trefoil, Quatrefoil, Cinquefoil, and Sixfoil.

Of the various Artificial Figures and Devices that

Heralds have charged upon Shields of Arms, it will be unnecessary for me to give detailed descriptions, except when either the heraldic name may require explanation, or some special circumstances connected with any particular figure or device may impart to it peculiar claims for attention. Again I refer to the "Glossary" for notices and examples of all Charges of this class — Annulets, Buckles, Castles, Crowns, Cups, Horseshoes, Keys, Knots, Sickles, Stirrups, Trumpets, and many others.

In blazoning Charges of various classes, Heralds employ *appropriate Epithets and descriptive Terms*, of which the following are characteristic examples:—The *Sun* is "*in splendour.*" The *Moon*, when full, is "*in her complement*": she is a "*Crescent*" when she appears in No. 166, A: she

A | B | C
Crescent. | Increscent. | Decrescent.
| No. 166. |

is "*Increscent*" when as in No. 166, B: and she is "*Decrescent*" when as in No. 166, C. Animals and Birds of prey are said to be "*armed*" of their talons, teeth, and claws. All horned animals, also, except Stags and Antelopes, are "*armed*" of their horns; and a Cock is "*armed*" of his spurs; whilst Griffins and birds of prey are "*armed*" of their beaks and claws (*i.e.* the part of the leg which is unfeathered). Animals are "*hoofed*" or "*unguled*" of their hoofs; and "*langued*" of their tongues. Fierce animals are "*vorant*" of their prey, when represented in the act of devouring it. Deer, when reposing, are "*lodged*," Nos. 25 and 26: when standing, and looking out from the Shield, No. 167, "*at gaze*": when in easy motion, they are termed "*trippant*," or sometimes the word "*tripping*" is substituted, No. 168: and when in rapid motion, they are "*courant,*" "*at speed,*" or sometimes described as "*in full course,*" No. 169. The male Stag is sometimes termed a "*Hart,*" and the female a "*Hind.*"

No. 167.—At Gaze

No. 169.—At Speed

There is really a distinction between the Buck and the Stag, but it is very usually disregarded in Heraldry. The antlers of the Hart are "*Attires,*" their branches are "*Tynes*"; and they are said to be "*attired*" of their

No 168.—Tripping

No. 170.—Stag's Head Cabossed.

antlers. A Stag's head full-faced, but without the neck, as No. 170, is "*cabossed*" or "*caboshed.*"

Eagles and Hawks with expanded wings, as in Fig. 206, are "*displayed.*" Expanded wings may be "*elevated,*" or, if drooping, "*inverted*" or "*in lure.*" Birds about to take wing are "*rising*"; when in flight, they are "*volant*"; when at rest, they are "*close.*" A Bird "*trusses*" its prey. A Peacock having its tail expanded is "*in its pride*"; and this same expression is applied to the Turkey. A Pelican, when feeding its young, is said to be "*in her piety,*" but may be merely "*vulning herself*" if the young are not represented. A Swan, when blazoned "*proper,*" is white with red legs and black beak.

F

Fish, represented swimming in fesse, are "*naiant*"; if they are in pale, they are "*hauriant*," No. 164; but if their heads are to the base, the term "*urinant*" is said to apply, but I cannot say I have so far come across an authenticated instance of the use of this word; if their bodies are bent, as the Dolphin is generally represented, they are "*embowed*," No. 163. Fish, also, are said to be "*finned*" of their fins. Insects are "*volant*." Reptiles are "*gliding*"; or, if they are twined into knots, "*nowed*." Trees of mature growth are "*accrued*"; when with leaves, "*in foliage*" (but these two terms are so seldom used that they may be entirely disregarded); with fruit or seeds, "*fructed*" or "*seeded*"; if without leaves, "*blasted*"; and if their roots are exposed, "*eradicated*." Branches or leaves torn off are "*slipped*."

The terms which denote the attitudes of Lions, all of them described in the next chapter, are equally applicable to other animals. Some other descriptive terms, not noticed here, will be found in the "Glossary" in Chapter X.

CHAPTER IX

THE GRAMMAR OF HERALDRY

SECTION VI

The Lion and the Eagle in Heraldry

" The LION and a King of Beasts."—SHAKESPEARE, *Richard II.*

" The EAGLE, ennobled by Nature in as high a degree of nobility as the chiefest of the terrestrial animals, is the most honourable bearing of Birds."—GWILLIM (*Edition of* 1724).

THE regal dignity of the LION amongst the creatures that are quadrupeds, like himself, would naturally secure for him a position of corresponding eminence in Heraldry. From the dawn of the heraldic era, accordingly, the Lion is blazoned on the Shields of Sovereigns, Princes, and Nobles. The tressured Lion has been already noticed upon the Royal Shield of SCOTLAND, No. 138; and a crowned Lion has also appeared in the same attitude, borne by an English Prince, RICHARD, Earl of CORNWALL, No. 140. From the time that they first possessed any true armorial insignia, the Sovereigns of the Realm of ENGLAND have borne Lions upon their Royal Shield. A Lion was the Ensign of the Native Princes of WALES, as he was of the Kings of LEON, of NORWAY, and of DENMARK, and of the Counts of HOLLAND, HAINAULT, EU, &c. And, in like manner, the Lion was in high favour with the most noble and powerful Barons of England—the MOWBRAYS, BOHUNS, LONGESPEES, FITZ-ALANS, LACIES, PERCIES, SEGRAVES, and such as they.

It was a necessary consequence of his great popularity

that the Lion of Heraldry should be blazoned in various
attitudes, and also variously tinctured, otherwise it would not
be possible duly to distinguish the Lions of different Shields.
Heralds of all countries appear readily to have permitted
their Lions to lay aside their natural tawny hue, and in its
stead to assume the heraldic *or, argent, azure, gules*, and
sable ; but Continental Heralds were not generally disposed
to recognise in their Lions any other attitude than the one
which they held to be consistent with their Lion character,
instincts, and habits—erect, that is, with one hind paw only
on the ground, looking forward towards their prey, so as to
show but one eye, and evidently in the act of preparing to
spring.   This undoubtedly most characteristic attitude is
rampant, No. 171 : and only when he was in this rampant
attitude did the early Heralds consider any Lion to be a
Lion, and blazon him by his true name.   A Lion walking
and looking about him, the early Heralds held to be acting
the part of a leopard : consequently, when he was in any
such attitude, they blazoned him as "*a leopard*."   The animal
bearing that name bore it simply as an heraldic title, which
distinguished a Lion in a particular attitude.   These heraldic
"leopards" were drawn in every respect as other heraldic
"lions," without spots or any leopard*ish* distinction whatever.   This explains the usage, retained till late in the fourteenth century, which assigned to the Lions of the Royal
Shield of England the name of "leopards."   They were so
called, not by the enemies of England for derision and
insult, as some persons, in their ignorance of early Heraldry,
have been pleased both to imagine and to assert; but the
English Kings and Princes, who well knew their "Lions"
to be Lions, in blazon styled them "leopards," because
they also knew that Lions in the attitude of their "Lions"
were heraldic "leopards."   When at length the necessity of
varying the attitude of their Lions was admitted by all
Heralds, in consequence of the greatly increased numbers

of the bearers of Lions, some strict adherents to the original distinctive nomenclature blazoned any Lion that was *not rampant* by the compound term of a "*lion-leopard*," or a "*lion-leopardé*." But that controversy has long been at rest.

The following terms are now in use to denote the various attitudes of the Lion in Heraldry:—

Rampant : erect, one hind paw on the ground, the other three paws elevated, the animal looking forward and having

No. 171.	No. 172.	No. 173.
Rampant.	Rampant Guardant.	Passant.

his tail elevated, No. 171. *Rampant Guardant :* as before, but looking out from the Shield, No. 172. *Rampant Reguardant :* as before, but looking backwards.

Passant : walking, three paws on the ground, the dexter fore-paw being elevated, looking forward, the tail displayed over the back, No. 173. *Passant Guardant :* as before, but

No. 174.	No. 175.	No. 176.
Passant Guardant.	Statant.	Statant Guardant.

looking out from the Shield, No. 174. *Passant Reguardant :* as before, but looking backwards.

Statant : standing, his four paws on the ground, and looking before him, No. 175. *Statant Guardant :* as before, but looking out from the Shield, No. 176: in this example the Lion has his tail extended, but this would be specified in the blazon, as it is an unusual position.   In like manner, if the tail of a Lion in any other attitude be extended, there must be a statement to that effect.

Sejant: sitting down with his head elevated, No. 178.

No. 177.
Couchant.

No. 178.
Sejant.

No. 179.
Dormant.

If he looks out from the Shield, the word *Guardant* is to be added.   A Scottish Lion sejant usually has his fore paws raised in the air, and in English terms of blazon would be described as " *Sejant erect*" or " *Sejant rampant.*"

Couchant: is at rest, the fore legs stretched on the ground, as No. 177.

Dormant: asleep, head resting on fore paws, No. 179.

Salient: in the act of springing, the hind paws on the ground, both the fore paws elevated, No. 180.

No. 180.
Salient.

No. 181.
Double-queued.

No. 182.
Coward.

Queue fourchée: having a forked tail.

Double-queued: two tails, as No. 181, which is a *Lion rampant double-queued.*

Coward: passant reguardant, his tail between his legs, No. 182.

Two Lions rampant, when face to face, are *Counter rampant,* or *Combatant:* when back to back, they are *Addorsed:* when passant or salient in contrary directions, they are *Counter passant* or *Counter salient.*

Lions, whatever their tincture, except it be red, or they are charged on a field of that tincture, are *armed and langued gules;* but *azure* in the case of either of these exceptions, unless the contrary be specified in the blazon. When

No. 183.—Lion's Head.

No. 184.—Lion's Face.

No. 185.—Lion's Jambe.

several Lions appear in one composition, or when they are drawn to a comparatively very small scale, they are sometimes blazoned as "*Lioncels.*" This term "*Lioncel,*" it must be added, when used alone, denotes a *small Lion rampant.*

A Lion's *head* is a Charge: it may be *erased,* as in No. 183; or cut off smooth, when it is *couped.* A Lion's *face* also is a Charge, No. 184; so is his *jambe* or *paw,* No. 185.

No. 186.—Demi-Lion Rampant.

No. 187.—England.

A *demi-lion rampant* is the upper half of his body and the extremity of his tufted tail, as in No. 186.

The LIONS OF ENGLAND are *golden Lions leopardé,* three in number, placed one above the other on a red Shield. They are blazoned—*Gu., three Lions pass. guard., in pale, or,* No. 187.

A Lion in this attitude, of this tincture, and on a field gules, may be blazoned as a "Lion of England." These three Lions *first* appear upon the second Great Seal of RICHARD I., A.D. 1194, on the Shield of the King, No. 188. An earlier Seal, used by Prince JOHN before his brother's accession, has a Shield charged with *two* Lions only, and they are *passant*, No. 189. The first Great Seal of the lion-hearted King has a Shield, bowed in its contour, and charged with a *single* Lion rampant facing to the sinister, or *counter-rampant*, No. 190; and it has been conjectured that, were the whole face of this Shield visible, a

No. 188.   No. 190.   No. 189.
Richard I. : 2nd Gt. Seal.   Richard I. : 1st Gt. Seal.   Prince John : Seal.

second Lion rampant facing to the dexter would appear, thus charging the Shield with *two Lions combattant;* this, however, is a conjecture which is not supported by the authority of many Shields of the same form. A red Shield charged with *two golden Lions passant guardant in pale* (No. 22), and therefore closely resembling No. 189, as I have already shown, has been assigned to WILLIAM I., and his two sons and his grandson, WILLIAM II., HENRY I., and STEPHEN. The Shield bearing the three Lions, No. 187, has been assigned to HENRY II., but it first makes its appearance on the Great Seal of his son. The probability is that up to this period the device was simply a lion, indeterminate in position or numbers. This same Shield has continued, from the time of RICHARD I., to display the ROYAL ARMS of the REALM OF ENGLAND: how, in the course of ages, these Arms become grouped with other insignia, I shall presently have to show.

The *Lion passant* is carefully distinguished in the earliest Rolls as a different Charge from the *Lion passant guardant.* Thus (H. 3), for HAMON LE STRANGE—*Gu., two Lions passant arg.*, No. 191 ; and for JOHN GIFFARD—*Gu., three*

No. 191.—Le Strange.   No. 192.—Giffard.   No. 193.—Mowbray.

Lions pass. arg., No. 192 : for Sir NICHOLAS CAREW (E. 2), —*Or, three Lions pass. sa.*

From the numerous early Shields which bear *Lions rampant*, I select the following examples, associated with names illustrious in English History. For ROGER DE MOWBRAY (H. 3)—*Gu., a Lion rampt. arg.*, No. 193 : this Coat is quartered by the present Lord MOWBRAY, SEGRAVE and

 STOURTON. For FITZ-ALAN, Earl of ARUNDEL —*Gu., a Lion rampt. or* (H. 3), No. 193. For DE LACI, Earl of LINCOLN— *Or, a Lion rampt. purpure* (E. 2), No. 194. For Sir JOHN DE SEGRAVE (E. 2)

No. 194.—De Lacy.

No. 195.
De Segrave.

—*Sa., a Lion rampt. arg., crowned or*, No. 195. For PERCY, Earl of NORTHUMBERLAND—*Or, a Lion rampt. az.*, No. 196 : this Shield is drawn from the fine counter-seal of Sir HENRY DE PERCY, first Lord of Alnwick, who died A.D. 1315.

Two Shields of the DE BOHUNS, Nos. 114, 115, already described, exemplify the display of Lioncels as heraldic charges. An earlier Shield, charged with six Lioncels, but without any Ordinary, was borne by FAIR ROSAMOND'S son, WILLIAM LONGESPÉE, Earl of SALISBURY, A.D. 1226: it is boldly sculptured with his noble effigy in Salisbury Cathedral, and it also appears upon his Seal—*Az., six Lioncels or*, No. 197. The Roll of Edward II., confirmed by his Seal, gives for Sir WM. DE LEYBOURNE the same composition, with a difference in the tincturing—*Az., six Lioncels arg.* Other members of the same family change these tinctures for *gules and or, gules and argent*, and *or and sable* (E. 2).

No. 196 —De Percy.   No. 197.—Longespée.

Examples of Shields which bear Lions or Lioncels with various other charges will be described and illustrated in succeeding chapters.

Lions also fulfil important duties of high honour in English Heraldry as *Crests* and *Supporters*, and also as *Badges*. From the time of EDWARD III. a Crowned Lion, at the first standing on a Cap of Estate, and afterwards upon the Crown, has been the Royal Crest of ENGLAND; a Lion also has always been the Royal Crest of SCOTLAND (see Chapter XVIII.). The Princes of the Royal Houses of England, in like manner, have always borne the Royal Lion distinguished by some "Mark of Cadency" (see

Chapter XII.): No. 198 is the Lion Crest of the BLACK PRINCE, from his Monument at Canterbury, the Lion differenced with the Prince's silver label. The Lion also appears as the Crest of many noble and distinguished families, as the DE BOHUNS, the PERCIES, and the HOWARDS. The Lion Crest of RICHARD. II., sculptured *statant guardant* upon his helm, with a chapeau and mantling, and with the Badge of two Ostrich feathers, in Westminster Hall, is without any crown: No. 199.

As a Royal Supporter of the Arms of *England*, the Lion appears in company with some other creature from the time of HENRY VI., EDWARD IV. sometimes having

No. 198.—Crest of Black Prince.

No. 199.—Crest of Richard II.

his Shield supported by two Lions. On the accession of JAMES I. of Great Britain, the Royal Lion Supporter formed that alliance with the Unicorn of Scotland which still continues, and will continue, it is to be hoped, throughout all time. Lions, as I shall point out more in detail in Chapter XVI., were frequently introduced into the composition of Seals before true heraldic Supporters were in use. In more recent Heraldry the Lion is a favourite Supporter: he now appears supporting the Shields of the Dukes of NORFOLK, ARGYLL, ATHOLL, BEDFORD, GRAFTON, NORTHUMBERLAND, PORTLAND, and WELLINGTON; also, with many others, those of the Marquesses

of BATH, EXETER, HEADFORT, and SALISBURY; of the
Earls of ALBEMARLE, BROWNLOW, CARLISLE, CARNARVON,
CORK, ESSEX, and HARDWICK; of the Viscount HARDINGE;
and of the Barons ARUNDEL, CAMOYS, DUNBOYNE, MONSON,
MOWBRAY, PETRE, and SOUTHAMPTON. As a Supporter
the Lion is represented *rampant, rampant reguardant*,
and *sejant rampant*. Lions also, and Demi-Lions, are
frequently borne as modern Crests.

In our own treatment of the Lions of Heraldry, whatever their attitude or tincture, whatever also the position
they may occupy or the heraldic duty they may discharge,
we are always to draw and to blazon them as true *heraldic
Lions*, while, at the same time, in their expression and
general characteristics they are to be *genuine Lions*.

In becoming fellowship with the Lion, the EAGLE
appears in the earliest English Rolls and examples of Arms.
The Royal bird, however, does not occur in English blazon
so frequently as the Lion; and his appearance often
denotes an alliance with German Princes. A Roll of Arms
(printed in "Archæologia," XXX.) of the year 1275 commences with the Shields of the "EMPEROR OF GERMANY,"
and of the "KING OF GERMANY," which are severally
blazoned as,—"*Or, an Eagle displayed having two heads
sa.*," and, "*Or, an Eagle displayed sable.*" In York Cathedral, in stained glass, there are Shields with both the
double-headed and the single-headed Eagles, all of them
German, which may be considered to have been executed
before the year 1310. In the north choir-aisle at Westminster, the Shield (now mutilated) of the Emperor FREDE-
RICK II. is boldly sculptured by an heraldic artist of the
time of our HENRY III., No. 200; here the Eagle had one
head only. The German Emperors naturally adopted the
Eagle for their heraldic Ensign, in support of their claim to
be successors to the Roman Cæsars; and the Russian
Czars, with the same motive, have also assumed the same

ensign. The Eagle having two heads, which severally look to the dexter and the sinister, as in No. 201, typified a rule that claimed to extend over both the Eastern and the Western Empires; as the Eagle with a single head, No.

No. 200.—In Westminster Abbey.

202, might be considered to have a less comprehensive signification. The Eagles of the Princes of Germany are frequently to be found, blazoned for them, in England.

RICHARD, the second son of King JOHN, in the year

No. 201.—Imperial Eagle.

No. 202.—Royal Eagle.

1256 was elected King of Germany (he is generally styled "King of the Romans"), when he bore the Eagle of the Empire: but the only Seals of this Prince that are known to exist in England display the Shield of his English Earldom of Cornwall, No. 140. His Son EDMUND, who succeeded to his father's Earldom, on his Seals has represented an *Eagle bearing in its beak his Shield of Cornwall*, as in No. 203: this is a peculiarly interesting example of an heraldic usage of striking significance, and it also illustrates the early existence of the sentiment which at a later period led to the adoption of "Supporters" to Shields of Arms. In the early Heraldry of Scotland, a single displayed Eagle is occasionally found supporting an armorial Shield; as in the Seals of ALEXANDER STEWARD, Earl of MENTEITH, A.D.

No. 203.—Cornwall.

No. 204.—Seal of Euphemia Leslie.

1296, and WILLIAM, Earl of DOUGLAS and MAR, A.D. 1378 (SETON's "Scottish Heraldry," Plates VIII. and XII.): sometimes also, as Mr. Seton has observed, "the Eagle's breast is charged with more than one Shield, as in the case of the Seals of MARGARET STEWART, Countess of ANGUS (1366), and EUPHEMIA LESLIE, Countess of ROSS (1381), on both of which *three* escutcheons make their appearance" ("Scottish Heraldry," p. 268, and Plate XII., No. 5): in No. 204 I give a woodcut of this interesting composition; the Shields are, to the dexter, LESLIE—*Arg., on a bend az., three buckles or ;* in the centre, the Arms of the Earl of Ross—*Gu., three*

Lions rampant arg., within a tressure; and, to the sinister, CUMMIN—*Az., three garbs or.* The Imperial Eagle is sometimes represented crowned; the heads also in some examples are encircled with a *nimbus* or glory, as in No. 212. I must add that in the Heraldry of the English Peerage the Imperial Eagle still supports the Shields of some few Peers of different ranks; as, for example, that of Baron METHUEN.

PIERS GAVESTON, who was created Earl of CORNWALL by EDWARD II., bore—*Vert, six Eaglets or,* No. 205, (E. 2

No. 205.—Shield of Piers Gaveston.

No. 206.—Montacute and Monthermer.

and York stained glass): on his Seal, however, the number of the Eaglets is reduced to *three*. Another early example is the Shield of that gallant and persevering knight, RALPH DE MONTHERMER—*Or, an Eagle displayed vert,* No. 206, who became Earl of GLOUCESTER in right of his wife, JOAN, daughter of EDWARD I., and widow of GILBERT DE CLARE, the " Red Earl " : this green Eagle of Monthermer long held a place of high distinction in the mediæval Heraldry of England, marshalled on the Shields of the Earls of SALISBURY and WARWICK; in which, as in the example, No. 206, the Eagle of Monthermer is quartered with the coat of Montacute, No. 20 (page 17). The

Eagle of early Heraldry was sometimes blazoned as an "*Erne*,"[1] and sometimes as an "*Alerion*," WILLIAM D'ERN-FORD (H. 3) bears—*Sa., an Erne displayed arg.*: and, at the same period WM. DE ERNFIELD bears a pair of Erne's or Eagle's Wings, called a "*Vol*," No. 207. From Shields of the fourteenth century which bear Eagles, and are blazoned in the Roll of Edward II., I select the following small group as good examples:—Sir WM. DE MONTGOMERIE—*Or, an Eagle displayed az.*: Sir NICHOLAS DE ETONE—*Gu., a Chevron between three Eaglets arg.*: Sir JOHN DE CHARLES-TONE—*Arg., on a Chevron vert three Eaglets or*: Sir PHILIP DE VERLEY—*Or, a Bend gu., between six Eaglets sa.*: Sir JOHN DE LA MERE—*Arg., on a Bend az. three Eaglets*

No. 207.—A Vol.

No. 209.—De la Mere.

or, No. 209: a Shield bearing a Bend charged with three Eagles, but with different tinctures, No. 88, I have shown to have been the Arms of the Grandisons.

Eagles, under their name of "*Alerions*" (which early Heralds represented without feet and beaks), are blazoned in the same disposition as in No. 209, in the Arms of the Duchy of LORRAINE,—*Or, on a Bend gu. three alerions arg.*: and this device the Dukes of Lorraine *are said* to have borne in commemoration of an exploit of their famous ancestor, GODFREY DE BOLOGNE, *who is also said*, when "shooting against David's tower in Jerusalem," to have "broched upon his arrow three footless birds called alerions." "It is impossible," remarks Mr. Planché upon this legend, "now to ascertain who broached this wonderful

[1] Query if this is not really a herne or heron.—A. C. F. D.

story; but it is perfectly evident that the narrator was the party who drew the long bow, and not the noble GODFREY." Mr. Planché adds, that the Alerions of Lorraine may indicate an alliance with the Imperial House; and he directs attention to "a similarity in sound between 'Alerion' and 'Lorraine,'" and also to a singular Anagram produced by the letters ALERION and LORAINE, which are the same ("Pursuivant of Arms," p. 87). The Arms of Lorraine

No 210.—Shield at St. Albans.   No. 211.—The Austrian Eagle.

are still borne by the Emperor of AUSTRIA : and in England they were quartered by Queen MARGARET of Anjou.

The Roll of Edward II. gives also for Sir HUGH DE BILBESWORTH these arms—*Az.*, *three Eagles displayed or*. A similar Shield, the tinctures changed to—*Arg.*, *three Eagles displayed gu.*, *armed or*, was borne by ROBERT DE EGLESFIELD, Confessor to PHILIPPA of Hainault, Queen of EDWARD III., who in the year 1340 founded Queen's College, Oxford: this Shield of the Founder is borne by the College. One of the Shields in the Chantry of Abbot RAMRYGE in St. Albans Abbey Church bears the same charges—*three eagles displayed*, No. 210: the drawing of the

G

eagle in this Shield is remarkable, and the form of the Shield itself is singularly characteristic of the close of the fifteenth century. Another Shield in the same monument bears a single Eagle, drawn in the same manner, and sculptured with extraordinary spirit. The German Heralds, and also their brethren of France, delight in exaggerations of what I may distinguish as the Westminster Eagle, No. 200. The Austrian Eagle, besides having both its heads crowned, has a large Imperial Crown placed between and above the two heads, as in No. 211. The Imperial Eagle (Holy Roman Empire) sometimes has a nimbus or glory about each head,

No. 212.
Imperial Eagle, with Nimbus.

No. 213.
Eagle "displayed," with Wings erect.

which dignified accessory is represented by a circular line, as in No. 212. In some examples of Eagles, as well in our own Heraldry as in that of continental countries, the wings are represented as *erect* (the more usual form in England), and having the tips of all the principal feathers pointing upwards, as in No. 213. The Eagle borne as the Ensign of Imperial FRANCE was represented grasping a thunder-bolt, in an attitude of vigilance, having its wings displayed, but with the tips of the feathers drooping, as they would be in the living bird; No. 214.

EDWARD III., as a Second Crest, bore an Eagle. An Eagle also was borne for his Crest, as the imperial bird was displayed upon his Shield (No. 206), by Earl RALPH

DE MONTHERMER. In the more recent Heraldry of England, the Eagle is a Supporter to the Shields of the Earls of CLARENDON, COVENTRY, and MALMESBURY; the Viscounts BOLINGBROKE and ST. VINCENT; and the Barons HEYTESBURY, RADSTOCK, WYNFORD, and others. Eagles also and Demi-Eagles are borne as Crests in the English Heraldry of our own day.

In drawing our heraldic Eagles, we can scarcely improve upon some of the examples in which early English Heralds expressed their ideas of the king of birds.

No. 214.—French Imperial Eagle.

CHAPTER X

THE GRAMMAR OF HERALDRY

Section VII

Glossary of Titles, Names, and Terms

"The several denominations given to these tokens of honour . . . with the terms of art given to them."—RANDLE HOME: "Academy of Armoury," A.D. 1688.

In this Glossary, which obviously must be as concise as possible, I shall include no word that is ordinarily well understood, unless some special signification should be attached to it when it is in use in armorial blazon.

Abased. Said of a charge when placed lower than its customary position.

Abatement. A supposed sign of degradation. (See Chapter XII.)

Accollée. Placed side by side.

Accosted. Side by side.

Achievement, or *Achievement of Arms.* Any complete heraldic composition.

Addorsed. Back to back.

Affrontée. So placed as to show the full face or front.

Alerion. A name sometimes given by early Heralds to the heraldic *Eagle,* which, when blazoned under this title, was also sometimes drawn without legs or beak. (See p. 97.)

Ambulant. In the act of walking.

Annulet. A plain ring; sometimes blazoned as a "*false roundle*": in modern English cadency, the difference of the fifth son or brother: No. 154.

Annulettée. Ending in Annulets.

Antelope. Depicted by early Heralds in a conventional manner, but now generally rendered more naturally, the earlier type being termed the heraldic antelope.

Anthony, St. His cross is in the form of the letter T, No. 93.

Antique Crown. See *Eastern Crown.*

Appaumée. Said of a hand, when open, erect, and showing the palm : No. 215.

Arched. Bent, or bowed.

Archbishop. A prelate of the highest order in the English Church ; his heraldic insignia are his *Mitre, Crozier,* and *Pall.* Next to the Royal Family, the Archbishop of Canterbury is the first subject in the realm ; he is styled " Most Reverend

No 215
Badge of Ulster.

Father in God," " by Divine Providence," and " Your Grace." The Archbishop of York is third in rank (the Lord Chancellor being second), and his style is the same, except that he is Archbishop " by Divine permission." Archbishops impale their own arms with those of their see, the latter being marshalled to the dexter.

Argent. The metal silver.

Arm. A human arm. When a charge, crest, or badge, it must be blazoned with full particulars as to position, clothing, &c. If couped between the elbow and the wrist, it is a *cubit arm.*

Armed. A term applied to animals and birds of prey, to denote their natural weapons of offence and defence : thus, a Lion is said to be " *armed* of his claws and teeth " ; a Bull, to be " *armed* of his horns " ; an Eagle, " of its beak and talons."

Armory. Heraldry. Also, a List of Names and Titles, with their respective Arms.

Arms, Armorial Bearings. Heraldic compositions, and the Figures and Devices which form them. (See Chapter I.)

Arms of Community. Borne by Corporate and other Bodies and Communities, as cities, colleges, &c.

Arms of Dominion. Borne by Sovereign Princes, being also the Sovereign arms of the realms over which they rule.

Arms of Office. Borne, with the personal arms, to denote official rank.

Armes Parlantes. Such as are allusive to the Name, Title, Office, or Property of those who bear them: thus, *Leaves* for *Leveson*, a *Castle* for *Castile*, a *Cup* for *Butler*, *Fish* for those who derive revenues from Fisheries, &c. The more usual term is, however, "canting arms." (See *Rebus :* also page 15.)

Arrow. Is *barbed* of its head, and *flighted* of its feathers ; a bundle of arrows is a *sheaf ;* with a blunt head, it is a *bird-bolt.*

At Gaze. A term applied to animals of the chase, to denote their standing still, and looking straight forward: No. 167.

Attires, Attired. The antlers of a Buck, Stag, or Hart : having antlers. A Reindeer is represented in Heraldry with double attires, one pair erect, and the other drooping forward.

Augmentation. An honourable addition to a Coat of Arms, specially granted with a peculiar significance : thus, the "Union" Device of the British Empire, blazoned on an inescutcheon, is the "*Augmentation*" specially granted to the great Duke of WELLINGTON, to be borne on the honour point of his paternal shield.

Augmented. Having an "Augmentation."

Avellane. A variety of the heraldic Cross : No. 109.

Azure. The colour *blue* (indicated by horizontal lines): No. 52.

Badge. A figure or device, distinct from a crest, and capable of being borne without any background or other accessory. Badges are, however, often depicted upon a standard or roundle of the livery colour or colours.

Badges were depicted as a sign of ownership upon property; were worn by servants and retainers, who mustered under the standards on which badges were represented. (See Chapter XV.)

Banded. Encircled with a band.

Banner. A flag, charged with the coat of arms of the owner, displayed over its entire surface. (See Chapter XVII.)

Banneret. A Knight who had been advanced by the King to that higher military rank which entitled him to display a banner.

Bar. One of the Ordinaries: Nos. 81, 82.

Bars Gemelles. Barrulets borne in pairs: Nos. 83, 84.

Barbed. Pointed, as an arrow. The term is also applied to the small green leaves between the petals of heraldic roses. (See *Rose.*)

Barbel. A Fish borne as an allusive device by the family of DE BARRE: No. 162.

Barded. Having horse-trappings.

Bardings. Horse-trappings, often enriched with armorial blazonry. On the Great Seal of EDWARD I. the Bardings of the King's charger for the first time appear adorned with the Royal arms. On both sides of the horse, the head is supposed to be to the dexter. An example is represented in the Seal of ALEXANDER DE BALLIOL, in Chapter XIV.

Barnacles, Breys. An instrument used in breaking horses. A rebus of Sir REGINALD BRAY, architect of St. George's Chapel, Windsor, and repeatedly represented there: No. 216.

Baron. The lowest rank in the British Peerage. A Baron is "Right Honourable," and is styled "My Lord." His coronet, first granted by Charles II., has on a golden circlet six large pearls, of which four appear in representations, as in No. 217. An Irish Baron has no coronet. All a Baron's children are "Honourable."

Baron. A purely heraldic term signifying a *husband*, a *wife* in Heraldry being *femme*.

Baroness. A lady in whom a Barony is vested by inheritance in her own right; also, the wife of a Baron. In either case she is "Right Honourable"; is styled "My Lady," and her coronet is the same as that of a Baron.

Baronet. An hereditary rank, lower than the peerage, instituted in 1612 by JAMES I., who fixed the precedence of Baronets before all Knights, those of the Order of the Garter alone excepted. As originally created, all

No. 216.—Breys.

No. 217.—Circlet of a Baron's Coronet.

Baronets were "of Ulster," or "of Nova Scotia"; afterwards all new creations were "of Great Britain"; now all are "of the United Kingdom." The "Badge of Ulster," generally borne as an augmentation upon a canton or small inescutcheon, is—*Arg., a sinister hand, couped at the wrist and appaumée, gu.,*—No. 215. The arms of Nova Scotia, which may be (but seldom are) similarly borne on a canton or inescutcheon, are—*Arg., on a saltire az., the Royal arms of Scotland.* (See No. 138.) By letters patent of JAMES I., the wives of Baronets have the titles of "*Lady, Madam,* or *Dame,*" at their pleasure prefixed to their names.

Barrulet. The diminutive of a Bar.

Barrulée, Barruly. Barry of ten or more pieces.

Barry. Divided into an even number of Bars, which all lie in the same plane: Nos. 85, 86.

Barry Bendy. Having the field divided by lines drawn *bar-wise,* which are crossed by others drawn *bend-wise:* No. 119.

Bar-wise. Disposed after the manner of a Bar,—crossing

the field, that is, horizontally.   The term *fessways* is
more usually employed.

Base. The lowest extremity : No. 27, B.

Basilisk. A cockatrice having its tail ending in a dragon's
head.

Basinet. A helm fitting close to the head.

Baton. A diminutive of the bend, couped at its extremities.

Battled, or *Embattled*. Having battlements, or bordered, as
No. 38, F.

Beacon, or *Fire Beacon*. An iron case of burning combus-
tibles set on a pole, against which a ladder is placed.

Beaked. Applied to birds, not of prey.

Bearer. An old Scottish term for a *Supporter*.

Bearing, Bearings. Armorial insignia, borne on shields.

Bell. Drawn, and generally blazoned as a *church-bell*, unless
specified to be a *hawk's-bell*.

Belled. Having bells attached.

Bend. One of the Ordinaries : Nos. 111–115.

Bendlet. The diminutive of a bend : No. 117.

Bend-wise, or *In Bend*. Placed in the position of or arranged
in the direction of a bend.

Bendy. Parted bend-wise into an even number of divisions :
No. 116.

Bezant. A golden "Roundle" or disc, flat like a coin : No.
151, and No. 140.

Billet. An oblong figure of any tincture : *Billetée*—strewn
with "Billets" : Nos. 130, 146.

Bird. Many Birds appear in blazon, and they are represented both in heraldic tinctures and "proper"—in
their natural aspect.   (See Chapters VIII. and IX.)

Bird-bolt. An arrow with a blunt head.

Bishop. The Bishops are "by Divine permission," and are
styled "Right Reverend Father in God," and "My Lord
Bishop."   The Bishops of England and Wales are not
Peers but are all "spiritual lords" of Parliament, some

of the junior Bishops, however, having no seats. The Suffragan Bishops are merely assistant Bishops, and are not Lords of Parliament. The heraldic insignia of Bishops consist of *a mitre* and *pastoral staff;* they impale their official and personal arms, as do the Archbishops; and, like them also, they bear no crests, but they ensign their shields with a mitre.

Blasted. Leafless, withered.

Blazon. Heraldry: Armorial Compositions. "To blazon" is to *describe* or to *represent* any armorial Figure, Device, or Composition in an heraldic manner. *Blazoning—Describing* in heraldic language: also, *representing* in an heraldic manner. *Blazonry—*the representation of

No. 218.—Water Bouget.   No. 219.—Bourchier Knot.

any heraldic Figure, Device, or Composition. But the distinction is in practice usually made to employ the word "emblazon" in cases of representation.

Boar. In Heraldry occasionally termed *Sanglier.*

Bordure. A Subordinary: Nos. 139, 140. Also, an important "Difference." (See Chapters XII. and XIII.)

Botoneé, Botoneé Fitcheé. Varieties of the heraldic Cross: Nos. 103, 110. This Cross is also termed *Trefleé.*

Bouget, or *Water Bouget.* A charge, representing the vessels used by the Crusaders for carrying water. The word is an early form of Bucket. Fine early examples occur in the Temple Church, at Beverley Minster, and in a monument at Blyborough, Lincolnshire: No. 218.

Bourchier Knot. The badge of the Bourchier family represented in No. 219.

Bourdon. A palmer's or pilgrim's staff. (See *Pilgrim's Staff.*)

Bow. The archer's weapon, in all its varieties of form, is a charge.

Bowed. Having a convex contour.

Bowen Knot. No. 220.

Braced. Interlaced.

Breys. Barnacles, *q.v.*

Brisure, or *Brizure.* Any difference or mark of cadency.

Buckle. See *Fermaile.*

Burgonet. A helm worn in the sixteenth century.

Cabossed, or *Caboshed.* The head of a stag, or other horned animal, represented full-faced, so as to show the face only : No. 170. In the case of a lion or leopard when the head is so represented it is termed the face.

No. 220.—Bowen Knot.

No. 221.—Caltrap.

Cadency, Marks of. Figures and devices, introduced into armorial compositions, in order to distinguish the different members and branches of the same family. (See *Difference,* and Chapter XII.)

Cadet. A junior member or branch of a family.

Caltrap. An implement formerly strewn on the ground in war to maim horses : No. 221.

Canting Heraldry. Refer to *Armes Parlantes.*

Canton. One of the Subordinaries : Nos. 129, 130.

Cantoned. Placed in the quarters of a shield.

Carbuncle. The same as *Escarbuncle.*

Cartouche. No. 46.

Castle. Generally represented with two or three turrets, as in the shield of Queen Alianore, of Castile : No. 222. Refer to *Tower.*

Celestial Crown. No. 223.

Centaur. Also blazoned as a *sagittary*, and supposed to have been a badge of King Stephen.

Cerceleé, or *Recercelee.* A descriptive term to denote a variety of the heraldic Cross: No. 98.

Chapeau. Also entitled *a cap of dignity, of maintenance,* or

No. 222. – Castle.

No. 223.—Celestial Crown.

of estate. An early symbol of high dignity, and in England of right of Peerage. In addition it is now more frequently met with supporting certain crests: No. 224.

Chaplet. A garland or entwined wreath of leaves and flowers, or of flowers alone. A *chaplet of rue,* sometimes called a *crancelin,* is blazoned bend-wise in the shield of Saxony—

No. 224.—Chapeau.

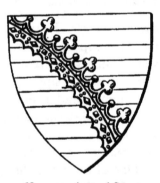

No. 225.—Arms of Saxony.

Barry of ten or and sa., over all a chaplet of rue vert: No. 225. (See *Crancelin.*)

Charge. Any heraldic figure or device. *Charged*—placed on a shield, banner, &c., as any heraldic figure or device may be.

Chequeé, Chequy, Checky. Divided into three, or into more

than three, contiguous rows of small squares, alternately of a metal (or fur) and a colour : No. 68.

Chess rook. A piece used in the game of Chess : borne by *Roke*wood and others : No. 226.

Chevron. One of the Ordinaries : Nos. 123, 125.

Chevronel. A diminutive of the Chevron : No. 124.

Chevroneé, Chevrony. A field composed of a number of pieces divided and disposed *per Chevron :* No. 124A.

Chief. One of the Ordinaries : Nos. 71–75. *In Chief—* placed in the upper part of the shield, or arranged in a horizontal row across the upper part of the field.

No. 226.
Chess Rook.

No. 227.
Cinque-foil.

No. 228.—Clarions.

Cinque-foil. A flower or leaf of five foils : No. 227.

Civic Crown. A wreath of oak-leaves and acorns.

Clarenceux. See *Herald.*

Clarion. An ancient musical instrument, a badge, apparently, of the DE CLARES. By some this charge is supposed to represent a *lance-rest*, and is sometimes so blazoned : No. 228, which shows two varieties of form.

Clecheé. A variety of the heraldic Cross : No. 105.

Close. With closed wings.

Closet. A Diminutive of the Bar, one half its width.

Cloueé. Fastened with Nails, and showing the Nail-heads : No. 150.

Coat Armour. True armorial or heraldic bearings, duly granted or inherited, and rightly borne : so entitled, from having been depicted by warriors of the Middle Ages upon their *surcoats*, worn by them over their armour.

Coat of Arms. A complete armorial composition, properly what would be charged upon a Shield or Banner, but often used as an alternative for *Achievement, q.v.*

Cockatrice. A fabulous creature, represented in No. 229.

Collar. One of the insignia of Orders of Knight-hood, worn about the neck. Also any ornament or distinction worn in the same manner. Knights occasionally wore collars charged with their own badge. In addition to their badges of the Red and White Rose, examples exist showing that adherents of the rival houses of York and Lancaster some-

No. 229.
Cockatrice.

times wore collars, the former formed of alternate *Suns and Roses*, No. 230; and the latter, of the letter S continually repeated, No. 231. No certain origin has been discovered for the Lancastrian "Collar of S.," but it has been suggested that it represents the word

No. 230.—A Collar of York.

No. 231.—A Collar of Lancaster.

SOVERAYGNE, the motto of HENRY IV. No. 230 is from the Brass to HENRY BOURCHIER, K.G., Earl of Essex, at Little Easton, Suffolk, A.D. 1483; and No. 231 from the Brass to Lord CAMOYS, K.G., at Trotton, Sussex, A.D. 1424.

College of Arms, or *Heralds' College.* (See *Herald.*)

Colour. See Chapter V., page 41. The term "*Colours*" is applied to Flags, particularly to those of infantry regi-ments, and to such as are displayed at sea. (See Chapter XVII.)

Combatant. Two lions, or other animals of prey, rampant and face to face.

Compartment. In Scottish Heraldry, "a kind of carved

panel, of no fixed form, placed below the escutcheon, bearing the supporters, and usually inscribed with a motto or the name and designation of the owner."—*Seton.* Other objects placed below the shield are met with under this description.

Componée, Compony, or *Gobony.* A single row of small squares alternately of two tinctures or furs: No. 66. (See *Counter Componée.*)

Complement, In her. Applied to the moon when full.

Compound Quartering. The quartering of a quarter, or division of a quartered Coat-of-Arms. (See page 34.)

Compound Arms. Arms formed from the combination of the bearings of two or more distinct coats, to produce a single compound coat.

Conjoined in Lure. Two wings united, their tips in base.

Contoise. A flowing scarf, worn attached to the helm before 1350. Two examples occur in effigies in Exeter Cathedral, and another in Westminster Abbey.

Contournée. Facing to the sinister.

Cornish Chough. A bird like a crow, black, with red beak and legs.

Coronet. An ensign of rank worn upon the head, in use in England from about the middle of the fourteenth century, but without any distinctive tokens of gradations of rank until a later period. In modern times English Coronets have enclosed a velvet cap with a bullion tassel. This cap originated in the cap of estate worn by Peers. (See *Prince, Duke, Marquess, Earl, Viscount,* and *Baron.*)

Cotise. A diminutive of the Bend or other Ordinary, being one-fourth of their width. *Cotised.* When a Bend or Chevron is placed between two Cotises, or when a Fesse or Bar is placed between two Barrulets. Nos. 114, 115.

Couchant. In repose. No. 177.

Couchée. Said of a Shield when suspended from the sinister extremity of the chief, or when placed as if it were so suspended. No. 49.

Count, Countess. *Count,* in Latin "Comes," the same as Earl. *Countess,* the wife of an Earl: she is "Right Honourable," and styled "My Lady": her coronet is the same as that of an Earl.

Counter. Reversed or opposite.

Counter-changing. See page 44, and Nos. 70, 126.

Counter Componée. Double *Componée,* or two conjoined rows of alternately tinctured squares. No. 67.

Counter-Embattled. A term in use for a fesse, bar, or chevron when embattled on both edges.

Counter-seal. Early seals were generally impressed on both sides; and the seals thus were produced from two dies or matrices. The two sides were severally called the *seal* and the *counter-seal,* the latter being termed the *reverse* of the compound composition. Every such double impression constituted a single seal. Both seal and counter-seal were sometimes used alone; and the counter-seal was regarded as a private seal, or *secretum.*

Couped. Cut off *smoothly*—the reverse of "erased."

Couple-close. Half a *chevronel.*

Courant. Running.

Courtesy, Titles of. Nominal degrees of rank, conceded to, and borne by, the Eldest Sons of Dukes, Marquesses, and Earls, and other titles used by their younger children and all children of Viscounts and Barons.

Coward, Cowed. A term applied to an animal with its tail between its legs. No. 182.

Crampet. The decorated end of a sword-scabbard.

Crancelin. From the German *kranzlein,* "a small garland," applied to the chaplet that crosses the shield of Saxony, No. 225: this charge is also blazoned as *a bend treflée vert, a bend archée coronettée,* or *a coronet extended in bend:* it is said to be an augmentation conferred, with the

Dukedom of Saxony, on BERNHARD of Ascania, by the Emperor BARBAROSSA. The Emperor took from his head his own chaplet of rue, and threw it across the shield of Duke Bernhard. This story is probably untrue.

Crenellated. Embattled.

Crescent. No. 166. In modern English cadency, the difference of the second son, or house.

Cresset. A beacon.

Crest. A figure or device originally worn upon a helm, and now generally represented above a Shield of arms. Crests at first were ensigns of high honour, and their use was restricted to a few persons of eminence: they

No. 232.—Crest-Coronet.

No. 233.—Crest-Wreath.

were attached by a *wreath,* or *torse,* or by a *coronet,* to the helm or basinet; and sometimes a crest stood upon a cap of estate. Crests are still represented standing upon either a wreath, or a cap, or issuing from a coronet: but in our own Heraldry a *crest-coronet* must always be carefully distinguished from those coronets that are insignia of princely and noble rank. Crests are not borne by ladies, a reigning Sovereign only excepted. (See *Panache, Rebus,* and Chapter XIV.)

Crest-Coronet. A coronet from which issues, or which supports, a crest. No. 232.

Crest-Wreath, or *Torse.* In the Middle Ages, of rich materials and costly workmanship; now represented as being formed of two rolls of silk of the principal metal and colour in the arms, which are twisted to show

H

the metal and colour alternately. The earliest examples are about A.D. 1375. No. 233 shows three varieties of representation. (See Chapter XIV.)

Crined. Having a mane or hair.

Cross. One of the Ordinaries. Nos. 90–110.

Crown. The ensign of Royal and Imperial dignity; in Heraldry borne as a charge, and also used to denote the rank of a Sovereign Prince. The Crown that is generally borne as a charge is represented without arches, and resembling No. 232. Certain other crowns, each distinguished by an appropriate title, are also sometimes borne on shields, or introduced as heraldic accessories. (See *Celestial, Eastern* or *Radiated, Mural, Naval,* and *Vallary* Crowns.) The different forms assumed at different periods by the Royal Crown of England are faithfully exemplified in the seals and the coinage of the successive Sovereigns, and several fine examples are preserved in the Royal effigies. The adornment of the regal circlet was arbitrary before the fifteenth century; still, it always was enriched with gems and surmounted by golden foliage. HENRY V. first arched his crown; and by HENRY VI. the circlet was first heightened with alternate crosses-patée and fleurs de lys. This arrangement has since been retained, the subsequent alterations being restricted to changes in the number and in the contour of the arches. The crown of His Majesty the KING has the circlet heightened with four crosses and as many fleurs de lys; from the crosses rise the arches, which are surmounted by a mound and a cross-patée. No. 234. This, the heraldic crown, is not an exact reproduction of the actual crown of the King.

Crozier. Strictly, the cross-staff of an archbishop; distinguished by its form from the pastoral-staff with a crook-head, of bishops; but the term is loosely and very generally applied also to the crook-headed pastoral-staff.

Crusilee, Crusily. Having the field semée of crosses-crosslets, or of other small crosses, their peculiar form (when not crosslets) being specified.

Cubit-arm. A human arm couped between the elbow and the wrist.

Cup, Covered Cup. A vessel formed like a chalice, and

No. 234.
Crown of H. M. The King.

No. 235.
Dacre Knot and Badges.

having a raised cover; borne by the BOTILERS, BUTLERS, &c.

Cushion, Pillow, Oreiller. Unless described of another form, square or oblong, and with a tassel at each corner.

Dacre Knot. No. 235. (See *Knot.*)

Dancetté. No. 38B. In early blazon, a fesse dancetté is styled simply "a *dancette*" or "a *danse.*" Nos. 78, 146; and No. 20A, page 70.

Debruised. When an ordinary surmounts an animal or another charge.

Decrescent. A half-moon having its horns to the sinister. No. 166C.

Deer. In general practice very little if any differentiation is made between the *Stag,* the *Buck,* and the *Hart;*

the female is a *Hind*, and of course is without attires. (See Chapter VIII.)

Degrees. A term applied to the steps upon which a Cross Calvary is represented.

Demembered, *Dismembered*. Cut into pieces, but without any alteration in the form of the original figure.

Demi. The half. The upper, front, or dexter half, unless the contrary be specified. No. 186.

Depressed. Surmounted.

Dexter. The right side. No. 27C.

Diaper, *Diapering*. Surface decoration. No. 68.

Difference, *Differencing*. An addition to, or some change in, a Coat-of-Arms, introduced for the purpose of distinguishing Coats which in their primary qualities are the same. (See Chapters XII. and XIII.)

Dimidiated. Cut in halves per pale, and one half removed: No. 250. (See Chapter XI.)

Disclosed. With expanded wings, in the case of birds that are *not* birds of prey. The contrary to *Close*.

Displayed. Birds of prey with expanded wings. No. 200.

Disposed, *Disposition*. Arranged, arrangement.

Dividing Lines. No. 38: also Nos. 27–37.

Dolphin. A favourite fish with Heralds. The heraldic Dolphin of antiquity is exemplified in No. 8; that of the Middle Ages in No. 163.

Dormant. Asleep, as in No. 179.

Double-queued. Having two tails. No. 181.

Doubling. The lining of a Mantle or Mantling.

Dove-tail. No. 381.

Dragon. A winged monster having four legs. No. 236.

Duke. The highest rank and title in the British Peerage; first introduced by EDWARD III. in the year 1337, when he created the BLACK PRINCE the first English Duke (in Latin, "*Dux*"). A Duke is "Most Noble"; he is styled "My Lord Duke," and "Your Grace"; and all his younger sons are "Lords," and all his daughters "Ladies," with the prefix "Right Honourable." His eldest son bears, by courtesy, his father's "second title"; and, accordingly, he generally bears the title of Marquess. Whatever his title, however, the rank of the eldest son of a Duke is always the same, and it assigns to him precedence between Marquesses and Earls. The Coronet of a Duke, arbitrary in its adornment until the sixteenth century was far advanced, is now a circlet, heightened with eight conventional strawberry-leaves, of which in representations three and two half-leaves are shown; No. 237. It encloses a velvet cap. The

No. 236.—Dragon.

No. 237.—Circlet of a Duke's Coronet.

present ducal coronet is represented in the portrait of LUDOVICK STUART, K.G., Duke of RICHMOND and LENNOX, who died in 1624; the picture, the property of the Crown, is at Hampton Court.

Ducal Coronet. A term commonly, but not very accurately, applied to a *Crest Coronet.* No. 232.

Duchess. The wife of a Duke. She is "Most Noble," and is styled "Your Grace." Her coronet is the same as that of a Duke.

Eagle. See Chapter IX., page 92.

Eaglet. An Eagle on a small scale.

Earl. In Latin, "Comes"; in French, "Comte" or "Count." Before 1337, the highest, and now the third degree of rank and dignity in the British

Peerage. An Earl is "Right Honourable"; he is styled "My Lord"; his eldest son bears his father's "second title," generally that of Viscount; his other sons are styled "Honourable," but all his daughters are "Ladies." The circlet of an Earl's Coronet has eight lofty rays of gold rising from the circlet, each of which supports a large pearl, while between each pair of these rays there is a golden strawberry-leaf. In representations five of the rays and pearls are shown; No. 238. Elevated clusters of pearls appear in an Earl's coronet —that of THOMAS FITZ ALAN, Earl of ARUNDEL—as early as 1445; but the present form of the coronet may be assigned to the second half of the following century.

No. 238.—Circlet of an Earl's Coronet.　　　No. 239.—Eastern Crown.

Eastern, Radiated, or *Antique Crown.* No. 239.

Electoral Bonnet. A cap of crimson velvet guarded with ermine, borne, in the Royal Arms, over the inescutcheon of the arms of Hanover from 1801 till 1816. No. 240.

Embattled, and *Counter-Embattled.* A term applied to a fess or bar when so depicted both above and below.

Embowed. Bent. An arm embowed has the elbow to the dexter, unless blazoned to the contrary.

Embrued. Stained with blood.

Endorse. A diminutive of the pale.

Enfiled. Pierced, *e.g.* with a sword, or surrounded, *e.g.* with a coronet.

Engrailed. The border-line, No. 38D.

Enhanced. Raised towards the chief. Thus the arms of BYRON, No. 241, are—*Arg., three bendlets enhanced gu.*

Ensigned. Adorned; having some ensign of honour placed above—as a coronet above a shield.

Entire. Said of a charge when it is necessary to express that it extends to the border lines of a shield, coat, or banner; also of a shield, coat, or banner of arms, when borne without any difference or mark of cadency.

Entoire, Entoyre. A bordure charged with a series of inanimate figures or devices, as crosslets, roundles, &c.; to a similar bordure of living figures the term *Enaluron* is applied. These are not terms ordinarily in use.

Enveloped, Environed. Surrounded.

Equipped. Fully armed, caparisoned, or provided.

Eradicated. Torn up by the roots.

No. 240.—Electoral Bonnet.　　　No. 241 —Shield of Byron.

Erased. Torn off with a ragged edge; the contrary to *Couped.*

Ermine, Ermines, Erminois. Nos. 57–60 and 57A. The animal, the ermine, sometimes appears in blazon, and an ermine spot is borne as a charge.

Erne. An eagle. (See p. 96.)

Escarbuncle. No. 19.

Escroll. A ribbon charged with a motto; also a ribbon, coiled at its extremities, borne as a charge.

Escutcheon. An heraldic shield: Nos. 39–40: also No. 27. An Escutcheon, when borne as a charge, is usually blazoned as an "*Inescutcheon*": thus, the Arms of HAY are,—*Arg., three inescutcheons gu.:* see also Nos. 131, 133.

Escutcheon of Pretence. A shield charged upon the centre of the field of another shield of larger size, and bearing a distinct Coat-of-Arms.

Escallop, or *Escallop-Shell.* A beautiful and favourite charge; No. 165.

Esquire. A rank below that of Knight. Besides those Esquires who are personal attendants of Knights of Orders of Knighthood at their installations, this title is held by most attendants on the person of the Sovereign, and all persons holding or having held the Sovereign's commission in which they are so styled.

Estate. Dignity and rank.

Estoile. A star with wavy rays or points, which are six, eight, or sometimes even more in number: No. 242. (See *Mullet.*)

No. 242
Estoile.

False. Said of any charge when its central area is removed—thus, an *Annulet* is a "false roundle."

Fan, or *Winnowing Fan,* or *Vane.* The well-known implement of husbandry of that name, borne by the Kentish Family of De Sevans or Septvans—*Az., three fans or* (E. 2). This shield appears in the Brass to Sir R. DE SEVANS, A.D. 1305, at Chartham, in Kent, and in the cloisters at Canterbury.

Fan Crest. An early form of decoration for the knightly helm, exemplified in the 2nd Great Seal of RICHARD I., and in many other Seals, until about A.D. 1350. (See Chapter XIV.)

Feathers. Generally those of the Ostrich, sometimes of the swan, the turkey, and a few other birds, borne generally as Crests and Badges, both singly and in plumes or groups. (See *Ostrich Feather, Panache,* and Chapter XIV.)

Femme. The Wife, as distinguished from the "Baron," the Husband.

Fer-de-Moline, or *Mill-rind.* The iron affixed to the centre of a mill-stone; No. 243: a modification of the *Cross-moline;* No. 97.

Fermail (plural *Fermaux*). A buckle: No. 244. Several varieties of form appear in blazon, it being usual to specify them as round, oval, square, or lozenge-shaped. They are always blazoned as buckles.

Fess, or *Fesse.* One of the Ordinaries: Nos. 76–80. *Fesse-wise, In Fesse.* Disposed in a horizontal line, side by side, *across the centre* of the field, and over the *Fesse-Point* of a shield: No. 27, M.

Fetter-lock. . A shackle and padlock—a Yorkist Badge: No. 245; is from the Brass to Sir S. DE FELBRIGGE, K.G., at

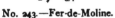

No. 243.—Fer-de-Moline.   No. 244.—Fermails.   No. 245.—Fetter-lock.

Felbrigg, Norfolk, A.D. 1414; this, however, being a very unusual shape.

Field. The entire surface of a Shield or Banner, or of an Ordinary.

File. A Label, from the Latin *filum,* a narrow ribbon.

Fillet. A diminutive of a Chief.

Fimbriated. Bordered—the border (which is narrow) lying in the same plane with the object bordered: No. 89.

Fish. Numerous Fish appear in blazon, and generally in their proper tinctures. They are borne as allusive charges, and also as types of some connection between those persons who bear them and the sea or lakes or rivers. Mr. Moule has published an admirable volume on the "Heraldry of Fish," beautifully illustrated with examples drawn by his daughter. (See p. 77.)

Fitchée. Pointed at the base, as in No. 110.

Flanches, Flasques. Subordinaries: Nos. 141, 142.

Fleur de lys. The beautiful heraldic device so long identified
with the history of France: No. 246 (from the
monument of EDWARD III.). The fleur de lys,
derived, it would seem, from the flower of a lily
resembling the iris, was adopted by LOUIS VII.
(A.D. 1137–1180) as his royal ensign, and in due
time it was regularly charged upon a true Shield
of Arms. Originally the Royal Shield of France was
—*Az., semée of fleurs de lys, or ;* the fleurs de lys scattered

No. 246.
Fleur de lys.

No. 247.—France Ancient.　　　No. 248.—France Modern.

freely over the field, and the Shield itself having the
appearance of having been cut out of a larger object,
over the whole surface of which the flowers had been

No. 249.
Edmund, Earl of Lancaster.

No. 250.
Margaret, Queen of Edward I.

semée. This Shield of France is distinguished as "*France
Ancient*": No. 247. About A.D. 1365, CHARLES V. of
France reduced the number of the fleurs de lys to three;

and this Shield is now known as "*France Modern*":
No. 248. In the year 1275, EDMUND, first Earl of Lancaster, the second son of HENRY III., married BLANCHE of Artois, when he differenced his shield of England with *a label of France—a blue label charged on each point with three golden fleurs de lys :* No. 249 ; thus, for the first time

No. 251.—Seal of Margaret, second Queen of Edward I.

did the armorial insignia of England and France appear together upon the same Shield. In 1299 EDWARD I. married his second Queen, MARGARET of France, and then this royal lady placed on one of her Seals a Shield of England and France dimidiated: No. 250. On another of her Seals, a very noble example of the Seal-engraver's art, Queen MARGARET displayed the Shield of King EDWARD I., her husband, *surrounded*,

on the field of the Seal, with her father's fleurs de lys:
No. 251. On the Seals of ISABELLE of France, Queen
of EDWARD II., the same dimidiated shield, and another
shield quartering the arms of England with *France Ancient*
and two other French coats (*Navarre* and *Champagne*)
appear. Then Prince JOHN of ELTHAM charged a
"bordure of France" *upon his shield*, No. 24; thus
applying the suggestion of the Seal of Queen MARGARET,
No. 251, in such a manner as was consistent with the
advanced condition of heraldic art. On his accession
in 1327, EDWARD III. placed a fleur de lys on each

No. 252.
Shield of Edward III., A.D. 1340.

No. 253.
Shield of Henry IV., about A.D. 1405.

side of the Shield of England upon his Great Seal : and
in 1340, when he claimed the crown of France, EDWARD
quartered France Ancient with his lions of England:
No. 252. Shortly after his accession, perhaps in 1405,
in order to conform to the altered blazonry of the
French sovereigns, HENRY IV. quartered *France Modern*
on his shield: No. 253. The position of the three
fleurs de lys was more than once changed in the Royal
Shield of England (as I shall hereafter show more particularly) after the accession of the STUARTS; and they
were not finally removed till the first year of the nine-
teenth century. The fleur de lys is also borne on many
English Shields, disposed in various ways. In modern

cadency the fleur de lys is the difference of the sixth son, or house.

Fleurettée, Florettée. Terminating in, or bordered with, fleurs de lys; also, *semée de lys.*

Fleurie, or *Fleury.* Ending as No. 100; also, *semée de lys.*

Flexed. Bowed, bent.

Flighted. Feathered, as arrows are.

Fly. The length, and also the side of a flag farthest from the staff.

Foliated. Crisped, or formed like a leaf.

Fountain. No. 153.

Fourchée, Queue Fourchée. A term applied to a lion with a forked tail.

Fret, or *Frette.* A subordinary: No. 148. *Frettée, Fretty*: covered with fretwork: No. 149

Fructed. Bearing fruit or seeds.

Furs. See p. 41: Nos. 57–65.

Fusil. An elongated Lozenge: No. 20A, p. 70. *Fusillée,* or *Fusilly.* A field entirely composed of Fusils, all lying in the same plane.

Fylfot. A peculiar cruciform figure, supposed to have a mystic signification, found in military and ecclesiastical decorations in England, and on Eastern coins, &c.: Nos. 254, 255; the latter example is from the monument of Bishop BRONSCOMBE, in Exeter Cathedral.

No. 254   No. 255.
Fylfot.

Gad, Gadlyng. A spike, knob, or other figure, projecting from the knuckles of gauntlets.

Galley. An ancient ship. (See *Lymphad.*)

Garb. A sheaf of wheat; if of any other grain, this to be specified.

Garnished. Adorned in a becoming manner.

Garter, Order of the. See Chapter XIX.

Garter King-of-Arms. The chief of the official Heralds of England, and officer of arms of the Order of the Garter. (See *Herald.*)

Gemelles. See *Bars Gemelles.*

Gem-Ring. A ring for the finger, set with a jewel.

Genet. A spotted animal, somewhat like a marten: a badge of Queen JOANNA of Navarre.

George, Saint. The Patron Saint of England. The circumstances which led to his association with England are unknown. His Shield of arms, *a red cross on a silver field*, first appears in English Heraldry in the fourteenth century: No. 1.

George, The. A mounted figure of the Saint in the act of piercing the dragon with his lance, and worn as a pendant to the collar of the Order of the Garter; added to the insignia of the Order, with the Collar, by HENRY VII. The *Lesser George* has the same group on an enamelled field, and surrounded by the Garter of the Order, the whole forming a "jewel," generally oval in shape: it was introduced by HENRY VIII., and is now worn pendent from the dark-blue ribbon of the Order, the ribbon passing over the left shoulder and the jewel hanging on the right side of the wearer. Originally, this "Lesser George" was worn from either a gold chain or a black ribbon: by Queen ELIZABETH the colour of the ribbon was changed to sky-blue, and it assumed its present darker hue in the reign of CHARLES II.

Gerattyng. Differencing by the introduction of small charges. It is an early term, now obsolete.

Gimmel-ring. Two annulets, interlaced.

Girt, Girdled. Encircled, or bound round.

Gonfannon. A long flag, pointed or swallow-tailed at the fly, and displayed from a transverse bar attached to a staff.

Gorged. Encircled round the throat.

Gouttée, Guttée. Sprinkled over with drops either of gold —*gouttée d'or;* of silver—*d'eau;* of blue—*de larmes* (tears); of red—*de sang* (blood); or of black—*de poix* (pitch).

Grand Quarters. The four primary divisions of a Shield, when it is divided *quarterly:* Nos. 30, 36, 37. The term "Grand Quarter" may be used to signify a primary quarter or division of a quartered Shield or Coat, and to distinguish such a quarter when *it is quartered.*

Grieces. Steps.

Guardant. Looking out from the field: Nos. 172, 174, 176, 187.

Guige. A Shield-belt, worn over the right shoulder, and frequently represented in heraldic compositions as if sustaining a Shield of arms: Nos. 48, 49.

Gules. Red: No. 53.

Gurges, or *Gorges.* A charge formed of a spiral line of blue on a white field, and supposed to represent a whirlpool: borne (H. 3) by R. DE GORGES: No. 256.

Gyron. A Subordinary. *Gyronny.* A field divided into Gyrons: No. 147. (See page 70.)

Habited. Clothed.

Hames, Heames. Parts of horses' harness.

No. 256.
Shield of R. de Gorges.

Hammer, or *Martel.* Represented in blazon much in the same shape as the implement in common use (H. 3).

Harp. A device and badge of Ireland. The Irish Harp of gold with silver strings on a blue field forms the third quarter of the Royal Arms.

Hart. A stag, with attires; the female is a *Hind:* page 81.

Hastilude. A tournament.

Hatchment. An achievement of arms in a lozenge-shaped frame, placed upon the front (generally over the principal entrance) of the residence of a person lately deceased. In the case of the decease of an unmarried person, or of a widower or widow, the whole of the field of the hatchment is painted black ; but in the case of a married person, that part only of the field is black which adjoins the side of the achievement occupied by the armorial insignia of the individual deceased. Thus, if a husband be deceased, the dexter half of the field of the hatchment is black, and the sinister white ; and so,

No. 257.—Hawk's Lure.

No. 258.—Hawk's Bells and Jesses.

in like manner, if the wife be deceased, the sinister is black and the dexter white.

Hauriant. A fish in pale, its head in chief.

Hawk's bells, jesses, and lure. A falconer's decoy, formed of feathers with their tips in base, and joined by a cord and ring, No. 257; also bells with straps to be attached to hawks, No. 258.

Heightened. Raised ; placed above or higher.

Heights. Applied to plumes of feathers which are arranged in rows or sets, one rising above another. See *Panache.*

Helm, Helmet. Now placed as an accessory above a Shield of arms, and bearing its Crest after the fashion in which, in the Middle Ages, both Helm and Crest were actually

worn in tournaments. A modern usage distinguishes
Helms as follows:—The Sovereign—Helm of gold,
with six bars, set *affrontée*, No. 259; Noblemen—
Helm of silver, garnished with gold, set in profile, and
showing five bars, No. 260; Baronets and Knights—
of steel with silver ornaments, without bars, the vizor
raised, set *affrontée*, No. 261; Esquires and Gentlemen

HELMS
OF

No. 259.—The Sovereign.   No. 260.—Nobles.

No. 261.   No. 262.   No. 263.
Baronets and Knights.   Esquires and Gentlemen.

—of steel, the vizor closed, and set in profile, Nos.
262, 263. The Helms that appear on early Seals and
in other heraldic compositions till about A.D. 1600,
are all set in profile, and the shield generally hangs
from them *couchée*, as in No. 49. In these early compositions, the shield is small in proportion to the helm
and its accessories.

I

Hemp-brake, Hackle. An instrument having saw-teeth, used for bruising hemp.

Heneage Knot. No. 264.

Herald. An officer of arms. The Heralds of England were incorporated by RICHARD III.; and from Queen MARY, in 1555, they received a grant of Derby House, on the site of which, between St. Paul's Cathedral and the Thames, stands their present official residence, HERALDS' COLLEGE, or the COLLEGE OF ARMS. The college now consists of three KINGS-OF-ARMS—*Garter,*

No. 264.—Heneage Knot.

No. 265.—Arms of the Heralds' College.

Clarenceux, and *Norroy;* six HERALDS, who have precedence by seniority of appointment—*Chester, Lancaster, Richmond, Windsor, York,* and *Somerset;* and four PURSUIVANTS—*Rouge Dragon, Portcullis, Rouge Croix,* and *Bluemantle.* The official habit is a *Tabard,* emblazoned with the Royal Arms, and the Kings and Heralds wear a *Collar of SS.* The Kings have a Crown, formed of a golden circlet, from which rise sixteen oak-leaves, nine of which appear in representations; and the circlet itself is charged with the words, *Miserere mei Deus secundum magnam misericordiam tuam* ("Have mercy on me, O God, according to thy great loving-kindness").

The supreme head of the English Heralds, under the

SOVEREIGN, is the EARL MARSHAL, an office hereditary in the family of the DUKE OF NORFOLK.   The Arms of the College are—*Arg., a cross gu., between four doves their dexter wings expanded and inverted az.*: No. 265 ; Crest—*From a crest-coronet or, a dove rising az.* ; Supporters—*Two lions ramp. guard. arg., ducally gorged or.* Each of the Kings has his own official arms, which he impales with his paternal coat on the *dexter* side of the shield.   The Arms of Garter are—*Arg., a cross gu. ; on a chief az., a ducal coronet encircled with a Garter of the Order, between a lion of England and a fleur de lys, all or.* · Clarenceux and Norroy have the same shield, but the former has *a lion of England only, crowned, on a chief gules ;* and the latter, *on a chief per pale az. and gu.,* has *a similar lion between a fleur de lys and a key, all of gold.*

There is also another King styled " Bath," who is specially attached to the Order of the Bath ; he is not a member of the College.

" Lyon King-of-Arms " is the chief Herald of Scotland ; and the establishment over which he presides is styled the " Lyon Office."   The Arms of the Office are—*Arg., a lion sejant erect and affronté gu., holding in his dexter paw a thistle slipped vert, and in the sinister an escutcheon of the second ; on a chief az., a saltire of the first :* No. 266.

No. 266.
Arms of Lyon Office.

Ireland is the heraldic province of " Ulster King-of-Arms." His official armorial ensigns differ from those of Garter only in the *charges of the chief,* which are *a lion of England between a golden harp and a portcullis.*

Herison. A hedgehog.

Hill, Hillock. A mound of earth.

Hirondelle. A swallow.

Hoist. The depth of a flag from chief to base. See *Fly.*

Honour Point. No. 27, L.

Humettée. Cut short at the extremities.

Hurst. A clump of trees.

Hurt. A blue roundle.

Illegitimacy. See Chapter XII.

Imbrued, or *Embrued.* Stained with blood.

Impaled. Conjoined per pale.

Impalement. The uniting of two (or more) distinct coats per pale, to form a single achievement.

Imperially Crowned. Ensigned with the Crown of England.

Incensed, Inflamed. On fire; having fire issuing forth.

Increscent. No. 166, B. See *Decrescent.*

Indented. No. 38, A.

Inescutcheon. An heraldic Shield borne as a charge. This term is sometimes used to denote an *Escutcheon of Pretence.*

In bend. Disposed in the position of a bend; *In Chevron, In Chief, In Cross, In Fesse,* &c. Disposed after the manner of a chevron, or in the chief of the shield, or in the form of a cross, &c.

In Foliage. Bearing leaves.

In Lure. Wings conjoined in the form of a hawk's lure.

In her piety. A term applied to a pelican feeding her young.

In Pretence. A term applied to a single inescutcheon placed upon and in the centre of a larger escutcheon.

In Pride. Having the tail displayed, as a peacock's.

In Quadrangle. When four charges are so disposed that one is in each quarter of the shield.

In Splendour. The sun irradiated.

Irradiated. Surrounded by rays of light.

Issuant. Proceeding from, or out of.

Jambe, Gambe. The leg of a lion, or other beast of prey: No. 185.

Jelloped. Having wattles and a comb, as a cock.

Jesses. Straps for hawk's bells.

Jessant. Shooting forth. *Jessant de lys.*—A combination of a leopard's face and a fleur-de-lys : No. 267.

Joust. A tournament.

Jupon. A short, sleeveless surcoat, worn over armour from about 1340 to about 1405. It is often charged with armorial insignia, and thus is a true " coat of arms."

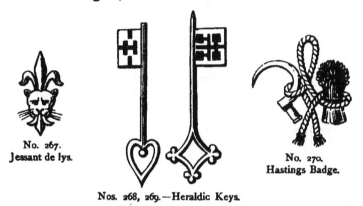

No. 267.
Jessant de lys.

Nos. 268, 269.—Heraldic Keys.

No. 270.
Hastings Badge.

Key. When represented in early blazon, Keys have always elegant forms. No. 268 is from Peterborough Cathedral, and No. 269 from Exeter.

King-of-Arms. See *Herald.*

Knighthood, Orders of: Knights. See Chapter XVI.

Knot. An intertwined cord, borne as a badge. The varieties of this device are—The *Bourchier*, No. 219 ; the *Bowen*, No. 220 ; the *Harington* (the same as a *Frette*), No. 148 ; the *Heneage*, No. 264 ; the *Lacy*, No. 274 ; the *Stafford*, No. 304 ; and the *Wake and Ormond*, No. 313. Cords were sometimes intertwined about other figures and devices, and so formed what may be regarded as *Compound Badges*, which significantly declared the union of two houses : thus, the knot of EDWARD Lord HASTINGS unites the Hungerford sickle with the Peverel garbe :

No. 270; and the *Dacre knot* is entwined about the
Dacre escallop and the famous "ragged staff" of
Beauchamp and Neville : No. 235.

Label, or *File.* A narrow ribbon placed across the field of a
shield near the chief, and having three, five, or sometimes other numbers of *points* depending from it, its
object being to *mark Cadency.* In the early Labels the
number of the points was arbitrary, the usual numbers
being five and three; and, subsequently, three points
were almost universally used; the object always was to
render the Label conspicuous. In blazon a Label is
supposed to have three points; but, if more, the number
is to be specified; thus, No. 271 is simply "*a Label,*"
but No. 272 is "*a Label of five points.*" Labels appear

Labels.—No. 271.   No. 272.   No. 273.

early in the thirteenth century, and in the next century
they are in constant use. Various charges may be
placed on the "points" of Labels to extend their
capacity for "differencing." Since the time of EDWARD
the BLACK PRINCE the Label of the PRINCE OF WALES
has been plain silver. The Label is almost exclu-

sively (now without any exception) used
in Royal Cadency; but, in modern
Heraldry, in the case of all other
persons it is the peculiar mark of the
eldest son. The Label is also found as
a charge. It has become a usage in the
degenerate days of Heraldry to repre-

No. 274.—Lacy Knot.   sent the Label as in No. 273, instead
of the earlier and far preferable forms of Nos. 271, 272.

Lacy Knot. No. 274.

Lambrequin. A mantling.

Langued. A term which refers to the tincture of an animal's tongue.

Leaves. Their peculiarities are to be blazoned, as *laurel leaves, oak leaves,* &c.

Leopard, Leopardé. See page 84.

Letters of the Alphabet sometimes are Charges.   Thus, the Arms of the Deanery of Canterbury are—*A z., on a cross arg., the letter " x " surmounted by the letter " i " sable :* the " x " is on the cross at the intersection of its limbs, and the " i " is above it.

Line, or *Border Line.* No. 38.

Lined. Having a cord attached : also, having a lining.

Lion. See page 83.

Lioncel. A lion drawn to a small scale, and generally rampant, Nos. 114, 115, 197.

Livery Colours. Of the PLANTAGENETS, as one family, *white and scarlet ;* of the house of YORK, *blue and murrey ;* of the house of LANCASTER, *white and blue ;* of the house of TUDOR, *white and green.*   The present Royal Livery is *scarlet and gold.*   In the Middle Ages, all great families had their own livery colours, which had no necessary relation to the tinctures of the shield.

Lodged. A term denoting animals of the chase when at rest or in repose, Nos. 25, 26.

Lozenge. A square figure set diagonally, No. 47 (also see page 69).   The armorial insignia of unmarried ladies and widows, with the sole exception of a Sovereign, are blazoned on a Lozenge instead of an Escutcheon.

Lozengy. A field divided lozengewise : No. 145.

Luce, or *Lucy.* The fish now called pike.   See page 77 and No. 164.

Lure. See *In Lure.*

Lymphad. An ancient galley, No. 275.   It was the feudal ensign of the Scottish lordship of LORN, and as such quartered by the Duke of ARGYLL.

Maintenance, Cap of. See *Chapeau.*

Manche, Maunche. A lady's sleeve with a long pendent lappet, worn in the time of HENRY I., and borne as an armorial charge by the families of HASTINGS, CONYERS, and some others. HASTINGS (H. 3)—*Or, a manche gu. :* No. 276.

Mantle. A flowing robe worn over the armour, or over their ordinary costume, by personages of distinction of both

No. 275.—Lymphad.

No. 276.—Arms of Hastings.

sexes: the mantles of ladies were commonly decorated with armorial blazonry.

Mantling, or *Lambrequin.* A small mantle of some rich materials, attached to the knightly basinet or helm, and worn hanging down. It is usually represented with jagged edges, to represent the cuts to which it would be exposed in actual battle: No. 199. (See *Panache.*) Mantlings blazoned with achievements of arms are sometimes adjusted in folds to form a background to the composition, and they are also occasionally differenced with various charges.

Marquess, Marquis. The second order of the British Peerage, in rank next to that of Duke. This rank and title were introduced into England in 1387, by RICHARD II., who then created his favourite, ROBERT DE VERE, Marquess of DUBLIN. The next creation was by HENRY

VI. A Marquess is "Most Honourable"; he is styled "My Lord Marquess": all his younger sons are "Lords," and his daughters "Ladies"; his eldest son bears his father's "second title." The Coronet, apparently contemporary in its present form with that of Dukes, has its golden circlet heightened with four strawberry leaves and as many pearls, arranged alternately: in representations two of the pearls, and one leaf and two half-leaves are shown, No. 277. The wife of a Marquess is a

No. 277.—Circlet of the Coronet of a Marquess.

"Marchioness"; her style corresponds with that of her husband, and her coronet is the same.

Marshalling. The disposition of more than one distinct coat of arms upon a shield, so forming a single composition; or the aggroupment of two or more distinct shields, so as to form a single composition; also the association of such accessories as the helm, mantling, crest, &c., and of knightly and other insignia with a shield of arms, thus again forming a single heraldic composition. See Chapter XI.

Martel. A hammer.

Martlet. The heraldic Martin, usually represented without feet: Nos. 160, 161, and 70 and 86.

Mascle. Lozenge voided: No. 143. *Masculée.* A field divided mascle-wise.

Masoned. Representing brickwork.

Membered. To denote the legs of a bird.

Merchant's mark. A device, adopted as early as 1400 by merchants, as a substitute for heraldic ensigns which were not conceded to them. Such marks are the predecessors of the *Trade-brands* and *Marks* of after times.

Mermaid, Merman, or *Triton.* The well-known fabulous creatures of the sea, borne occasionally as charges, but more frequently as supporters, badges, or crests. A mermaid was the device of Sir WILLIAM DE BRIVERE, who died in 1226, and it is the badge of the BERKELEYS.

Metal. The Tinctures *Or* and *Argent:* Nos. 50, 51.

Mill-rind. See *Fer-de-Moline.*

Mitre. The ensign of archiepiscopal and episcopal rank, placed above the arms of prelates of the Church of England, sometimes borne as a charge, and adopted by the BERKELEYS as their crest. The contour of the mitre has varied considerably at different periods, the early examples being low and concave in their sides, the later lofty and convex. See No. 159.

Moline. A cross terminating like a Fer-de-moline, No. 97. In modern cadency it is the difference of the eighth son.

Moon. No. 166, page 80.

Motto. A word, or very short sentence, placed generally below a shield but sometimes above a crest, an idea perhaps derived from the "war-cries" of early times. A motto may be emblematical, or it may have some allusion to the person bearing it, or to his name and armorial insignia; or it may be the epigrammatic expression of some sentiment in special favour with the bearer of it. As a matter of course, allusive mottoes, like allusive arms, afford curious examples of mediæval puns. I give a few characteristic examples:—" *Vero nil verius*" (*nothing truer than truth,* or, *no greater verity than in Vere*)—VERE; " *Fare, fac*" (*Speak—act;* that is, *a word and blow*)—FAIRFAX; " *Cave*" (*beware*)—CAVE; " *Cavendo tutus*" (*safe, by caution,* or *by Cavendish*)—CAVENDISH; " *Set on,*" says SETON; " *Fight on,*" quoth FITTON; " *Festina lente*" (*On slow—push forward, but be cautious,* that is), adds ONSLOW. Again: JEFFERAY says, " *Je feray ce que je diray*" (*I shall be true to my word*); SCUDAMORE—*Scutum amoris divini* (*the shield of Divine love*); says JAMES—" *J'aime jamais*" (*I love ever*);

says ESTWICK—"*Est hic*" (*he is here*); and POLE—
"*Pollet virtus*" (*valour prevails*); and TEY—"*Tais en
temps*" (*be silent in time*). The crest of CHARTERIS, an
arm with the hand grasping a sword, has over it—
"*This our charter is.*" In his arms the Marquess
CHOLMONDELEY bears *two helmets*, and his motto is—
"*Cassis tutissima virtus*" (*valour is the safest helm*); the
crest of the MARTINS of Dorsetshire was an ape, with
the significant motto—"*He who looks at Martin's
ape, Martin's ape shall look at him!*" The motto of
PERCEVAL is—"*Perse valens*" (*strong in himself*); but,
"*Do no yll,*" quoth DOYLE. Some "lippes," as Camden
remarks, have a taste for "this kind of lettuce."

Mound. A globe, encircled and arched over with rich

No. 278.—Mullet.

No. 279.—Mullet, pierced.

bands, and surmounted by a cross-patée, the whole an
ensign of the royal estate. A mound or orb forms part
of the regalia, and the same form appears upon the
intersecting arches of the crown of the SOVEREIGN; and
it also surmounts the single arch of the coronet of the
PRINCE OF WALES: Nos. 234, 289.

Mount. A green hill.

Mullet. A star, generally of five, but sometimes of six or
more points (if more than five the number to be
specified), always formed by right lines, as No. 278. A
mullet is sometimes "pierced," as in No. 279, when the
tincture of the field is generally apparent through the
circular aperture. In modern cadency an unpierced
mullet is the difference of the third son. See *Estoile.*

Mural Crown. Represents masonry, and is embattled:
No. 280.

Naiant. Swimming in fesse.   See *Hauriant.*

Naissant. Equivalent to *Issuant,* but applied only to living creatures.

Naval Crown. Has its circlet heightened with figures of the stern and the hoisted sail of a ship alternating: No. 281.

Nebulée, or *Nebuly.* No. 38, H.

No. 280.—Mural Crown.   No. 281.—Naval Crown.

Nimbus. A glory about the head of a figure of a sainted personage: sometimes used to denote sanctity in a symbolical device.

Norroy. See *Herald.*

Nova Scotia, Badge of. See *Baronet.*

Nowed. Coiled in a knot, as a snake.

Ogress. A *Pellet,* or black roundle.

Opinicus. A fabulous heraldic monster, a dragon before, and a lion behind with a camel's tail.

Oppressed. An alternative for *Debruised.*

Or. The metal gold: No. 50.

Ordinary. An early principal charge of a simple character.   See Chapter VI., and Nos. 71–128: see also page 14.

Ordinary of arms. A list of armorial bearings, classified or arranged alphabetically, with the names of the bearers. See *Armory.*

Oreiller. A cushion or pillow, generally with tassels.

Orle. A Subordinary formed of a border of a Shield, which is charged upon another and a larger shield, as in No. 134.   *In Orle.* Arranged after the manner of an Orle, forming a border to a Shield, as in No. 86.

Ostrich feathers. A Royal Badge: also a Device in a few instances charged by Royal and some other personages on an Armorial Shield. See Chapter XV.

Over all, or *Sur tout.* To denote some one charge being placed over all others.

Overt. With expanded wings.

Pale. One of the Ordinaries: No. 87. *Pale-wise,* or *In Pale.* Disposed after the manner of a Pale—that is, set vertically, or arranged vertically one above another, as are the Lions of England in No. 187, page 87.

Pall, Pallium. A vestment peculiar to Archbishops of the Roman Church: in Heraldry, as a charge, half only of the pall is shown, when it resembles the letter Y; it is borne in the arms of the Sees of CANTERBURY, ARMAGH, and DUBLIN.

Pallet. Half a *Pale.*

Palmer's Staff, Pilgrim's staff, or *Bourdon.* No. 282. JOHN BOURDON (H. 3) bears—*Arg., three palmer's staves gu.*

Paly. Divided per pale into an even number of parts, which all lie in the same plane, as in No. 88. *Paly Bendy.* Divided evenly pale-wise, and also bend-wise, No. 118.

No. 282. Bourdon.

Panache. A plume of feathers, generally of the ostrich, set upright and born as a crest. A panache sometimes consists of a single row of feathers; but more generally it has two or more rows or "heights" of feathers, rising one above the other. In the greater number of examples the tips of the feathers are erect; in others they wave, or slightly bend over. A panache may be charged with some device or figure, "for difference," as by the TYNDALLS, with an *ermine circlet,* a *martlet,* and a *fleur de lys.* In Nos. 283, 285, from the seals of EDWARD COURTENAY, and EDMUND MORTIMER (A.D. 1400 and 1372) the "heights" both expand and rise in a curved pyramidal form. No. 284, from the seal of WILLIAM LE LATIMER (A.D. 1372), shows a remarkable variety of both panache and mantling. Waving plumes formed of distinct feathers first appear near the end of the fifteenth century, and are prevalent during the sixteenth century.

Party, Parted. Divided.

Passant. Walking and looking forward: No. 173. *Passant Guardant.* Walking and looking out from the shield,

PANACHE CRESTS:

| No. 283. | No. 284. | No. 285. |
| Edward Courtenay. | William le Latimer | Edmund Mortimer. |

No. 174. *Passant Reguardant.* Walking and looking back. *Passant Repassant,* or *Passant and Counter Passant.* Walking in opposite directions.

Pastoral Staff. The official staff of a bishop or abbot, having a crooked head, and so distinguished from an archbishop's *crozier.*

Patée, or *Formée.*
Patonce.
Patriarchal.
} Varieties of the heraldic Cross, Nos. 106, 99, and 95.

Pean. The Fur, No. 60.

Peer. That general title, expressing their equality as members of a distinct "order" in the realm, which is applied to Dukes, Marquesses, Earls, Viscounts, and Barons of England, Scotland, Great Britain, Ireland, and the United Kingdom.

Peerage. The hereditament of a Peer: also rank of a Peer; a list of the Peers.

Pegasus. A horse with wings—a classic as well as an heraldic imaginary creature.

No. 288.—A Portcullis.   No. 286.—A Pennon.   No. 287.—A Pheon.

Pelican. Blazoned "in her piety," when feeding her young with her own blood.

Pellet. A black roundle.

Pendent. Hanging.

Pennon. An armorial lance-flag, pointed or swallow-tailed at the fly. No. 286 is from the Brass to Sir JOHN D'AUBERNOUN, A.D. 1279; the arms are—*Az., a chevron or.*

Per. By means of, or after the manner of.

Pheon. A pointed arrow-head, borne with the point in base, unless the contrary is specified, No. 287.

Phœnix. A fabulous eagle, always represented as issuant from flames.

Pile. One of the Ordinaries, in form like a wedge, Nos. 126, 127, 128. *In Pile.* Arranged after the form of a pile.

Planta Genista. The broom-plant badge of the Plantagenets, No. 21.

Plate. A silver roundle.

Plenitude. The moon when full. See No. 166.

Plume. See *Panache.*

Points of Shield. No. 27. *In Point* is the same as *In Pile.*

Pomme. A green roundle.

Popinjay. A parrot (H. 3).

Port. A gateway, as the entrance to a castle: No. 222.

Portcullis. A defence for a gateway, No. 288: the badge of the Houses of BEAUFORT and TUDOR, borne by the former with the significant motto, "*Altera securitas*" (additional security).

Potent. A variety of the heraldic cross, No. 108; also a Fur, No. 64.

Powdered, Poudrée. The same as *Semée.*

Preying. When an animal devours its prey. See *Trussing.*

Prince, Princess. In this country the rank and title of the members of the Royal Family. Their style is "Your Royal Highness." The coronet of the Prince of Wales differs from the crown of the King, only in having a single arch instead of two intersecting arches: No. 289. The coronets of the Princes and Princesses, the sons and daughters of the King, are the same as the coronet of the Prince of Wales, but without any arch: No. 290. The coronets of the Princes and Princesses, the grand-children of the Sovereign, differ in having the circlet heightened with two crosses patée, as many strawberry leaves, and four fleurs-de-lys, No. 291. Other Royal coronets have the circlet heightened with four crosses patée, and as many strawberry leaves. No. 292. For the arms of their Royal Highnesses, see Chapter XVIII.

Purfled. Lined and bordered or garnished.

Purpure. A colour: No. 56.

Pursuivant. A Herald of the lowest rank. In the Middle Ages, these officers were attached to the households of personages of high rank, and bore titles generally taken from the armorial insignia of their lords.

Quadrate. A form of cross: No. 94.

Quarter. The first (from the dexter chief) of the divisions of a shield that is parted per cross, as in No. 30; also any other division of a shield, to be specified in blazoning. See No. 36, and *Canton.*

Quartering. Marshalling two or more coats of arms in the different quarters of the same shield. When two coats are thus quartered, the one in the first quarter is repeated in the fourth, and the one in the second in the third; when three are quartered, the first quartering is repeated

CIRCLETS OF ROYAL CORONETS:

No. 289.
Prince of Wales.

No 290.
King's Daughters and Younger Sons.

No. 291.—King's Grandchildren.

No. 292.—Royal Dukes.

in the fourth quarter. Any required number of coats may be quartered on the same principle. This same term is also applied to denote the dividing a shield "*quarterly,*" as in No. 30, or into more than four divisions, as in No. 36.

Quarterly. A shield divided into four divisions, as in No. 30: each division to contain a complete coat of arms, or a distinct heraldic device or composition. Should the shield be divided into more than four sections, the number is to be specified: thus, No. 36 is "*quarterly of eight,*" &c. See Nos. 252, 253.

K

Quarterly Quartering and *Quartered.* The quartering of a
"quarter" of a shield that is divided "quarterly"; also
distinguished as "*Compound Quartering.*" See page 34.

Quatrefoil. A flower or figure having four foils or conjoined
leaves, No. 293. In modern cadency a *Double Quatrefoil* is the difference of the ninth son.

Queue Fourchée. Having a forked tail; No. 181.

Quilled. Used to blazon the quills of feathers: thus, a blue

No. 293.—Quatrefoil.   No. 294.—The Ragged Staff Badge.

feather having its quill golden is blazoned—*A feather
az., quilled or.*

Radiant. Encircled with rays.

Rayonée. Formed of Rays.

Ragulée, Raguly. Serrated, as No. 38, G. A "ragged staff,"
No. 294, is a part of a stem from which the branches
have been cut off roughly. This "ragged staff," or
"*staff ragulée,*" is the famous badge of the BEAU-
CHAMPS, and, derived from them, of the NEVILLES.
No. 294 is from the monument of the great Earl,
RICHARD DE BEAUCHAMP, K.G., who died in 1439, at
Warwick.

Rampant, Rampant Guardant and *Reguardant.* Nos. 171,
172; when *reguardant,* the animal looks backward.

Rebus. An allusive charge or device. A cask, or *tun,* to
represent the final syllable "*ton*" of many surnames, is
frequently found. I give a few examples of several
varieties of Rebus:—JOHN OXNEY, Canterbury—An

eagle (the emblem of *St. John* the Evangelist, to denote
"*John*") standing on an *ox*, charged on its side with
the letters *N E*.   JOHN WHEATHAMSTEDE, St. Albans—
An eagle and an Agnus Dei (the emblems of *St. John*
the Evangelist and *St. John* the Baptist, to denote
"*John*"), and clusters of *ears of wheat*.   JOHN RAMRYGE,
St. Albans—A *ram*, gorged with a collar inscribed with
the letters *R Y G E*.   WOODSTOCK—The stump or *stock
of a tree*.   Abbot ISLIP, Westminster—A man falling from
a tree, exclaiming, "I slip!" and a human *eye*, and a
slip (small branch of a tree).   WALTER LYHART, Norwich
—A *hart* (stag) *ly*ing down in *water*.   An *owl*, with the
letters *D O M* on a scroll in its beak, for Bishop OLDHAM,
at Exeter.   A church ("*kirk*") on a *tun*, with a pastoral
staff and the initial R, for Abbot ROBERT KIRTON, No.
295; and a *bird* on a *tun*, and a *tree* growing out of
a *tun*, for BURTON and ASHTON, all at Peterborough.
At Wells, with an initial T, a fire-*beacon* planted *in*
a *tun*, for Bishop THOMAS BECKYNGTON, No. 296; and
at Lullinstone, Kent, in stained glass, the shield of Sir
JOHN PECHÉ, A.D. 1522—*Az., a lion rampt. queue
fourchée erm., crowned or*—is encircled by *peach-branches
fructed and in foliage, each peach being charged with the
letter É*, No. 297; the crest-wreath also is formed of a
similar peach-branch.

Recercelée. A variety of the heraldic cross: No. 98.

Reflexed, Reflected. Curved and carried backwards.

Reguardant. Looking backwards: see No. 182.

Rein-deer. Heraldically drawn with double antlers, one pair
erect, the other drooping.

Respecting. Face to face—applied to creatures not of a
fierce nature.

Rest. See *Clarion*, No. 228.

Ribbon, Riband. A diminutive of a *Bend*.

Rising, Roussant. About to fly.

Rompu. Broken.

Rose. Represented in blazon as in Nos. 298, 299, and

No. 295.
Rebus of Abbot Kirton.

No. 296.
Rebus of Bishop Beckyngton.

No. 297.—Arms and Rebus of Sir John Peché.

without leaves. The five small projecting leaves of the calyx, that radiate about the flower itself, are styled *barbs*, and when they are blazoned "proper" these barbs are green, as the "seeds" in the centre of the flower are golden. Both the "red rose" of LANCASTER and the "white rose" of YORK, but more especially the latter, are at times surrounded with rays, and each is termed a "*rose-en-soleil*," No. 300. The rose, the emblem of ENGLAND, is generally drawn like the natural flower; or with natural stem, branches, leaves, and buds, but with heraldic rose-flowers. In modern cadency the heraldic rose is the difference of the seventh son.

Roundle. See page 72.

Rustre. A mascle pierced with a circular opening: No. 144.

Sable. The colour black: No. 54.

Sagittary. The fabulous centaur, half man and half horse.

Nos. 298, 299.—Heraldic Roses.   No. 300.—Rose-en-Soleil.

Salamander. An imaginary being, supposed to live in flames of fire; it is represented sometimes as a kind of lizard, and at other times (as in the crest of Earl DOUGLAS, A.D. 1483) as a quadruped somewhat like a dog, breathing flames.

Salient. Leaping or bounding.

Saltire. An ordinary, in form a diagonal cross: Nos. 120, 121. 122. *Saltire-wise*, or *in saltire*. Arranged after the form of a saltire.

Sanglier. A wild boar.

Sans. Without. "*Sans nombre*," without any number fixed or specified.

Savage-man, or *Wood-man*. A wild man, naked except large wreaths of leaves about his head and loins, and carrying a club.

Saw, or *Frame-saw*. Borne as the crest of HAMILTON, Duke of HAMILTON, which is thus blazoned—*Out of a ducal crest-coronet or, an oak-tree fructed and penetrated transversely in the main stem by a frame-saw ppr., the frame gold; above the crest the motto,* "THROUGH!" This device is said to commemorate the escape into Scotland, in **1323**, of Sir GILBERT HAMILTON, a reputed ancestor of the present ducal house. At the court of EDWARD II. Sir Gilbert had unadvisedly expressed admiration for ROBERT BRUCE, on which JOHN LE DESPENCER struck him. Despencer fell in single combat the next day, and Hamilton fled, hotly pursued, northward. Near the border the fugitive and a faithful esquire joined some wood-cutters, assumed their dress, and commenced working with them on an oak, when the pursuers passed by. Hamilton, saw in hand, observed his esquire

anxiously watching their enemies as they passed, and at once recalled his attention to his woodman's duties by the word, "Through!"—thus, at the same time, appearing to consider the cutting down the oak to be far more important than the presence of the strangers. So they passed by, and Hamilton followed in safety. This crest does not appear in the Hamilton seals till long after the days of Bruce and his admirer, Sir Gilbert: No. **301**.

No. 301.—Crest of Hamilton.

Scarpe, Escarpe. A diminutive of a *Bend sinister.*

Scintillant. Emitting sparks.

Seax. A Saxon sword.

Seeded. Having seeds or seed-vessels, as in the centre of an heraldic rose. See Nos. 298–300.

Segreant. A term applied to a griffin when rampant.

Sejant. Sitting.

Semée. Sown broadcast or scattered, without any fixed

number, over the field; parts of the charge thus semée appearing at the border-lines of the composition. See Nos. 247, 250, 252.

Shake-fork. Resembles the letter Y, but does not extend to the margin of the shield, and is pointed at its extremities.

Shamrock. A trefoil plant or leaf, the badge of IRELAND.

Shield, or *Escutcheon.* The Shield of Heraldry is fully described at page 32. See also Nos. 27, 39–49.

Ship. Sometimes blazoned as a modern vessel, but sometimes also as an ancient galley. See *Lymphad.*

Shoveller. A species of duck.

Simple Quartering. Dividing a shield quarterly, with the quartering of any of the quarters. See *Quartering*

Sinister. The left side. No. 27.

Sinople. The colour *vert* in French Heraldry.

Sixfoil. A flower of six leaves: No. 302.

Slipped. Having a stalk, as a leaf or branch: No. 309.

Spear. The spear or lance is not of common occurrence in blazon; but it appears, with heraldic propriety, in the arms granted in 1596 to the father of the great poet, who bore—*Or, on a bend sa. a spear gold, the head arg.* —the arms of SHAKESPEARE, No. 303. (In the woodcut the bend is accidentally shaded for *gules*, instead of *sable.*)

No. 303.
Arms of Shakespeare

Spur. Not common as an heraldic charge. Before about 1320 the spur had a single point, and was known as the "pryck-spur"; about that time appeared a "rouelle-spur" of simple form; in the middle of the fifteenth century spurs of extravagant length were introduced.

SS., Collar of. See *Collar*, and No. 231.

Stafford-knot. No. 304.

Stall-plate. A plate bearing the arms of a knight and placed

in his stall. The stall-plates of the Knights of the
GARTER and the BATH are severally placed in the
Chapels of ST. GEORGE and of HENRY VII., at Windsor
and Westminster. The earliest plates now in existence
at Windsor, though many of them bear arms of an
earlier date, were executed about 1430.

Standard. A long narrow flag, introduced for the purpose of heraldic display, in the time of EDWARD III.,
but not in general use till a later period. Standards
generally had the Cross of ST. GEORGE next the staff,

No. 302.—Sixfoil. No. 304.—Stafford Knot. No. 305.—Stapleton Badge.

to which succeeded the badge or badges and the motto
of the owner. See Chapter XVII.

Staple. Borne by STAPLETON : No. 305 represents a badge
formed of two staples.

Statant. Standing.

Star. See *Estoile* and *Mullet;* also a knightly decoration.

Stirrup. Borne, with appropriate straps and buckles, by
SCUDAMORE, GIFFARD, and a few others.

Stock. The stump of a tree.

Stringed. As a harp or a bugle-horn ; or, suspended by, or
fastened with, a string.

Sun. When represented shining and surrounded with rays,
he has a representation of a human face upon his disc,
and is blazoned "*In splendour.*" *Sunbeams,* or *Rays,* are
borne in blazon, and form an early charge. See *Collar.*

Supporter. A figure of whatsoever kind that stands by a
Shield of arms, as if *supporting* or guarding it. Single
Supporters occasionally appear, but the general usage is
to have a pair of Supporters—one on each side of the

supported Shield. They came gradually into use in the course of the fourteenth century, but were not regularly established as accessories of Shields till about 1425, or rather later. At first they were generally alike, being then duplicate representations of the badge, but subsequently the more prevalent custom was that the two Supporters should differ, as in the case of the Royal Supporters, the Lion and the Unicorn, famous in History as in Heraldry. See *Bearer*, *Tenant*, and also Chapter XVI.

Surcoat. Any garment worn over armour; but especially the long flowing garment worn by knights over their armour until about 1325, when its form was modified by cutting it short in front, and it was distinguished as a *Cyclas.* See *Jupon.*

Surmounted. Placed over another.

Swan. When blazoned "*proper*," white with black beak and red legs. It is the badge of the BOHUNS, and of their descendants the LANCASTRIAN PLANTAGENETS, the STAFFORDS, and some others. This Swan has his neck encircled with a coronet, from which a chain generally passes over his back. By HENRY V., the Swan badge of his mother, MARY DE BOHUN, was borne with the wings expanded.

Sword. When borne as a charge, straight in the blade, pointed, and with a cross-guard. All the appointments of the weapon are to be blazoned. It appears, as a spiritual emblem, in several episcopal coats of arms; in the arms of the CITY OF LONDON, No. 306, the first quarter of a Shield of ST. GEORGE (*arg.*, *a cross gu.*) is charged with *a sword erect gules*, the emblem of ST. PAUL, the special patron of the English metropolitan city. The sword is also borne in blazon in its military capacity.

No. 306.
Arms of City of London.

Tabard. A short garment with sleeves, worn in the Tudor
era. It has the arms blazoned on the sleeves as well
as on the front and back: No. 307, the Tabard of
WILLIAM FYNDERNE, Esquire, from
his brass, A.D. 1444, at Childrey in
Berkshire: the arms are—*Arg., a
chevron between three crosses patée
sable,* the ordinary being charged
with *an annulet of the field* "for
Difference." A similar garment
is the official habit of heralds.

No. 307.
Tabard; A.D. 1444.

Tau, Tau-Cross. A cross formed like
the letter T, so called in Greek,
No. 93; borne as a charge in the
arms of DRURY, TAWKE, and some
others: this charge is also called
the Cross of ST. ANTHONY: it is
sometimes borne on a badge, as in the Bishop's Palace
at Exeter. See Chapter XV.

Templars, Knights. See Chapter XIX.

Tenent, Tenant. Used by French Heralds to distinguish
human figures from animals, as *supporters.*

Tennée, or *Tawney.* A deep orange-colour; in
use in the Middle Ages as a *livery-colour.*

Thistle. The national Badge of SCOTLAND,
represented after its national aspect,
and tinctured *proper.* JAMES I. of
Great Britain, to symbolise the union
of the two realms of England and
Scotland, compounded a Badge from
the *Rose* of one realm, and the *Thistle*
of the other, united by impalement under a single crown:
No. 308. The impaled rose and thistle is borne by the
Earl of KINNOULL, repeated eight times upon a bordure.

No. 308.
Badge of James I.

Timbre. In the early Heraldry of England, this term denotes the true heraldic *crest*: but, in the modern Heraldry of France, the "timbre" is the *Helm* in an armorial achievement. *Timbred*. Ensigned with a Helm; or, if referring to an early English achievement, with a Crest. It is a term very seldom met with in use.

Tiercée. *In tierce*, *Per tierce*. Divided into three equal parts.

Tinctures. The two *metals* and the five *colours* of Heraldry: Nos. 50–56. See page 40. It was one of the puerile extravagancies of the Heralds of degenerate days to distinguish the Tinctures by the names of the *Planets* in blazoning the arms of Sovereign Princes, and by the names of *Gems* in blazoning the arms of Nobles.

Torse. A crest-wreath.

Torteau, plural *torteaux*. A red spherical Roundle: No. 152.

Tower, *Turret*. A small castle. *Towered*. Surmounted by towers, as No. 222, which is a "*Castle triple towered.*"

Transposed. Reversed.

Trefoil. A leaf of three conjoined foils, generally borne "slipped," as in No. 309.

Treflée, or *Botonée*. A variety of the cross: No. 103. *Treflée* also implies *semée* of trefoils.

No. 309.
Trefoil Slipped.

Treille, *Trellis*. See page 71, and No. 150.

Tressure. A subordinary. See pages 66, 67; and Nos. 135–8

Tricked. Sketched in outline.

Trippant, or *Tripping*. In easy motion, as a stag. See page 81; and No 168.

Triton. See *Mermaid*.

Trivet. A circular or triangular iron frame, with three feet, borne by the family of TRYVETT.

Trogodice. An animal like a reindeer.

Trumpet. In blazon usually a long straight tube, expanding at its extremity: No. 310, from the brass to Sir R. DE TRUMPINGTON, at Trumpingdon, near Cambridge; A.D. 1272.

No. 310.
Trumpet.

Trussed. With closed wings. *Trussing*. Devouring —applied to birds of prey.

Tudor Rose. An heraldic rose, *quarterly gu. and arg.;* or a white heraldic rose, *charged upon* a red one.

Tun. A cask ; the rebus of the final syllable T O N in many surnames. See *Rebus.*

Tynes. Branches of a stag's antlers. See *Attires.*

Ulster. See *Baronet* and *Herald.*

Undy, Undée. Wavy: No. 38, c.

Unguled. Hoofed.

Unicorn. A well-known fabulous animal, famous as the sinister supporter of the Royal Shield of England,

Union Jack. The National Ensign of the United Kingdom of Great Britain and Ireland, fully described in Chapter XVII. It is borne on an inescutcheon upon the arms of the Duke of WELLINGTON as an augmentation.

Uriant. A term said to be applied to a fish when it swims in a vertical position, head downwards. The reverse of *Hauriant, q.v.*

Vair. A Fur: Nos. 61, 62, 63.

Vane. See *Fan.*

Vert. In French Heraldry, *Sinople.* The colour green: No. 55.

Vervels, Varvals. Small rings.

Vested. Clothed.

Viscount. The *fourth* degree of rank and dignity in the British Peerage, in Latin *Vice-Comtes*, introduced by HENRY VI., A.D. 1440. *Vice-comes* is also the Latin word for the office of Sheriff. A Viscount is " Right Honourable," and is styled " My Lord." All his sons and daughters are " Honourable." His Coronet, granted by

No. 311.—Circlet of a Viscount's Coronet.

JAMES I., has a row of sixteen pearls, of comparatively small size set on the circlet; in representations nine are shown: No. 311. The wife of a Viscount is a *Viscountess,* whc has the same rank, style, and coronet as her husband.

Vivre. An early term, fallen into general disuse; but apparently denoting a *Barrulet* or *Cotise Dancettée;* as in No. 312, at St. Michael's Church, St. Albans.

Voided. Having the central area removed.

Voiders. Diminutives of *Flanches.*

Volant. Flying. *Vorant.* Devouring.

Vol. Two bird's wings conjoined, having the appearance of an eagle displayed without its body: No. 207.

Vulned. Wounded.

Wake Knot. No. 313.

No. 312.
Shield at St. Michael's Church, St. Alban's.

Walled. Made to represent brick or stone-work. The term *masoned* is, however, usually employed.

No. 313.—Wake Knot.　　No. 315.—Wyvern.　　No 314.—Catherine Wheel

Water Bouget. No. 218.

Wattled. Having a comb and gills, as a cock.

Wavy, Undée. No. 38, c.

Wheat-sheaf. See *Garb.*

Wheel, Catherine Wheel. Has curved spikes projecting from its rim: No. 314: from a shield upon a boss, about A.D. 1400, in the south choir-aisle of the church of Great Yarmouth.

Wreath, Crest-Wreath. See *Crest-Wreath,* and No. 233; also Chapter XIV.

Wreathed. Adorned with a wreath, chaplet, or garland; or twisted into the form of a wreath, &c.

Wyvern, Wivern. A fabulous creature, being a species of dragon with two legs: No. 315.

CHAPTER XI

MARSHALLING

*Aggroupment—Combination—Quartering—Dimidiation—Impalement
—Escutcheon of Pretence—Marshalling the Arms of Widowers,
Widows, and others ; Official Arms ; and, the Accessories of Shields.*

" Marshalling is a conjoining of diverse Coats in one Shield."—GUILLIM.

UPON this concise definition, Guillim, in another part of his
work, adds the following comment :—" *Marshalling* is an
orderly disposing of sundry Coat Armours pertaining to
distinct Families, and their contingent ornaments, with their
parts and appurtenances, in their proper places."   Hence it
is apparent that this term, " Marshalling," implies—

1. First, the bringing together and the disposition of two
   or more distinct " Coats in one Shield " :
2. Secondly, the aggroupment of two or more distinct Coats
   to form a single heraldic composition, the Shields being
   still kept distinct from one another: and,
3. Thirdly, the association of certain insignia with a Shield
   of arms, so as to produce a complete heraldic achievement.

The association of " Arms " with Names, Dignities, and
Estates would necessarily require, at an early period in the
history of Heraldry, the establishment of some regular and
recognised system for the combination and aggroupment of
various distinct coats and insignia, whenever a single individual became the representative of more than one family,
or was the hereditary possessor of several dignities and
properties.

Again: it would be equally necessary that this system should extend to the becoming heraldic declaration and record of *Alliances* of every kind, including (a matter of no little importance in the Middle Ages) *feudal dependence*.

In another, and a secondary sense, this same term, *Marshalling*, is used by Heralds to denote the general arrangement and disposition of heraldic charges and insignia in blazon upon the field of a Shield.

In its simplest form, MARSHALLING is effected by *Aggroupment* without Combination—by placing two or more Shields of arms, that is, in such positions as to form a connected group of distinct Shields, either with or without various accessories. Seals afford excellent examples of Marshalling of this order. These Seals may be classified in two groups,—one, in which an effigy appears; and a second, in which the composition does not include any effigy. Here I may observe that the same armorial blazonry that was displayed upon their military surcoats by Princes, Nobles, and Knights, was adopted by Ecclesiastics for the decoration of their official vestments, and also (towards the close of the thirteenth century) by Ladies of rank, as an appropriate style of ornamentation for their own costume: and many examples of the effigies of Ladies, with a few of Ecclesiatics, adorned in this manner with heraldic insignia, exist in Seals and in Monumental Memorials. In Beverley Minster there is a noble effigy of a priest, a member of the great family of PERCY (about A.D. 1330), the embroideries of whose vestments are elaborately enriched with numerous allied shields of arms. Upon his episcopal seal, LEWIS BEAUMONT, Bishop of Durham from 1317 to 1333, has his effigy standing between two Shields of Arms (to the dexter, *England;* to the sinister, a cross potent between four groups of small crosses patées, three crosses in each group), while his chasuble is semée de lys and also charged with a lion rampant—the arms of the house of Beaumont. The

obverse of the Seal of MARGARET, daughter of PHILIP the
Hardy, King of France, the second Queen of our EDWARD
I., illustrates this usage in the instance of ladies : No. 316.
Upon her tunic the Queen has emblazoned the three lions
of her royal husband ; on her right side is a shield of *France*,
the arms of her royal father ; and on the left side a corre-

No. 316.—Seal of Margaret, Queen of Edward I.

sponding shield is charged with a lion rampant. I have
already shown the reverse of this fine Seal (No. 251), which
in the original is one inch more in depth than it appears in
these woodcuts.[1]   Other characteristic examples are the
Seals of AGNES DE PERCY, whose effigy, having the arms of
Louvaine upon the tunic, holds two armorial shields, one in

[1] In No. 251 the initial A of the word AQVITANNIE has been
omitted.

each hand : and of MARGARET, Countess of LINCOLN and
PEMBROKE (about 1241), who blazons the old arms of DE
LACI—*quarterly or and gu., a bend sa., over all a label
vert*—upon the tunic of her effigy, and has the same arms
on a Shield to the dexter, while another Shield to the sinister
is charged with the *lion rampant,* borne by the DE LACIES
as Earls of LINCOLN. The effigies of illustrious Ladies,
which appear on Seals with allied Shields of arms, are not
always represented in heraldic costume : good examples are
the Seals of ISABELLE of FRANCE,
Queen of EDWARD II., and of
ELIZABETH, daughter of EDWARD
I., who was Countess, first of
HOLLAND, and afterwards of
HEREFORD : both are engraved
in Sandford's "Genealogical History of England," page 121. The
Seal of MARGARET BRUCE, of
Skelton, Lady DE ROS, attached
to a deed, dated 1820, has the
effigy of the noble lady, wearing
her ermine mantle, and supporting two Shields of arms—the
Shield of DE ROS, *gu., three
water-bougets arg.,* to the dexter,
and a Shield of BRUCE, *a lion
rampant :* No. 317. I am in-

No. 317.—Seal of Margaret, Lady
de Ros. (*Laing.*)

debted, for the use of the excellent woodcut of this very interesting seal, to Mr. Laing of Edinburgh, the talented author
of the two noble volumes on the *Early Seals of Scotland,*
which occupy a foremost position amongst the most valuable
as well as the most beautiful heraldic works that have ever
been published in Great Britain. (See page 11.) In the
Monumental Brasses and also in the Sculptured Monumental Effigies of Ladies of the fourteenth and fifteenth cen-

L

turies, heraldic costume is frequently represented, and the figures are constantly associated with groups of Shields of arms. As most characteristic examples I may specify the effigy of a Lady, about A.D. 1325, at Selby in Yorkshire; and the Brass in Westminster Abbey, A.D. 1399, to ALIANORE DE BOHUN, Duchess of GLOUCESTER.

The aggroupment of various armorial ensigns upon a Seal, without the presence of any effigy, is exemplified in the characteristic Seal of JOAN, daughter of HENRY Count DE BARRE, and of ALIANORE, daughter of EDWARD I., the

No. 318.—Seal of Joan, Countess of Surrey.

widow of JOHN DE WARRENNE, Earl of SURREY, A.D. 1347. In this remarkable composition, No. 318, the arms, blazoned on lozenges, are, in the centre, *Warrenne*; in chief and base, *England*; and to the dexter and sinister, *De Barre* (No. 162): also, at the four angles of the group, the lion and castle of *Leon* and *Castile*, in direct allusion to the descent of the Countess from ALIANORE, first Queen of EDWARD I. In the original, this elaborate composition is only one and a half inches in diameter. Still smaller, measuring no more than one and a quarter inches in diameter, and yet no less rich in either its Heraldry or its Gothic traceries, is the beautiful little Counter-seal of MARY DE SAINT PAUL, wife of AYMER DE VALENCE, Earl of Pembroke, which is faithfully shown on an enlarged scale, in order to render the details more effectively, in No. 319. This illustrious lady, who founded Pembroke College, Cambridge, A.D. 1373, was the daughter of GUY DE CHASTILLON, Count of ST. PAUL, by his wife MARY, daughter of JOHN DE DREUX, Duke of BRITTANY, and of BEATRICE, sister of EDWARD I. On her Seal, accordingly, the Countess of Brittany marshals, in the centre, the arms of her husband (*De Valence:* No. 86), and those of her father (*De Chastillon—gu., three pallets vair, on a chief or a label of three points az.*), united upon a single shield by " Dimidiation "—a process presently to be described : to the dexter, the arms of her Royal relatives of *England* are blazoned in a circular compartment : to the sinister, in a similar compartment, are the fleurs de lys of *France Ancient*, No. 247, at that time so closely allied with the English lions : and, finally, in a third roundle, in the base of the composition, are the arms of *De Dreux* (*chequée or and az., within a bordure gu. ;* [1] *over all a canton of Brittany*, No. 15, borne by the maternal grandfather of the Countess : the legend is, + S . MARIE . DE . SEYN . POVL . COMITISSE . PEMPROCHIE. The original impression of this Seal, from which the woodcut, No. 319, was drawn, is appended to a charter, dated 1347, which is preserved amongst the muniments of Pembroke College. A very good example of the aggroupment of Shields upon a Seal, under conditions differing from those that now have been illustrated, I have already given in No. 204. Another beautiful and most interesting example, now unfortunately partially mutilated, is the Seal of MATILDA of LANCASTER, the wife, first, of WILLIAM DE BURGH, Earl of ULSTER (and

---

[1] In No. 319 the bordure of *De Dreux* in the roundle in base is charged with Lions of England, as borne by JOHN DE DREUX ; but the presence of these in the Seal of the Countess is uncertain. See No. 322

by him mother of ELIZABETH, the wife of Prince LIONEL
OF CLARENCE), and, secondly, of Sir RALPH DE UFFORD.
This seal, of circular form, No. 320, displays to the dexter
a shield of *De Burgh—or, a cross gu.*; to the sinister, a
shield of *Ufford—or, a cross engrailed sa.*, in the first
quarter *a fleur de lys, for difference*: in base there is a
lozenge of *De Chaworth* (the mother of the Countess was
MATILDA DE CHAWORTH)—*barrulée arg. and gu., an orle of
martlets sa.*; and in chief there remains part of another

No 319.
Seal of Mary, Countess of Pembroke.

No. 320.
Seal of Matilda of Lancaster.

lozenge of *Lancaster*, to complete this remarkable heraldic
group. Of the legend there remains only . . ILLV
MATILD' . . . . SE . . . The introduction of *Badges*,
with a Shield or Shields of arms, in the composition of a
Seal, is another variety of this same system of Marshalling.
No. 321, the Seal of OLIVER DE BOHUN, exemplifies this
usage, having the *white swan Badge* of the noble house of
BOHUN thrice repeated about the Shield. See No. 114.
Also see, in the frontispiece, the Seal of Earl RICHARD DE
BEAUCHAMP, No. 449, which is described in Section II. of
Chapter XXII

Marshalling by Aggroupment was practised under another form by placing Shields of arms in the different panels of the same architectural monument.

MARSHALLING *by Combination* is effected by actually forming, for the blazonry of a single Shield, a composition which includes the principal charges of two or more allied Shields. The composition of the Shield borne by the house of DE DREUX, to which I have just referred in describing the Seal of the Countess of Pembroke, No. 319, is a most striking example of this variety of Marshalling: and this

No. 321.
Seal of Oliver de Bohun.

No. 322.
Shield of Earl John de Dreux.

Shield was borne by JOHN DE DREUX, created Earl of RICHMOND by his uncle King EDWARD I., who lived and died in England, as it is represented in No. 322—the *field, chequée or and azure*, being for De Dreux; the *canton ermine* for Brittany; and the *bordure, gules charged with golden lions of England*, representing the royal Shield of England, and showing the close connection existing between the Earl of Richmond and his Sovereign. The shield of Prince JOHN of ELTHAM (No. 24), *England within a bordure of France*, is another characteristic example of this Marshalling by Combination.

For many reasons, except in particular instances, these

methods of Marshalling were not considered to be altogether satisfactory. Accordingly, a fresh arrangement was
devised which would preserve intact the original integrity of
each coat of arms, would imply a definite systematic method
of arrangement, and would admit into a single composition
any required number of distinct coats. This MARSHALLING
by Quartering, naturally suggested by such simple bearings
as Nos. 16 and 17, consists in dividing the Shield, as in No.
30, into four parts, and placing in each of these divisions or
quarters one of the coats to be marshalled on a single
Shield. If two coats only are thus to be "*quartered*," the
most important of the two occupies the first quarter, and is
repeated in the fourth ; and, the other coat is placed in the

second quarter, and repeated in the
third. The earliest example known
in England is the quartered Shield
of *Castile and Leon—quarterly: first
and fourth, gules, a castle triple-towered
or ; second and third, argent, a lion
rampant gu.*, No. 323. This shield
is sculptured upon the monument in
Westminster Abbey to ALIANORE,
daughter of FERDINAND III., King

No. 323.
Shield of Castile and Leon.

of CASTILE and LEON, and Queen of EDWARD I. : the date
is 1290.   This form of Marshalling began gradually to be
adopted during the first half of the fourteenth century, and
in the second half of that century it became generally
adopted.   Other examples of quartered shields I have
already given in Nos. 252 and 253.

Should there be *three* Coats to be quartered, they would
severally occupy the first, second, and third quarters of the
Shield, in due order, and the first quarter would be repeated
in the fourth.   In quartering *four* coats, no repetition would
be necessary.   If more than four coats would require to be
quartered, the Shield would be divided into whatever num-

ber of sections might be necessary, as in No. 36, and the required arrangement would be made; should any repetition be necessary, the first quarter is to be repeated in the fourth. This process, whatever the number of the coats thus marshalled (and their number sometimes is very great), is always entitled "*quartering*"; and each of these divisions of a Shield, for the purpose of Marshalling, is distinguished as a "Quarter." Occasionally a *quartered coat* would have to be marshalled with others. In the "grand quartering" which then takes place, the quartered coat is treated precisely as any other member of the group. See No. 37. For example, the Shield, No. 324 (R. 2), of HENRY, first Earl of NORTHUMBERLAND, is—I. and IV. Grand Quarters,—*first and fourth, or, a lion rampt. az.*, for Louvaine, or Percy modern: *second and third, gu., three lucies haurient arg.* (No. 164) for Lucy: II. and III. Grand Quarters,—*az., five fusils conjoined in fesse or*, for Percy ancient.

No. 324.—Shield of Henry, Earl of Northumberland.

When a Shield to be quartered has a very numerous array of Quarterings, Grand Quartering is seldom adopted; but, in its stead, the new quarterings are marshalled in their proper succession, with the original quarterings of the Shield.

In this Marshalling the first quarter is occupied by the most important quartering, which is determined (without any fixed rule) by the original grant or licence: the other quarterings follow, in the order in which they may have been "brought in" to the composition.

To denote and record ALLIANCE BY MARRIAGE, two distinct Coats were first marshalled upon a single Shield by *Dimidiation*. This process is accomplished in the following manner. The Shield to be charged with the two Coats in union is divided *per pale*, as in No. 28: on the dexter half the corresponding half, or generally somewhat more than that half, of the arms of the husband is marshalled : then,

in like manner, the sinister half is charged with the corresponding portion of the arms of the wife. In the Shield, No. 250, from another Seal of Queen MARGARET, *England* dimidiates *France ancient*, Nos. 187 and 247. This Dimidiation in most cases produces a singular effect; as in No. 325, a Shield from the Seal of the Mayor of Winchelsea, one

No. 325.—Shield of Mayor of Winchelsea.

of the famous Sussex Cinque Ports, which bears *England* dimidiating *azure, three hulls of ships, in pale, or :* here the dimidiated lions and ships appear to unite for the purpose

No. 326.—De Valence, dimidiating Claremont Nesle.

of forming the most extravagant of compound monsters. The Seal of the Borough of Great Yarmouth substitutes *three herrings*, in allusion to the staple fishery of the port, for the ships, and dimidiates them with the national lions. In the central Shield of the Seal, No. 319, I.have shown *De Valence* dimidiating *De Chastillon*. In No. 326, from the monument of WILLIAM DE VALENCE, *De Valence* appears dimidiating the French Coat of *Claremont Nesle — gu.*, *semée of trefoils, two barbels haurient addorsed or :* the Dimidiation here cuts off and removes one-half of the De Valence martlets and also one of the two barbels of Claremont.

The characteristic features of one or of both of the united Coats, as I have just shown, being commonly rendered indistinct and uncertain by Dimidiation, that form of marshalling was generally superseded by IMPALEMENT in the course of the third quarter of the fourteenth century. This process, at once simple and effectual, marshals the whole of the husband's arms on the dexter half of a Shield divided per pale, as No. 28; and the whole of the arms of the wife on the sinister half of it. Such an impaled Shield is borne by a husband and wife during their conjoint lives; and should the wife become a widow, by her the impaled arms are borne during her widowhood charged upon a lozenge. The dexter half only—the husband's arms—of an impaled Shield is hereditary. Fine examples of Shields that are both impaled and quartered, are preserved in the monuments of EDWARD III. and his Queen PHILIPPA, in the Brass to ALIANORE DE BOHUN, and in the monument to MARGARET BEAUFORT, all in Westminster Abbey. Other fine examples occur on the monument of Earl RICHARD BEAU-CHAMP, at Warwick. No. 327, from the Brass to THOMAS, LORD CAMOYS, K.G., and his wife, ELIZABETH MORTIMER (the widow of HENRY HOTSPUR), at Trotton, in Sussex, A.D. 1410, marshals *Camoys—arg., on a chief gu. three plates,* impaling *Mortimer,* No. 131. Again, at Warwick, the Brass to Earl THOMAS DE BEAUCHAMP and his Countess,

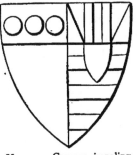

No. 327.—Camoys, impaling Mortimer.

MARGARET FERRERS of Groby, A.D. 1406, has a Shield of *Beauchamp—gu., a fesse between six crosslets or*, impaling *Ferrers—gu., seven mascles, three three and one, or.*

No. 328.—D'Aubigny, impaling Scotland.

It is to be observed that *Bordures* and *Tressures*, which are not affected by Quartering, are *dimidiated by Impalement*,—that is, that side of both a Bordure and a Tressure which adjoins the line of Impalement is generally removed: thus, one of the small Shields sculptured upon the canopy of the monument of Queen MARY STUART, at Westminster, is charged with *D'Aubigny* impaling *Scotland*,—that is, *az., three fleurs de lys or, within a bordure gu. charged with eight buckles gold*, impaling No. 138. This Shield, represented in No. 328, has both the bordure on its dexter half, and the tressure on its sinister half, dimidiated by the impalement. There are other excellent examples of this partial dimidiating in the monuments of MARGARET TUDOR and MARGARET BEAUFORT, in the same chapel of Westminster Abbey.

The husband of an *Heiress* or a *Co-heiress*, instead of impaling the arms of his wife, marshals them upon his Shield charged as an *Escutcheon of Pretence*. The son of an heiress, as heir to his maternal grandfather through his mother, as well as to his own father, *quarters* on his Shield, and transmits to his descendants, *the arms of both his parents*, his father's arms generally being in the first quarter. The Shield of RICHARD BEAUCHAMP, K.G., Earl of WARWICK (died in 1439), is a good example of the use of an Escutcheon of Pretence; it is represented in No. 329,

drawn from the garter-plate of the Earl, in St. George's
Chapel, Windsor. The Earl himself, as his hereditary coat,
quarters *Beauchamp* with *Newburgh—chequée or and az.,
a chevron erm.:* upon this, for his Countess, ISABELLE,
daughter and heiress of THOMAS LE DESPENCER, Earl of

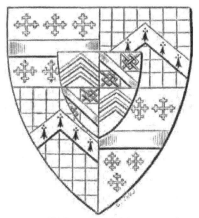

No. 329.—Shield of Earl Richard Beauchamp.

GLOUCESTER, he marshals an Escutcheon of Pretence
charged with *De Clare*, No. 124, quartering *Le Despencer—
quarterly arg. and gu., in the second and third quarters a
frette or, over all a bend sa.* In the monument of this great
Earl, at Warwick, upon the Escutcheon of Pretence the

No. 330.   No. 330.   No. 330.

arms of Bohun are quartered with those of Clare and
Despencer.

A few very simple diagrams will clearly elucidate the
principle of Marshalling the arms of Husband and Wife.
Suppose B (*Baron*) to represent the Husband, and F
(*Femme*) the Wife: then, No. 330 B may represent the arms

of the Husband, and No. 330 F the arms of the Wife.   If F
be *not* an heiress, the arms of B and F, as husband and wife,
are borne impaled, as in No. 330 B F ; and their son bears
No. 330 B only.   If F *be an heiress*, the arms of B and F, as
husband and wife, are borne as in No. 331—the arms of
the wife on an Escutcheon of Pretence ; and, in this case,

No 330.   No. 331.   No. 332

the son of B and F quarters the arms of both his parents, as
No. 332.   Now, suppose this son, whose arms are No. 332,
to marry a lady, *not* an heiress, whose arms are No. 330 F F,
he would simply impale the arms of his wife, as in No. 333,
and his son would bear No. 332 only, as his father bore
that quartered shield before his marriage.   But if the wife

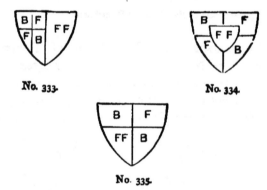

No. 333.   No. 334.

No. 335.

of the bearer of No. 332 were to *be an heiress*, he would
charge the arms of his wife in pretence upon his own
hereditary paternal Shield, as in No. 334 ; and his son, by
this heiress, as before, would quarter the arms of both his
parents, as in No. 335.   It is obvious that Marshalling on
this system (of which I here give the general outline) admits
of a widely-extended application.   Younger sons in all

cases place over all the quarterings of their Shield their own distinctive Mark of Cadency, until they inherit some different quartering from those to which the head of their house is entitled, and the quartering itself then forms sufficient difference.

A *Widower* who marries again places the arms of both his wives upon any permanent record, but for ordinary purposes of use, *e.g.* on a seal or carriage, bears only the arms of his living wife.

An *Unmarried Lady* bears her paternal arms on a *lozenge*, without any Helmet, Crest, or Motto.

A *Widow* bears on a *lozenge* the arms borne by her husband and herself. Should she marry again, a Widow ceases to bear the arms of her former husband.

A *Peeress in her own right*, if married to a Peer, has both her own arms and those of her husband fully blazoned, and the lozenge and the Shield, with all their accessories, are marshalled to form a single united group, the achievement of the husband having precedence to the dexter. If married to a Commoner, a Peeress in her own right bears her own arms on a lozenge as before, and her husband marshals her arms ensigned with her coronet in pretence on his Shield: and this lozenge and Shield are grouped together, the lozenge yielding precedence.

Prelates bear the arms of their see impaling their own paternal and hereditary arms, the insignia of the see occupying the dexter half of the Shield, this Shield being ensigned with a mitre only. A married Prelate bears also a second Shield, placed to the sinister of the other, on which are marshalled, in accordance with ordinary usage, his own personal arms with those of his wife. The mitre then is placed over the conjoined shields.

The *Kings of Arms*, in like manner, bear two Shields, disposed to form a single group: on the dexter Shield their official arms impale their personal; and on the sinister

Shield their personal arms are marshalled with the arms of their wives.

Again, the same usage obtains in marshalling the arms of *Knights of Orders of Knighthood* who, when married, bear two Shields grouped together. On the dexter Shield are blazoned the arms of the Knight himself alone; and around this Shield are displayed the insignia of his Order, or Orders, of Knighthood: and on the sinister Shield the arms of the Knight and of his wife are marshalled, but without the knightly insignia. This second Shield is generally environed with decorative foliage. This usage, prevalent in England, is not accepted or adopted by foreign Heralds: nor does it appear to be required by true heraldic principle, or to be strictly in accordance with it. The wife of a Knight shares his knightly title, and takes precedence from her husband's knightly rank; and a knight, with perfect heraldic consistency, might marshal his own knightly insignia about the Shield which is charged with his own arms and those of his wife, whether united by impalement, or when the latter are borne in pretence: and thus a single Shield would be borne, and there would cease to exist any motive for endeavouring to impart to a second Shield some general resemblance to its companion by wreaths or other unmeaning accessories. There are ancient precedents for the use of a single shield.

Official Arms are not hereditary.

Royal Personages, when married, bear their own arms on a separate Shield; and a second Shield bears the arms of the husband and wife conjoined.

The circumstances of every case must exercise a considerable influence in determining the Marshalling of the Accessories of any Shield, Lozenge, or Group. As a general rule, however, the *Helm* always rests on the chief of the Shield: Commoners, Knights, Baronets, and Peers place their *Crest* upon the Helm: Peers and Princes place their *Helm* upon the Coronet, and their Crest is placed upon the Helmet. The SOVEREIGN places the Crest upon the Royal Crown, which is a part of the Royal Crest, and it is unusual to duplicate the Crown by repeating it below the Helmet. The *Mantling* is displayed from the back of the Helm : it is most effective when simple in its form and adjustment, and when it droops behind the Shield. The *Motto* is usually placed below the Shield ; but if it has special reference to the Crest, above the Crest. A Scottish motto always goes over the Crest. *Supporters* are usually placed erect, as if in the act of really supporting the Shield : they ought to stand either on an appropriate ground, or on a Gothic basement to the entire Achievement. *Badges*, with all *Official* and *Knightly Insignia*, and all other *Honourable Insignia* of every kind, are rightly marshalled in an Achievement of Arms.

CHAPTER XII

CADENCY

Marks of Cadency are temporary or permanent—The Label—The Bordure—The Bendlet, Barrulet, and Canton—Change of Tincture—Secondary Charges—Single Small Charges—Differences of Illegitimacy—Cadency of Crests, Badges, &c.—Modern Cadency.

"Merke ye wele theys questionys here, now folowying!"
—BOKE OF ST. ALBANS, A.D. 1486.

AMONGST his comrades in arms, or in the midst of a hostile array, the last object that a mediæval Knight would expect or desire to observe, on the morning of a battle or a joust, would be an exact counterpart of himself. Occasions, indeed, might sometimes arise, when it might be highly desirable that five or six counterfeit "Richmonds" should accompany one real one to "the field"; or, when a "wild boar of Ardennes" might prefer to encounter the hunters, having about him the choice of his own "boar's brood," garnished at all points exactly after his own fashion. These, however, are rare and strictly exceptional cases. And the Knight, to whom distinction was as the breath of his nostrils, as he closed his vizor trusted confidently to his heraldic insignia to distinguish him, while, in the fore-front of the fray, with sword and lance and axe he would strive manfully to distinguish himself. This implies that Heraldry, besides assigning to different families their own distinct insignia, should possess the faculty of distinguishing the several members, and also the various branches of the same family, the one from the other. A faculty such as this Heraldry does possess, in its marks of CADENCY.

In "*marking Cadency*"—that is, in distinguishing the armorial insignia of kinsmen, who are members of the very same family, or of some one of its various branches, it is a necessary condition of every system of "Differencing" that, while in itself clear and definite and significant, it should be secondary to the leading characteristics of the original Coat of Arms which denotes the senior branch of the Family, and also declares from what fountain-head all the kinsmen of all the branches have derived their common descent.

Various methods for thus marking Cadency were adopted, and accepted as satisfactory, in the early days of Heraldry. Of these I now shall describe and illustrate such as are most emphatic in themselves, and in their character most decidedly heraldic,—such also as most advantageously may be retained in use in our own Heraldry of the present time. It will be seen that the "Differences" which mark Cadency necessarily resolve themselves into two groups or classes: one, in which the "Difference" is *temporary* only in its significance and use,—as, when an eldest son, on the death of his father, succeeds to the position in the family which his father had held, he removes his Mark of Cadency as eldest son from his Shield, assumes the unmarked Shield as his father had borne it before him, and tranfers to his own son the mark that previously had distinguished his Shield from that of his father. In the other group, the Marks of Cadency are more *permanent*, and consequently may become integral elements of the heraldic composition in which they appear: thus, the mark of Cadency which distinguishes any particular branch of a family, is borne alike by all the members of that branch, and in that branch it is transmitted from generation to generation.

More than one Mark of Cadency may be introduced into the same Coat of Arms; and, for the purpose of some

M

form of secondary distinction, it is quite correct Heraldry to *mark Marks of Cadency*—to charge one variety of mark, that is, upon another.

The LABEL, Nos. 271, 272, is blazoned as a Mark of Cadency in the earliest Rolls of Arms, and it appears discharging this duty in the earliest examples. The Label is generally borne with three points, as in No. 271; frequently with five, as in No. 272; and occasionally with four or with more than five points. It is quite certain that no significance was formerly attached to the number of the points, the object in all cases being to make the Label

No. 336.—Eldest Sons of Edward I. and II.   No. 337.—Black Prince.

distinctly visible, and to adjust the points to the general composition of the Shield. Labels are of various tinctures. EDWARD I., EDWARD II., and EDWARD III., each one during the lifetime of his father, bore the Shield of England, No. 187, differenced with an *azure label*, sometimes of three points, as in No. 336, and sometimes having five points. EDWARD the BLACK PRINCE marked the Royal Shield of EDWARD III. with a *label argent*, as in No. 337; and a plain silver label has since been the Mark of Cadency of every succeeding heir-apparent to the English throne. The Label has been used in this manner by personages of all ranks who have borne arms, from the time of HENRY III.; and examples abound in all the early Rolls of Arms, in Monuments, and upon Seals.

The LABEL, borne as a Mark of Cadency, was sometimes, particularly in the cases of junior members of the Royal Family, charged with other figures and devices, as differences of a secondary rank. Or, when it is thus charged, the charges upon a Label may be considered to be elements of the Label itself, in its capacity of a Mark of Cadency. EDMOND, the first Earl of LANCASTER, as I have already shown, No. 249, differenced his father's Arms of England with a *Label of France*, No. 338—an azure label, that is, charged with golden fleurs de lys, to denote his French alliance; and thus by the same process he was Marshalling and Marking Cadency. JOHN OF GHENT, Duke of LANCASTER, differenced with an *ermine Label*, No. 339, derived

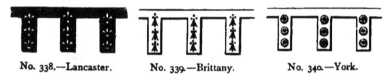

No. 338.—Lancaster.   No. 339.—Brittany.   No. 340.—York.

from the ermine shield of Brittany (No. 15): and the Plantagenet Dukes of YORK charged each point of their silver Label with *three torteaux*, No. 340, which may be considered to have been derived from the shield of Wake (No. 82). In order to show them on a larger scale, the Labels in Nos. 338–343 are represented without the Shields on which they were charged. All these Shields would be repetitions of the same blazonry of France and England quarterly: Nos. 252 and 253.

The Label, with various Differences, has generally been the Royal Mark of Cadency; and now differenced silver Labels are borne, to mark Cadency, by every member of our Royal Family.

Like the points of Labels, the Charges blazoned on those points had no fixed or determinate numbers. That both the Labels and their Charges should be distinct and conspicuous, was the special object with which they were blazoned. Accordingly, in different examples of the same

Label the number of the repetitions of the Charges sometimes is found to differ. At the same time, in the earliest
examples of charged Labels, the repetitions of the Charges,
while devoid of any special differencing aim or meaning,
may be considered to have been suggested by the sources
from which the Charges themselves were derived. For
example : the Label of Lancaster, No. 338, of Earl EDMOND,
derived directly from the Shield of *France ancient*, No. 247,
with its field *semée de lys*, has three fleurs de lys upon
each point, so that this Label has the appearance of being
also *semée de lys*. Had it been derived from the Shield of
France modern, No. 248, charged with three fleurs de lys
only, a single fleur de lys in all probability would have

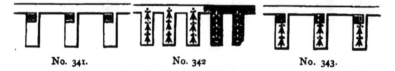

No. 341.   No. 342   No. 343.

been blazoned on each of the three points of this same
Label. Upon this principle the Label of Prince LIONEL,
DUKE of CLARENCE, second son of EDWARD III., which is
differenced with *cantons gules*, has a single canton on each
point, as in No. 341, evidently because only a single canton
can be blazoned on a Shield. The figures and devices that
are charged for secondary difference upon Labels vary widely
in their character; but, however difficult it now may be in
very many instances to trace these differencing charges to
their sources, and so to determine the motive which led to
their adoption, there can be no doubt that originally they
were chosen and adopted for the express purpose of denoting and recording some alliance or dependency. Some
early Labels are of a compound character; that is, they are
charged with two distinct groups of devices, which are at
once divided and conjoined by impalement. Such a Label
was borne by Prince HENRY, son of JOHN of GHENT, be-

tween the time of his father's death and his own accession as
HENRY IV. (Feb. 3 to Sept. 30, 1399): it was a *Label of
five points per pale of Brittany and Lancaster*, No. 342, being
his father's Label impaling that of his mother's father. The
second son of this Prince, THOMAS Duke of CLARENCE,
instead of adopting impalement, charged *a red canton
upon each point of an ermine Label*, as in No. 343: while
his brother, JOHN Duke of BEDFORD, bore their father's
Label, No. 342.

The BORDURE, both plain and charged, is a Mark
of Cadency borne by Princes and by personages of
various ranks. EDMOND, youngest son
of EDWARD I., differenced *England*
with a plain *silver bordure*, as in No.
344: the HOLLANDS, Earls of KENT,
did the same: and the same silver
bordure also was borne by THOMAS,
youngest son of EDWARD III., about
the quartered shield of *France ancient
and England;* and about the quartered

No. 344.—Holland, of Kent.

shield of *France modern and England* by HUMPHREY,
youngest son of HENRY IV. Prince JOHN of ELTHAM,
as I have already shown, and after him the HOLLANDS,
Dukes of EXETER, differenced *England with a Bordure
of France:* No. 24. Though not so numerous as Labels,
Bordures employed to mark Cadency exist in very many
early examples, and a variety of devices appear charged
upon them for secondary Difference. See No. 140. In
the Royal Heraldry of our own times the Bordure is
not used as a Royal Difference; but its use is retained in
Scotland for differencing Shields of less exalted rank.

In some few early Examples a BENDLET is charged
upon the paternal shield as a mark of Cadency: and a
BARRULET is found to have been also used for the same
purpose. Thus, HENRY, second son of EDMOND the first

Earl of LANCASTER, during the lifetime of his elder brother,

differenced *England* with an *azure Bendlet,* as in No. 345 : and, in the Seal of HENRY DE PERCY, son and heir of HENRY third Baron, the lion is debruised, for Difference, by a Barrulet which crosses the Shield in the honour-point. Possibly, this Barrulet may be a *Label without points.* A CANTON, plain, or more frequently

No. 345.
Henry of Lancaster.

charged, and in many examples of ermine, is also added to Shields to mark Cadency, but more frequently nowadays its use denotes absence of blood descent. See Nos. 128, 129, 130.

To mark Cadency by a *change of Tinctures* was a simple expedient, and such a one as would naturally be practised at an early period. It was effected, first, in the case of the *Field :* thus (H. 3) the brothers DE LA ZOUCHE severally bear—*Gu., bezantée,* and, *Az., bezantée ;* and the brothers FURNIVAL (H. 3) bear—*Arg., a bend between six martlets gu.,* and, *Or, a bend between six martlets gu.* Secondly, the change is effected in the *Charges :* thus, two William BARDOLFS (H. 3 and E. 2) severally bear—*Az., three cinquefoils or,* and, *Az., three cinquefoils arg.* Thirdly, the tinctures are *reversed :* for example, for two Sir JOHN HARCOURTS (E. 2)—*Gu., two bars or,* and, *Or, two bars gu.* Fourthly, there is a complete change in *all the tinctures :* and so, while Sir ANDREW LOTEREL (E. 2) bears—*Or, a bend between six martlets sa.,* Sir GEFFREY LOTEREL (E. 2) bears—*Az., a bend between six martlets argent.* Finally, this system of marking Cadency admits various modifications of the changes already described : thus, in the Arms of Mortimer, No. 131, *gules* is substituted for *azure ;* and, again, in the same Shield an *inescutcheon ermine* takes the place of the *inescutcheon argent.*

Another and a favourite method of marking Cadency, calculated to exercise a great and decided influence in the development of heraldic blazon, is the *addition of secondary Charges* of small size (not on a Label or a Bordure. but) semée over the field of a Shield, or charged upon an Ordinary, or disposed in orle. In a large number of examples, these small charges are found to have been gradually reduced to six or three, in order to admit of their being blazoned on a somewhat larger scale, and consequently made more distinct. Again: while the number and the tinctures of the secondary differencing charges remain the same, in order to carry out the Cadency still farther the secondary charges themselves are varied: and, once

No. 346.—Beauchamp of Elmely.   No. 347.—Beauchamp at Carlaverock.

more, in other cases the identity of the original secondary charges is retained, but their number is increased or diminished. I must be content to illustrate these various forms of Cadency with a few examples only. First, a group of shields of the BEAUCHAMPS:—Beauchamp of Elmely (H. 3)—*Gu.*, *a fesse or*, No. 346: Beauchamp at Carlaverock—*Gu.*, *crusilée and a fesse or*, No. 347: Beauchamp, Earl of Warwick—*Gu.*, *a fesse between six crosses crosslets or*, No. 348: and Beauchamp of Bletshoe—*Gu.*, *a fesse between six martlets or*, No. 349. Second, a corresponding group of shields of the BERKELEYS:—Maurice de Barkele (or Berkeley)—*Gu.*, *a chevron arg.* (H. 3): and then for other Berkeleys—*Gu.*, *a chevron between ten crosses pattées, six and four, arg.;* and the same Ordinary, with either *ten*

cinquefoils of silver, or the same number of *white roses*.
Three CORBETS bear severally (E. 2)—*Or, a raven sa.; Or,
two ravens sa.;* and, *Or, three ravens sa.* And, once more,
their original Shield—*Gu., a chevron or*, is differenced by the
COBHAMS by charging the Ordinary with three lioncels,
three eaglets, three crosslets, three mullets, three estoiles,
three crescents, or three fleurs de lys, all of them sable.
The particular devices and figures selected thus to mark
Cadency, like those charged upon Labels or Bordures, must
be considered to have a special significance of their own,
though this significance may frequently fail to be discerned
in consequence of our being no longer able to trace out
their association with the sources from which they were

No. 348.—Beauchamp of Warwick   No. 349.—Beauchamp of Bletshoe.

obtained. The alliances and the incidents that give these
various Marks of Cadency, when it is possible to ascertain
what they may have been, illustrate in a striking manner
the motives by which the early Heralds were influenced
when they differenced the Arms of Kinsmen.

Official Insignia sometimes become Marks of Cadency.
Thus, JOHN DE GRANDISON, Bishop of Exeter (A.D. 1327–
1369), on the bend in his paternal arms, No. 89, substitutes
a *golden mitre* for the central eaglet, as in No. 350. WILLIAM
COURTENAY, Archbishop of Canterbury (A.D. 1381–1396),
adopts a different course, and charges three golden mitres
upon each point of the Label of Courtenay—*Or, three torteaux, over all a label of three points az. charged on each
point with as many mitres gold.* And again, HENRY LE

Despencer, Bishop of Norwich (A.D. 1370–1406), places about his paternal shield an *azure bordure charged with eight golden mitres* (see the largest shield in No. 351). On his official seal the canopied effigy of the Bishop stands between this, his personal Shield, and the Shield of his see —*az., three mitres or :* but his Secretum, or private seal, is much more interesting, as an heraldic image of the man himself. Haughty, fierce, cruel, and pugnacious, his career not less inglorious as a military commander than as a churchman, this Henry le Despencer, a grandson of the unhappy favourite of the no less hapless Edward II.,

No. 350.—Bishop Grandison.   No. 351.—Secretum of Bishop le Despencer.

was one of the war-loving prelates who occasionally appear sustaining a strange, and yet as it would seem a characteristic, part in the romantic drama of mediæval history. His Secretum, No. 351, displays his Shield of *Despencer*, differenced with his bordure of mitres, couché from a large mantled helm, surmounted by a mitre, in place of a crest-coronet, which supports the Despencer crest, a silver griffin's head of ample size; on either side are the Shields of the *see of Norwich*, and of *Ferrers* (the Bishop's mother was Anne, daughter of William Lord Ferrers of Groby) —*Or, seven mascles, three three and one, gu.;* the legend is, S . HENRICI . DESPENCER . NORWICENSIS . EPISCOPI.

At an early period, Cadency was marked by *adding a single small charge* to the blazon of a Shield, or by charging some secondary device or figure upon any accessory of a Shield of arms.   Such a Mark of Cadency as this, obtained from some allied Shield, and charged upon an ordinary or principal bearing, or occupying a conspicuous position in the general composition, was in high favour with the Heralds of both the fourteenth and fifteenth centuries. From the early examples, which exist in great numbers and in as great variety, it will be sufficient for me to adduce only a few specimens—a single example, indeed, illustrates the system.   The Shield of *Ufford*, in the Seal of MATILDA of LANCASTER, which I have

No. 352.
Sir Fulk Fitz Warin.

already described (No. 320), is thus differenced with a single fleur de lys in the first quarter.   Precisely in the same manner Sir FULK FITZ WARIN differences the Shield of the head of his house, No. 17, by charging a *mullet sable* upon the first quarter, as in No. 352.   THOMAS LE SCROPE,

No. 354.

No. 355.

No. 353.—Thomas le Scrope.

on the other hand, for Cadency marks the golden bend upon his azure Shield, No. 111, with an *annulet sable*, as in No. 353.   Two members of the family of Beauchamp charge their golden fesse (see Nos. 346–349), the one with a *crescent sable,* and the other with a *pierced mullet* of the same tincture: Nos. 354, 355.   In like manner, in addition to various labels, the NEVILLES charge no less than eight different small figures upon their silver saltire, No. 121, to distinguish different members and branches of their powerful race: I give one of these Shields in No. 356, which was borne by GEORGE NEVILLE, Lord LATIMER, from the monument to Earl RICHARD DE BEAUCHAMP at Warwick—*Gu., on a saltire arg. a gimmel-ring az.* : another

No. 356.—Lord Latimer.   No 357.—Neville.

No. 358.—Sir William de Brewys.

differenced shield of Neville, No. 357, has *a cinquefoil* charged on the saltire: a third example from this group I have already given, No. 122, differenced with *a rose* : this shield, No. 122, is now borne by the Earl of ABERGAVENNY. Once more: Sir WILLIAM DE BREWYS (E. 2) bears—*Az., crusilée and a lion rampt. or*, No. 358, which coat another Sir WILLIAM DE BREWYS differences, to distinguish himself from his kinsman, while at the same time declaring their near relationship, by simply charging a *red fleur de lys* upon his lion's shoulder.

Differences of Illegitimacy, which rightly and indeed necessarily are included under the general head of "Cadency," do not appear at any time to have assumed a definite or decided character, and yet they bring before the student of Heraldry much curious matter for inquiry and investigation. Early in the true heraldic era illegitimate sons are found to have differenced their paternal arms, as other sons lawfully born might have done: and it does not appear that any peculiar methods of differencing were adopted, palpably for the purpose of denoting illegitimacy

of birth, before the fourteenth century had drawn near to
its close.   And even then, if any express heraldic rule on
this point ever was framed, which is very doubtful, it
certainly was never observed with any care or regularity.

The earliest known example of the arms of a man of
illegitimate birth is the fine Shield of WILLIAM LONGESPÉE,
Earl of SALISBURY, son of HENRY II. and FAIR ROSÁMOND,
No. 197.   This Shield is supposed to have been assumed
and borne by the Earl on his marriage with the daughter
and heiress of D'EVREUX, when in right of his wife he succeeded to the Earldom of Salisbury : but this theory does
not rest upon any solid foundation, since it would be very
difficult to show that the Shield with the six lioncels was
certainly borne, on his armorial ensign, by the father-in-law
of Earl William.   Also, if a Shield charged with an escarbuncle and many lioncels, which has been assigned to
GEOFFREY Count of ANJOU, was really borne by the
Founder of the House of PLANTAGENET, Earl WILLIAM
LONGESPÉE may have derived his own Shield from his
paternal grandfather.   Upon his Counterseal the Earl
displays his own "long sword" as his proper device.
In like manner, certain other personages, also illegitimate,
appear to have borne arms which were either expressly
assigned to themselves by the Sovereign, or such as they
assumed in right of their mothers or wives.   In all such
cases as these, the Arms were not the paternal coat in
any way differenced, but what now would be designated
"fresh grants."   Towards the beginning of the fifteenth
century, however, a peculiar kind of Differencing for
Illegitimacy gradually prevailed throughout Europe: thus,
illegitimate children either altered the position of the
charges in their paternal Shield ; or they marshalled the
entire paternal arms upon a bend or a fesse ; or they composed for themselves a fresh Shield, either using their
father's badges and the actual charges of his Shield, or

adopting devices evidently derived from the paternal bearings; or they bore the paternal Shield differenced in a peculiarly conspicuous manner with certain marks by which they might be readily and certainly distinguished.

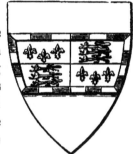

When the composition of the paternal Shield would admit of such an arrangement, the field not being argent, an illegitimate son sometimes bore his father's arms marshalled fesse-wise, so as to leave both the chief and the base of his Shield plain white. HENRY, Earl of WORCESTER, whose father was an illegitimate son of HENRY BEAUFORT, third Duke of

No. 359.
Henry, Earl of Worcester.

SOMERSET, bore the arms of Beaufort couped in this manner in chief and in base, as if they were charged upon a very broad fesse on the field: No. 359.

JOHN DE BEAUFORT (great-grandfather of HENRY, Earl of WORCESTER), eldest illegitimate son of Prince JOHN of

No. 360.—Beaufort before 1397.

No. 361.—Beaufort after 1397.

GHENT, *before* the Act for his legitimation was passed in the year 1397, bore his father's hereditary arms of *Lancaster— England with a label of France*, No. 249—*on a broad bend*, the field being *per pale arg. and az.*, the Lancastrian livery colours: No. 360. After their legitimation act had become a law, this same JOHN DE BEAUFORT, with his brothers, sons, and grandsons, bore the Royal quartered shield of France and England, No. 361, differenced, not with labels, but with *a bordure componé arg. and az.* (the Lancastrian colours): the different members of the Beaufort family slightly varied the bordure, but by the head of their house it was borne

No. 362.—Charles, Earl of Worcester.

as in No. 361. It will be seen that this is the coat that HENRY, Earl of WORCESTER (himself the legitimate son of an illegitimate son), bore fesse-wise, as in No. 359. The father of this Earl HENRY, CHARLES SOMERSET, Earl of WORCESTER (illegitimate son of the third Duke of SOMERSET), differenced *Beaufort*, No. 361, with a *silver bendlet sinister*, as in No. 362, the bendlet covering the quarterings, but being included within the bordure.

Since the fifteenth century, in English Heraldry, a narrow bendlet or baton sinister, couped at its extremities,

No. 363.—Sir Roger de Clarendon.

No. 364.—Radulphus de Arundel.

either plain or charged, has usually been the mark employed as difference by the illegitimate descendants of the Royal Family. It was borne by ARTHUR PLANTAGENET, Viscount LISLE, son of EDWARD IV.: by HENRY FITZ ROY, Duke of

RICHMOND, son of HENRY VIII., and, variously differenced, by illegitimate descendants of CHARLES II.—that is, it is borne at the present day, *argent*, by the Duke of BUC-CLEUCH ; *ermine*, by the Duke of CLEVELAND ; *componée arg. and az.*, by the Duke of GRAFTON ; and, *gules charged with three white roses*, by the Duke of ST. ALBANS.

Sir ROGER DE CLARENDON, illegitimate son of the BLACK PRINCE, bore *on a sable bend the three Ostrich Feathers* of his illustrious father's "*Shield of Peace*," the field of his Shield being golden, as in No. 363. Here the "Difference for Illegitimacy" is very emphatically marked in a singularly felicitous and beautiful Shield.

The paternal arms of illegitimate children have also sometimes been carried by them charged on a *canton*, either dexter or sinister, the rest of the Shield being left blank, or perhaps in some cases displaying the maternal arms ; of this usage I am not able to give any good example, in English Heraldry, of certain authority : one other variety of these singular Shields, however, I must add to my small group of examples, which was first noticed by Mr. MONTAGU ("Guide to the Study of Heraldry," p. 44). This is the Shield, No. 364, of RADULPHUS DE ARUNDEL ; and it bears the quartered arms of the Earls of ARUNDEL—*Fitz Alan* and *Warrenne* (*gu. a lion rampt. or*, and No. 68), "*flanched*," —that is, blazoned only upon the flanches (see No. 141) of the Shield, the central area being blank.

For a lengthy period the use of the *bend, bendlet,* and *baton sinister* was usual for the purpose of denoting illegiti-macy, but this has now given way to the use, in England, of a *bordure wavy ;* in Scotland, of a *bordure compony ;* whilst in Ireland both these *bordures* are used, more usually, however, the *bordure wavy* being employed. By a curious divergence the *bordure wavy* is not a mark of illegitimacy in Scotland, but a mark of perfectly legitimate cadency. The use of the *bendlet sinister* for the debruising of crests still exists in

England and Ireland, but crests are not usually differenced for any reason in Scotland.

In treating of this subject, some writers have maintained that the *bordure componée* is, in its heraldic nature, the most decided and unquestionable Difference for Illegitimacy : and this opinion these writers have derived from the singularly contradictory fact, that the BEAUFORTS differenced with a bordure componée when they became legally *legitimate*. A bordure componeé *may*, indeed, be used with such an intention, as it is used by the Duke of RICHMOND, who bears the arms of CHARLES II. within a *bordure componée arg. and gu., charged with eight roses of the last;* but by the BEAUFORTS it was used with an intention exactly the reverse of this. The bordure, however, whatever its aspect or modification of treatment, remains still, as it was of old, an honourable Difference, until some abatement of honour has been associated with its presence under special circumstances. But the stereotyped use of the *bordure wavy* in England with a set meaning, gives to the wavy variety a lack of desirability. Marks of illegitimacy are intended to remain upon a shield for all time, although in a few historic cases their use has been discarded. And precisely the same words may be applied to any other charge that has been employed, or may be required to mark Cadency.

Marks of Cadency, as they are borne on Shields of Arms, may also be charged on Badges, Crests, and Supporters. As a matter of course, they appear on Armorial Banners and Standards under the same conditions that they are blazoned upon Shields and Surcoats. Such examples as may be necessary to illustrate heraldic usage in these cases, I propose to describe in the following Chapters.

It cannot be necessary for me to adduce any arguments in order to impress upon Students of Heraldry the importance of investigating early Cadency, or to assure them that a special interest is inseparable from this inquiry : I may suggest, however, that it is most desirable that Students should arrange groups of allied Shields, and should carefully blazon them with their various "Marks of Cadency," being careful also to record their authorities for every example.

MODERN CADENCY is marked by the Label and by single small Charges, which take precedence in the following order :—

1. The *Label*, No. 271.
2. The *Crescent*, No. 166, A.
3. The *Mullet*, No. 278.
4. The *Martlet*, No. 161.
5. The *Annulet*, No. 154.
6. The *Fleur de lys*, No. 246.
7. The *Rose*, No. 298.
8. The *Cross Moline*, No. 99.
9. The *Octofoil*, or *Double Quatrefoil*.

When they are adopted, Marks of Cadency now are generally placed upon the Honour Point of the Shield, or in some other conspicuous position: one of these Marks also may be charged upon another, if desired,—as a Martlet may be charged upon a Crescent to denote the fourth son of a second son; and so in other cases.

No. 365.
Seal of William Fraser: appended to Homage Deed, A.D. 1295, preserved in H.M. Record Office.

The Seal of WILLIAM FRASER, No. 365, from Mr. Laing's Collection, exemplifies in a singular and interesting manner the early use of a differenced Label. Here the Label appears, without any Shield, borne as if it were a Badge: and it is charged, on each of its three points, with two devices that have the appearance of mullets of six points, but which really may be *fraises*—strawberry-leaves, the rebus-device of Fraser. (See pp. 182–185.)

N

CHAPTER XIII

DIFFERENCING

*Differencing to denote Feudal Alliance or Dependency: Differencing
without any Alliance—Augmentation—Abatement.*

"Differencing, which comprises in truth the growth and ramification of
Coat-Armour, and the whole system of its early development, has been
strangely lost sight of in the numerous treatises on Armory that have satis-
fied recent generations of Englishmen."

—HERALD AND GENEALOGIST, II. 32.

DIFFERENCING, using the term here as distinct from, or
perhaps as not identical with, the subject of CADENCY,
includes not only the treatment of Coats of Arms and
other armorial insignia, that denote and are based upon
Feudal Alliance or *Dependency*, but without blood-relation-
ship; but also implies a comprehensive system of distinguishing similar Arms, when they are borne by individuals
or families between whom no kind of alliance is known
to have existed. It is evident, on the one hand, that a
feudal influence would naturally lead to some degree of
assimilation to the Coat-Armour of the feudal Chief, in
the Arms of all allies and dependants: and, on the other
hand, it will readily be understood that, even in the early
days of its career, Heraldry would see the necessity for
providing for the constantly increasing demands upon its
resources; and, consequently, that it would organise a
system which would enable the same Ordinaries and the
same principal Charges to appear in distinct Shields, without either confusion or misapprehension.

It is highly probable, and indeed it may be assumed to be certain, that what I have called a "feudal influence," in the thirteenth and fourteenth centuries in no slight degree affected the general composition of Coats of Arms. In very many instances the working of this influence is still palpable; and it is always interesting to the student of Heraldry, as it must always be eminently useful to the student of History, to detect its presence and to explore its method of action. Like Cadency, feudal Differencing is expressed by various means, all of them indicating, in a greater or a less degree, the motive which suggested their adoption. I proceed at once to examples, which illustrate and explain the system so clearly and so fully, that prolonged introductory remarks are altogether superfluous.

No. 366.—Earl of Chester.

Upon his Seal, RANULPH DE BLON-DEVILLE, Earl of CHESTER (died in 1232) bears three garbs or wheat-sheaves; and Rolls of Arms of the time of HENRY III. blazon the Shield of the Earl of CHESTER as—*Az.*, *three garbs or*, No. 366. This Shield has been assigned to the Earls of CHESTER to this day: and, in token of feudal alliance, from the middle of the thirteenth century, "one or more garbs," in the words of Mr. PLANCHÉ, "are seen in the majority of Coats belonging to the nobility and gentry of the County Palatine of Chester." Thus, since the year 1390, the arms of GROSVENOR have been—*Az.*, *a garb or.*

A cinquefoil, said to have been borne by him on a red Shield, was the device of ROBERT FITZ-PERNEL, Earl of LEICESTER, who died in 1204. Accordingly, the cinquefoil, derived from him, as early as the thirteenth century, appears in token of feudal connection on the Shields of many families of Leicestershire. As I have already shown, (page 183) a BERKELEY, who was of Leicestershire, substituted *ten cinquefoils* for the ten crosses patée of the Berkeley Shield; and thus he combined feudal Differencing with Cadency.

Many a red chevron or chevronel, with other devices, charged upon a golden field, or a gold chevron on a red field, is a sign of feudal alliance with the great house of DE CLARE, whose Shield was—*Or, three chevronels gu.*, No.

No. 367.—Fitz Ralph.

124. For example, the FITZ-RALPHS, near neighbours of the De Clares at Clare in Suffolk, differenced the Shield of the Earls by charging *silver fleurs de lys* on each chevronel, as in No. 367 (E. 2); and, for secondary difference, they sometimes added a *bordure azure*, as in the fine early Brass at Pebmarsh, near Clare. Again: by a change of tinctures, without affecting the charges of the Shield, the Arms of L'ERCEDECKNE (now Archdeacon) are—*Arg., three chevronels sa.*

At Carlaverock, EDMUND DE HASTINGS, brother of the Earl, bore—*Or, a maunche gu., with a label of five points sa.*, the Earl himself bearing simply—*Or, a maunche gu.*, No. 276. And, close by the side of EDMOND DE HASTINGS was his friend and companion, the feudal ally, without doubt, of his house, JOHN PAIGNEL, a very proper comrade, as the chronicler testifies—

" Un bacheler jolif et comté,"

who differenced Hastings by change of tinctures, and bore —*Vert, a maunche or.*

The Shield of the noble house of DE LUTERELL, or LOTEREL, I have blazoned with changed tinctures for two near kinsmen bearing that name (page 182), thus showing in what manner they marked their Cadency. This same shield, No. 368—*Or, a bend between six martlets sa.*, was also differenced by other families to mark their feudal alliance with the house of Luterell. Thus, the DE FUR-NIVALS, themselves a powerful and distinguished family, who held their lands by feudal tenure under the Lute-rells, in token of this alliance bore the Shield of De Luterell with a fresh change of tinctures ; and, accordingly, the arms of the De Furnivals are well known as—*Arg., a bend between six martlets gu.* Then, while the FURNI-VALS, for Cadency, differenced these

No. 368.—De Luterell.

arms amongst themselves, *their* feudal allies and depen-dants, the ECCLESALLS or EKELESHALES, the MOUNTENEYS, the WADESLES or WADSLEYS, and the WORTELES or WORT-LEYS, all united in declaring their connection with their chief by assuming arms founded upon the Furnival Coat. These very inte-resting and characteristic examples of feudal Differencing are well blazoned, as follows, in the Roll of EDWARD II. For DE ECCLESALL—*Sa., a bend be-tween six martlets or :* for DE MOUN-TENEY—*Gu., a bend between six martlets or :* for DE WADSLEY—*Arg., on a bend between six martlets gu., three escallops*

No. 369.—De Wadsley.

or, No. 369: and for DE WORTLEY—*Arg., on a bend be-tween six martlets gu., three bezants*, No. 370.

The MOUNTENEYS further difference their common arms, for Cadency, after this manner. Instead of *gules*, Sir ERNAUF DE MOUNTENEY has the field of his shield *azure*, his bend and martlets being *golden :* Sir JOHN bears these same arms, but charges his bend with a *mullet gules*, No. 371 : Sir T. DE MOUNTENEY bears Sir John's arms, but with a *field gules :*

and another Sir JOHN cotises his bend thus—*Gu., a bend cotised between six martlets or*, No. 372.

Noith of the Tweed, also, the same principle is found to be exemplified in Scottish Heraldry.   "In Annandale," writes Mr. SETON, "the chief and saltire of the Bruces are carried (of different tinctures and with additional figures) by the Jardines, Kirkpatricks, Johnstons, and other families." The arms of BRUCE are—*Or, a saltire and a chief gu.*, No. 73: those of JARDINE are—*Arg., a saltire and a chief gu., the latter charged with three mullets of the field, pierced of the second:* and the arms of KIRKPATRICK are—*Arg., a saltire*

No. 370.   No. 371.   No. 372.
De Wortley.   Sir John de Mounteney.   Sir John de Mounteney.

and chief az., the latter charged with three cushions or.   This coat of Kirkpatrick is also borne by the JOHNSTONS, the tinctures differenced thus—*Arg., a saltire sa., and on a chief gu. three cushions or.*

Once more, returning to the southern side of the Scottish border, of RICHARD DE NEVILLE, the renowned "King-maker," we find it to be recorded that, so great was his popularity at Calais, of which city he was governor, that his Badges were universally adopted,—"no man esteeming himself gallant whose head was not adorned with his *silver ragged staff* (No. 294) ; nor was any door frequented, that had not his *white cross* (silver saltire, No. 121) painted thereon." This was an extravagant application of the earlier usage in denoting feudal alliance, such as was in keeping with the heraldic sentiment of the second half of the fourteenth century. Those good citizens of Calais, however, who were Neville-worshippers four hundred years ago, were not singular in exhibiting an armorial ensign at the entrance to their houses. Numerous, indeed, are the doorways in various parts of England, and particularly in the counties of Surrey, Sussex, and Norfolk, which in the "sign of the chequers" still display the insignia (*chequée or and az.*, No. 68) of the once mighty Earls of WARRENNE and SURREY; and thus show that relics of the old feudal influence are endowed with a tenacious vitality, which prolongs their existence for ages after the feudal system itself has passed away. But no doubt some cases must be referred to the less romantic explanation of the reckoning board of the Steward.

Differencing adopted, so far as now is apparent, *simply for the sake of distinction*, lays open before the student of Heraldry a wide and a diversified field of inquiry. All the miscellaneous charges that are associated in blazon with the Ordinaries, and also with the Subordinaries, thus are brought under consideration; and, without a doubt, it was for the express purpose of Differencing that many of these charges were introduced into English Heraldry. How far some remote degree of relationship, or some subordinate feudal motive now lost to sight and forgotten, may originally have affected the choice of Charges "for difference," it is not possible now to determine; nor can we always follow the rebus-loving search for a " Difference," that might speak through that allusive quality which is a primary element of the Herald's science. We do know that the act of bearing the same arms by different families, without some heraldic Difference, was of very rare occurrence; and that, when it did occur, it was regarded with marked surprise, and on more than one occasion led to a memorable controversy: and, further, we find great numbers of early differenced

Shields, which illustrate in a very effective manner the growth and development of English Heraldry. Shields of this order have strong claims on our attention. The examples that I am able here to place before students are to be regarded simply as specimens, few in number, and yet sufficient to show some of the varied forms under which early Differencing was effected.

The proceedings in the High Court of Chivalry in the suit between Sir RICHARD LE SCROPE and Sir ROBERT GROS-VENOR, relative to the right to the Arms—*Azure, a bend or*, No. 111—commenced on the 17th of August 1385, and the final judgment of the King himself upon the appeal of the defendant against the finding of the Court was not pronounced till the 27th of May 1390. On the 15th of May 1389 the judgment of the Court assigned the arms—*Azure, a bend or*—to Sir RICHARD LE SCROPE; and to Sir ROBERT GROSVENOR, these arms—*Az., a bend or, within a plain bordure argent*. Thus the Court confirmed to Sir Richard le Scrope the right to bear the Ordinary in its severe simplicity, without any other charge and without any Difference: and, at the same time, it was decided that these arms of Scrope should be differenced, in order that they might become the arms of Grosvenor, and the "Difference" was to be a *plain silver bordure*. The whole of the proceedings in this remarkable case are preserved, and have been published; and they derive a peculiar interest from the circumstance, that amongst the witnesses who gave evidence was the father of English Poetry, GEOFFREY CHAUCER. Appeal having been made to the Sovereign, RICHARD II. determined that a "plain bordure argent" was a Mark of Cadency, good and right, and perfectly sufficient as a Difference "between Cousin and Cousin in blood"; but that it was "not a sufficient Difference in Arms between two strangers in blood in one kingdom." The King, therefore, cancelled and annulled the sentence of the Court of Chivalry; and in so doing he gave a very clear definition of the distinction to be observed in Heraldry between kinsmen and strangers in blood. Then it was that the Shield, *Azure, a garb or*, was adopted as the arms of Grosvenor. We may assume, that the judgment of the Court would have been confirmed by the King, had Sir Robert Grosvenor been commanded to blazon his golden bend between two garbs, or charged with one or more garbs, or with three garbs on a chief, or with any other decided Difference which would be palpably distinct from a Mark of Cadency.

The examples of Differenced Shields which follow I have selected from the Roll of EDWARD II. It will be seen that in each small group of these examples some primary feature of the composition is common to every Shield, so that the distinction between the Shields in each group is effected either by a simple change of tinctures, or by the introduction of various secondary charges.

CHIEFS.—Sir JOHN DE ARDERNE—*Gu., crusilée and a chief or.* Sir THOMAS LE ROUS—*Erm., on a chief indented gu. two escallops arg.* Sir JOHN DE CLINTONE—*Arg., on a chief az. two fleurs de lys or*, No. 74. Sir JOHN DE CLINTONE, of Maxtoke—*Arg., on a chief az. two mullets or*, No. 75: here the Difference denotes Cadency as well as a distinct individuality.

BENDS.—Sir ROBERT POUTREL.—*Or, on a bend az. three fleurs de lys arg.* Sir WALTER DE BERMYNGHAM—*Arg., on a bend gu., cotised az., three esallops or.* OLIVER DE BOHUN —*Az., on a bend, cotised and between six lioncels or, three escallops gu.*, No. 321.

FESSES AND BARS.—Sir JOHN DE DAGEWORTH—*Erm., a fesse gu. bezantée*, No. 80. Sir G. DE WACHESHAM—*Arg., a fesse and in chief three crescents gu.* Sir R. DE COLEVILLE —*Or, a fesse gu., and in chief three torteaux.* Sir J. DE GEYTONE—*Arg., a fesse between six fleurs de lys gu.* Sir G.

DE OUSFLET—*Arg., on a fesse az. three fleurs de lys or.* Sir
R. DE LOMELYE (Lumley)—*Gu., on a fesse between three
popinjays arg., as many mullets sa.* Sir B. BADLESMERE—
Arg., a fesse between bars gemelles gu. Sir G. DE LA MERE—
Or, a fesse between bars gemelles az., No. 84. Sir J. DE
PREIERES—*Gu., a fesse between bars gemelles arg.* Sir J.
WAKE—*Or, two bars gu., in chief three torteaux*, No. 82.
Sir B. PYCOT—*Az., two bars or, in chief three bezants.* Sir
R. DE WEDONE—*Arg., two bars gu., in chief three martlets
sa.* Sir R. BORDET—*Az., two bars or, on the uppermost
three martlets gu.* Sir R. DE ROYINGE—*Arg., three bars
and an orle of martlets gu.* Sir N. DE ESTOTEVILLE—*Barry
arg. and gu., three lioncels sa.* Sir R. DE YNGELFELD—*Bar
rulée arg. and gu., on a chief or a lion pass. az.* Sir W. DE
MONECASTRE—*Barrulée arg. and gu., on a bend sa. three
escallops or.* Sir T. DE PONINGE—*Barry or and vert, on a
bend gu. three mullets arg.*

CROSSES.—Sir N. DE WEYLANDE—*Arg., on a cross gu.
five escallops or.* Sir R. BYGOD—*Or, on a cross gu. five
escallops arg.* Sir. WM. KIRKETOT—*Az., on a cross arg. five
escallops gu.* Sir WM. DE BERHAM—*Sa., a cross between four
crescents arg.* Sir R. DE BANNEBURY—*Arg., a cross patée
between four mullets gu.* Sir J. RANDOLF—*Gu., on a cross
arg. five mullets sa.* Sir G. DE DUREM—*Arg., on a cross gu.
five fleurs de lys or.* Sir P. DE GEYTONE—*Arg., crusilée and
three fleurs de lys az.* Sir R. DE HOFTOT—*Az., a cross patée
erm. between four roses erm.*

CHEVRONS.—Sir G. ROSSEL—*Or, a chevron az., between
three roses gu.* Sir J. DE CRETINGE—*Arg., a chevron between
three mullets gu.* Sir R. MALET—*Sa., a chevron between three
buckles arg.* Sir T. DE ANVERS—*Gu., a chevron between
three mullets or.* Sir WM. DE BERKEROLES—*Az., a chevron
between three crescents or.* Sir W. BLUET—*Or, a chevron
between three eagles vert.* Sir R. DE CAPLE—*Arg., a chevron
gu. between three torteaux.* Sir T. MALET—*Sa., a chevron*

between three buckles arg. Sir R. DE PEYVRE—*Arg., on a chevron az. three fleurs de lys or,* No. 125. Sir R. DE BOTERELS—*Chequée or and gu., on a chevron az. three horseshoes arg.*

LIONS.—The Earl of LINCOLN—*Or, a lion rampt. purp.,* No. 194. The Earl of ARUNDEL—*Gu., a lion rampt. or.* Sir HENRY DE PERCY—*Or, a lion rampt. az.,* No. 196. Sir

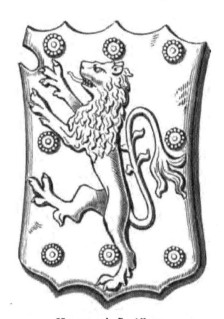

No. 373.—At St. Albans.

JOHN MOWBRAY—*Gu., a lion rampt. arg.,* No. 193. Sir R. DE SOTTONE (Sutton)—*Or, a lion rampt. vert.* Sir J. DE NORTONE—*Vert, a lion rampt. or.* Sir W. FAUCONBERG—*Arg., a lion rampt. az.* Sir G. DE HAUTVILLE—*Sa., crusilée, a lion rampt. arg.* Sir — DE MOUNTFORT—*Arg., crusilée gu., a lion rampt. az.* Sir WM. MAUFEE—*Arg., semée of escallops gu., a lion rampt. sa.* Sir J. DE CREPPINGE—*Gu., billetée or, a lion rampt. arg.* Sir R. DE ASSCHEBY—*Arg., a lion rampt. sa. billetée or.* Sir J. DE DEYVILLE—*Gu., semée de lys, a lion*

*rampt. arg.   Arg., within a bordure gu. bezantée, a lion rampt.
sa.*, for Sir T. DE PICKERING; and, *Arg., within an orle of
roses gu., a lion rampt. sa.*, for Sir R. PIERPOUND, both
apparently founded on the shield of the Earl of CORNWALL,
No. 140, which also is blazoned in this Roll.   Sir J. LE
STRANGE—*Gu., two lions pass. arg.*, No. 191.   Sir J. DE
SOMERI—*Or, two lions pass. az.*   Sir R. DE ST. WALY—
Or, two lions pass. gu.   Sir N. CARRU (Carew)—*Or, three
lions pass. sa.*   Sir J. GIFFARD—*Gu., three lions pass. arg.*, No.
192.   Sir R. LE FITZ PAYN—*Gu., three lions pass. arg., over all
a bendlet az.*   Sir G. DE CANVYLE—*Az., three lions pass arg.*
In the beautiful chantry of Abbot THOMAS RAMRYGE, at St.
Albans, one of the large sculptured Shields is charged with
a lion rampant within what may be considered to be
an *orle of roses*—the arms, as I have just shown, assigned
in the Roll of EDWARD II. to Sir R. PIERPOUND.   This
Shield, carefully drawn by the engraver himself from the
original in the Abbey Church of St. Alban, is represented in
No. 373.

AUGMENTATION, or AUGMENTATION OF HONOUR, is a
term employed to denote an addition to a Shield of arms,
specially granted by the Sovereign to commemorate some
worthy or illustrious deed, and forming an integral element
of the Shield as an hereditary bearing.   Such additions will
be found marshalled in the forms of Chiefs and Inescutcheons
as Cantons, or as Quarterings; or they may assume the
character of additional charges.   Also, this same term
denotes similar additions of Crests, Badges, or any other
accessories of Shields.

The Augmentation displayed upon the Ducal Shield of
WELLINGTON, a most honourable exception to the prevailing
degenerate heraldic feeling of the period in which it was
granted to the Great Duke, in characteristic and expressive
qualities is second to no other example of its own class and
order.   This true Augmentation of Honour is the *National*

Device of the British Empire, as it is blazoned in the " Union Jack," charged upon an inescutcheon, and displayed upon the honour point of the Duke's paternal Shield.

An equally significant Augmentation of an earlier date is borne in the Arms of HOWARD. These Arms before the battle of Flodden were—*Gu., a bend between six crosses crosslets fitchée arg.* To commemorate the great victory won by him at Flodden Field, Sept. 9, 1513, when JAMES IV. of Scotland was defeated and slain, HENRY VIII. granted to THOMAS HOWARD, Duke of Norfolk, and to his descendants, as an Augmentation of Honour, the *Royal Shield of Scotland* (No. 138), *but having a demi-lion only, which*

No. 374.—Howard, after Flodden.   No. 374A.—The Howard Augmentation.

is pierced through the mouth with an arrow, to be borne in the middle of the bend of his proper arms. This Shield is represented in No. 374; and in No. 374A the augmentation is shown on a larger scale.

A small group of additional examples will be sufficient to illustrate this most interesting class of historical Arms, and at the same time will not fail to excite in students a desire very considerably to extend the series through their own inquiries and researches. In memory of the devoted courage and all-important services of JANE LANE, after the disastrous battle of Worcester, CHARLES II. granted as an Augmentation a *Canton of England* (No. 187 marshalled on a canton), to be added to the hereditary Coat of Lane, which is—*Per fesse or and az., a chevron gu. between three mullets counterchanged.* The Crest of the family of DE LA BERE is said to have been conferred by the BLACK PRINCE upon Sir RICHARD DE LA BERE, as a memorial of the good service rendered by that gallant knight on the memorable field of Cressi. This Crest is—*Out of a crest-coronet a plume of five ostrich feathers per pale arg. and az.,* the Plantagenet colours—the device (as Mr. LOWER observes) being evidently derived from the Prince's own Badge, and also forming a variety of the "panache," the Crest then held in such high estimation. The heart charged upon the shield of DOUGLAS (see Nos. 156, 157, p. 74) is another remarkable Augmentation. So also is the adoption of the armorial insignia of the CONFESSOR, No. 2, by RICHARD II., and his marshalling it upon his own Royal Shield, impaled to the dexter with the quartered arms of France and England.

English Heraldry has been required to recognise another and a perfectly distinct class of "Augmentations," which consist of additions to the blazonry of a Shield or of additional quarterings or accessories, granted as tokens of Royal favour, for heraldic display, but without any particular "merit" in the receiver, or any special historical significance in themselves. Augmentations of this order may be considered to have been first introduced by RICHARD II., when he granted, "out of his mere grace," to his favourite ROBERT DE VERE, Earl of OXFORD, Marquess of DUBLIN and Duke of IRELAND, a differenced Coat of ST. EDMUND (No. 3)—*Az., three crowns or, within a bordure argent,* to be quartered with the DE VERE arms as the arms of IRELAND. In the same spirit, RICHARD II. granted, as similar Augmentations, the arms of the CONFESSOR to be marshalled, with Differences, on their Shields by THOMAS and JOHN HOLLAND, Dukes of SURREY and EXETER, and by THOMAS MOWBRAY, Duke of NORFOLK. It will be remembered that it was one of the capital charges against the then Earl of SURREY, a lineal descendant of this THOMAS MOWBRAY, the Duke of NORFOLK, in 1546, that he had assumed, without the special licence of HENRY VIII., the same arms of the CONFESSOR as an augmentation.

By EDWARD IV. similar augmentations, "by grace" and not "for merit," were granted; and by HENRY VIII. the system was carried to excess in the grants made to augment the armorial blazonry of ANNE BOLEYN, and of his English consorts, her successors.

ABATEMENT is a term which was unknown until it made its appearance in certain heraldic writings of the sixteenth century, when it was used to denote such marks or devices as, by the writers in question, were held to be the reverse of honourable Augmentation—*Augmentations of dishonour* indeed, and tokens of degradation. True Heraldry refuses to recognise all such pretended abatements, for the simple reason that they never did exist, and if they could exist at all, they would be in direct antagonism to its nature, its principles, and its entire course of action. Honourable itself, Heraldry can give expression only to what conveys honour, and it records and commemorates only what is to be honoured and held in esteem.

The very idea of an heraldic Abatement implies, if not a complete ignorance, certainly a thorough misconception of the character and the office of Heraldry. Even if Heraldry were to attempt to stigmatise what is, and what ought to be esteemed, dishonourable, who would voluntarily accept insignia of disgrace, and charge and display them upon his Shield, and transmit them to his descendants? And the believers in Abatement must hold that Heraldry can exert a compulsory legislative power, which might command a man to blazon his own disgrace, and force him to exhibit and to retain, and also to bequeath, any such blazonry. A belief in heraldic Abatement, however, is by no means singular or rare. A curious example of its existence was recently brought under my notice, in connection with one of the most renowned of the historical devices of English Heraldry. The *bear*, the badge of the BEAUCHAMPS, Earls of WARWICK, which appears at the feet of the effigy of Earl RICHARD in the Beauchamp chapel at Warwick, in accordance with a special provision to that effect, is "*muzzled*"; and, wearing a muzzle has this bear been borne, as their Badge, by the successors of the BEAU-CHAMPS in the Warwick Earldom, the Earls of the houses of NEVILLE, DUDLEY, RICH, and GREVILLE. But, it would seem that a legend has found credence at Warwick Castle itself, which would associate the muzzle of the bear with some dishonourable action of an Earl of the olden time; and, consequently, it was proposed that at length this Abatement should be removed from the bears still at Warwick! Earl RICHARD DE BEAUCHAMP was not exactly the man to have displayed upon *his* bear any ensign of dishonour; nor were his son-in-law, the "King-maker," and Queen ELIZABETH'S ROBERT DUDLEY, at all more probable subjects for any similar display; still, it is quite certain that they bore the muzzled bear, as he appears on the seal of the great Earl, No. 448.[1] That muzzle, doubtless, has its becoming heraldic significance, without in the slightest degree partaking in the assumed character of an Abatement. I hope eventually to be able to trace out conclusively what the muzzle may really imply, and I commend the research to other inquirers: meanwhile, neither at Warwick nor elsewhere is there any such thing as "Abatement" in English Heraldry.

[1] See Frontispiece.

CHAPTER XIV

CRESTS

"On high their glittering crests they toss."—LORD OF THE ISLES.

" Then he bound
Her token on his helmet."—ELAINE.

THE idea of a CREST, of some accessory specially designed
to form its crowning adornment, appears inseparable from
the existence and use of a Helm. The Warriors and Warrior
Divinities of classic antiquity are represented to us, wearing
head-pieces richly crested: and, in the Middle Ages, had no
other Heraldry ever been devised, assuredly ornaments of

No. 375.—Richard I.   No 376.—Henry de Perci.   No. 377.—Henry de Laci.

some kind would have been placed on helms and basinets,
and these insignia would have been held in high esteem and
honour. Accordingly, about the time that·Coat-Armour
became hereditary, having been reduced to a system and
accepted as an independent science, heraldic Crests began to
be worn as honourable distinctions of the most exalted
dignity by the mediæval chivalry.

Upon the Second Great Seal of RICHARD I. the cylin-
drical helm of the King appears surmounted by a kind of

O

cap or fan charged with a lion passant, the whole being arched over by a radiated ornament somewhat resembling a displayed fan, as in No. 375. Similar Crests, somewhat modified in their details, are represented in other seals of the same era, and with them the flowing Contoise or Scarf

No. 378.—Seal of Alexander de Balliol, A.D. 1292.

is sometimes associated, as in No. 376, from the seal of Baron HENRY DE PERCI, A.D. 1300. Similar ornaments were also placed by the knights of those ages upon the heads of their chargers. The seal of HENRY DE LACI, Earl of LINCOLN, A.D. 1272, shows the Fan-Crest both upon the helm of the Earl, No. 377, and the head of his war-horse. Another equally characteristic example is the Seal

of ALEXANDER DE BALLIOL, No. 378, appended to the
"General Release" given by JOHN BALLIOL to EDWARD I.,
2nd January, 1292: it will be observed that this knight
displays the arms of his house, No. 134, upon his Shield,
and also, in addition to the Fan-Crest, upon the barding of
his charger. Again I am indebted to the kindness and
liberality of Mr. Laing for the use of his admirable woodcut of this fine and interesting seal.

The flowing Contoise continued to be attached to
helms till about the middle of the fourteenth century;
unless, indeed, some veritable "lady's favour" were worn in
its stead by knights favoured as was Sir LAUNCELOT, who,
on a memorable day,—

> " Wore, against his wont, upon his helm
> A sleeve of scarlet, broidered with great pearls,
> Some gentle maiden's gift."

The seal of THOMAS, second Earl of LANCASTER, about A.D.
1320, gives an excellent example both of such figures as

No. 379.—Helm of Thomas, second Earl of Lancaster.

were beginning at that early time to supersede the Fan-
Crests, and also of the Contoise; No. 379. About this
same period the fashion was introduced of fixing two tall
spikes, one on each side of the Crest, upon the helm,
probably intended in the first instance to display the contoise. These singular spikes may have been derived by
the English Heralds from their brethren of Germany, who

delighted, as they still delight, in placing upon helms as Crests, or as the accessories of Crests, small banners displayed from staves set erect and surmounted by spear-heads. In German Heraldry also Crests are very frequently placed between tall upright horns or trumpets : and, sometimes, upon a German helm the Crest stands between horns shaped like two elephant's trunks (for which they have often been mistaken by English Heralds), placed

No. 380.—Helm and Crest of Sir Geoffrey Luterell : A.D. 1345.

No. 381.—Seal of Sir Robert de Marny : A.D. 1366.

in the same erect position, and, like the trumpets, so adjusted as to have the general aspect of the curved outline of a classic lyre. The helm of Sir GEOFFREY LUTERELL, A.D. 1345, No. 380, drawn from a celebrated illumination, between the tall spikes has a late example of the Fan-Crest ; and it exemplifies the practice sometimes adopted of charging armorial insignia upon Crests of this fan form. The Arms of Luterell—*Or, a bend and six martlets sa.*—were borne by Sir GEOFFREY thus differenced (E. 2)—*Az., a bend and six martlets arg.* A pair of lofty upright wings were held in much esteem in the Heraldry of both England and Scotland, to form the accessories of Crests. The Seal of Sir ROBERT DE MARNY, A.D. 1366, No. 381, shows his armorial shield—*Gu., a lion rampant arg.*, suspended from a tree, between two crested helms, the crest in both cases being a *winged chapeau*, having the wings very tall and very slender.

From the earliest times, Crests have occasionally been identical with the principal charge in the Shield of Arms, or they have repeated the principal charge with some slight modification of attitude or accessory : but, more generally, Crests have been altogether distinct. The Dragon and the Wyvern, the latter well exemplified in No. 315, are amongst the earliest figures that were borne as Crests in England. Other early Figure-Crests are the Lion, crowned and assumed for the first time by an English Sovereign by EDWARD III. ; and the Eagle, borne by the same Prince. Various devices and figures are found gradually to have been added to these earliest Crests. The graceful and peculiarly appropriate *Panache* soon joined them, with the heads of various animals and other creatures : and, as the fourteenth century advances, the *Crest-Coronet*, No. 232, the *Crest-Wreath*, No. 233, and the *Chapeau*, No. 224, assume their places in connection with Crests ; and the *Mantling* falls in rich folds from them, covering the back of the Helm. In the succeeding century, with Helms less dignified in form, but more elaborately enriched, and with strangely fantastic Mantlings, Crests become considerably larger in their proportions ; and they often are extravagant in their character, devices constantly being assumed and borne as Crests, which are no less inconsistent with true heraldic feeling, than with the peculiar conditions and the proper qualities of true heraldic Crests. The Crest of the Duke of HAMILTON, No. 301, is far from being one of the most inconsistent devices that were intended to be worn upon helms. And, as it is scarcely necessary for me to add, every really consistent Crest should be such a figure or device as might be actually worn upon his helm, by a mediæval knight, with dignity and with a happy effect.

Early examples of Panache-Crests exist in considerable numbers, and they show much variety of treatment. No. 285, already given at page 142, shows a Panache of several heights of feathers, the general outline having an oval contour. In No. 283, from the Seal of EDWARD DE COUR-TENAY, Earl of DEVON, A.D. 1372, there are three heights of feathers, and the outline has a square form. Again, the

No. 382.—Seal of William de Wyndesor.

Seal of WILLIAM LE LATIMER, A.D. 1415, gives the peculiar Panache, with the no less peculiar variety of mantling, shown in No. 284. A Panache of ample proportions, and of exceedingly graceful form, is represented in the Seal of WILLIAM DE WYNDESOR, A.D. 1381. The comparatively small size of the armorial Shield, as it generally appears when introduced into the composition of Seals in the fourteenth century, is shown in a striking manner in this same example, No. 382, which in the woodcut is slightly enlarged, in order to show the device more clearly: the arms are— *Gu., a saltire or.* Other fine examples of Panache-Crests may be seen in the effigies of Sir RICHARD DE PEMBRIDGE, K.G., A.D. 1375, in Hereford Cathedral; of Sir ROBERT DE

MARMION, A.D. 1400, at Tanfield, Yorkshire; and of Sir
THOMAS ARDERNE, about the same date, at Elford, in Staf-
fordshire. The very fine effigy of Sir EDWARD DE THORPE,
A.D. 1418, at Ashwelthorpe, in Norfolk, has a helm of rare
beauty of form, with a rich mantling, and a most graceful
Panache of peacock's feathers; and peacock's feathers also
form the Panache of Lord FERRERS of CHARTLEY, in his
Brass, A.D. 1425, at Merevale, in Warwickshire. And, once
more, upon the Seal of THOMAS DE HATFIELD, Bishop of
Durham, A.D. 1345, the Panache rises from the episcopal
mitre, after the same manner as it
does in No. 383 from a Coronet.

No. 383.—Crest of Sir Richard
Grey, K.G.; A.D. 1420.

Another episcopal Seal, that of
Bishop HENRY LE DESPENCER, No.
351, shows a Shield of small size
when compared with the helm and
crest, the latter being the favourite
device of a gryphon's head between
two tall upright wings. The Seals
of the FITZALANS, Earls of Arundel,
and the Seal of JOHN TIPTOFT, Earl
of Worcester, may be specified as
displaying fine examples of the same Crest. With them
may be grouped the Crest of Sir RICHARD GREY, K.G.,
Lord Grey of Codnor, A.D. 1420—*A peacock's head and
neck, between two wings erect, the feathers az., and their pens*
(quills) *arg.*, No. 383, from the Garter-plate at Windsor.
This Crest rises from such a Crest-Coronet as was borne on
their helms by noblemen in the time of HENRY V.

The use of the *Chapeau*, or Cap of Estate, instead of a
Crest-Coronet, to support a Crest upon a helm, I have
already illustrated with Nos. 198 and 199, severally the
Lion-Crests of the BLACK PRINCE and of his son
RICHARD II. Like No. 199, No. 384 is from one of the
unrivalled series of helms sculptured in Westminster Hall,

with the Crest and Ostrich-feather Badge of King RICHARD II. In both of these examples the adjustment of the *Mantling* is shown. Two famous Lion-Crests are those borne by the great families of HOWARD and PERCY, severally Dukes of Norfolk and Northumberland. The HOWARD lion, originally granted by RICHARD II. to THOMAS MOWBRAY, Earl Marshal, and now borne by the Duke of NORFOLK,

No. 384.

Helm, Crest, Mantling, and Badge of Richard II., from Westminster Hall.

is *a lion statant guardant, his tail extended or, and ducally gorged arg.*: the PERCY lion is *statant, his tail extended or:* each lion stands upon a chapeau. The Lion-Crest of the BLACK PRINCE, being charged with the *silver Label* (which he may be said to wear after the fashion of a collar), · exemplifies the prevailing practice of *differencing Crests with marks of Cadency.* Crests admit every variety of Difference: and Mantlings also are frequently differenced with small charges, or with badges; as in the Garter-plate of Sir JOHN BEAUMONT, K.G., and in the Brass at Little Easton, Essex, to Sir HENRY BOURCHIER, K.G., Earl of ESSEX.

The *Crest-Wreath* first appears about the middle of the fourteenth century. The earliest example to which I can refer is represented in the Brass to Sir HUGH HASTINGS, at Elsyng, in Norfolk, A.D. 1347. In this most remarkable engraven memorial, the finial of the principal canopy is surmounted by a helm with mantling, wreath, and the crest of HASTINGS—*a bull's head sable;* No. 385. In the effigy of Sir R. DE PEMBRIDGE, K.G., already noticed, the date of which is 1375, the crest is united to the great helm that supports the head of the knight by a wreath formed of a band of four-leaved flowers. A little later, A.D. 1384, at Southacre, in Norfolk, the Brass of Sir JOHN HARSYCK has a

Crest-Wreath formed of two rolls, probably of silk, twisted as in No. 386. In the second half of the next century, amongst many good examples of Crest-Wreaths I select as typical specimens those which appear in the Brasses to Sir WILLIAM VERNON, A.D. 1467, at Tong, in Shropshire, No.

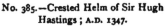

No. 385.—Crested Helm of Sir Hugh Hastings; A.D. 1347.

No. 386, 387, and 388.—Crest-Wreaths.

386; and to Sir ROBERT HARCOURT, K.G., No. 387, at Staunton Harcourt, Oxfordshire.

The Crest-Wreath in the form shown in the last examples, and now almost universally used in representations of such Crests as are without the Crest-Coronet and the Chapeau, may fairly be considered to have been derived from the rich ornamentation, generally, as it would seem, formed of costly textile fabrics, if not executed in jewelled or enamelled goldsmith's work, that was frequently wreathed about knightly basinets. These wreath-like ornaments are represented in numerous effigies both sculptured and engraven; and they are shown to have been worn either flat, as in No. 388, or wrought to high relief, as in No. 389. These two examples are severally from the effigies of a knight in Tewkesbury Abbey Church, about A.D. 1365, and of Sir HUMPHREY STAFFORD, A.D. 1450, at Bromsgrove, in Worcestershire. The enamelled effigy of Earl WILLIAM DE VALENCE, A.D. 1296, at Westminster, has a wreath of delicate workmanship in relief, which once was set with real or imitative jewels.

For many years after their first appearance, heraldic Crests were regarded as insignia of great dignity and exalted estate; and it was not till a considerably later period that the right to bear a Crest came to be regarded as an adjunct of the right to bear arms. Still later, when they were granted with Coat-Armour to corporate bodies, communities, and institutions, Crests altogether lost their original significance; and they became, in their use, Badges

No. 389.—Basinet with Crest-Wreath, Effigy of Sir Humphrey Stafford, A.D. 1450.

in everything except the habit of placing them, with their accessories of Wreath or Crest-Coronet, of Chapeau and Mantling, upon representations of helms.

When they were actually worn, Crests were undoubtedly constructed of some very light materials. It is probable that *cuir bouilli* (boiled leather), the decorative capabilities of which were so well understood by mediæval artists, was generally employed.

It has been sometimes held that Crests are personal bearings only; and, therefore, not hereditary, though capable of being bequeathed or granted by their possessors. This theory is not sustained by early or general usage; and, accordingly, Crests must be pronounced to be hereditary, as is Coat-Armour.

It is evident that as one person may inherit, and therefore may quarter, two or more Coats of Arms, so the same person might claim to bear *two or more Crests* by a similar right of inheritance. This in early times resulted in selection because no early British precedent exists for the simultaneous display of *two* Crests. But it was soon recognised that as no woman could bear a Crest, she ought not to transmit one, and the idea of the inheritance of the Crest with a quartering from a female ancestress ceased. At the present day, several Crests, each with its own helm and mantling, are occasionally represented above a Shield of arms: but, in England, by strict heraldic rule, two (or more than two) Crests can be borne by one individual, only when he has obtained the Royal licence to bear and use the *Surname and Arms* of another family *in addition* to those of his own family, or, by a special grant from the Crown.

CHAPTER XV

BADGES

" Might I but know thee by thy household Badge ! "
—SHAKESPEARE, *Henry VI.*, *Part 2.*

A BADGE, like a Coat of Arms, is an armorial ensign that is complete in itself, and possesses a definite signification of its own. In use with a decided heraldic significance long before the adoption of systematic Heraldry, Badges have always held a conspicuous position in the estimation of Heralds. A Badge resembles any single charge in Heraldry, in being a figure or device that is assumed as the distinctive cognisance of a particular individual or family : but, unlike a charge, it may be borne by itself, without any Shield, and also without any accompanying accessory, with the exception, in some instances, of a *Motto* (See " Motto," p. 138). Badges, however, are found depicted on roundels of the livery, and upon Standards, and for decorative purposes are often depicted upon mantlings. It will be evident that a Badge may be the very same figure or device as a Crest ; but, it must be remembered that a Badge always differs from a Crest, in usually being altogether without crest-wreath or coronet, in consequence of having no connection whatever with the knightly helm. There was, however, a period in which the Badge was much confused with the Crest, which has resulted in many devices which are really Crests being officially recorded as Badges.

After the establishment of a true Heraldry, Badges were generally used to commemorate remarkable exploits, or in reference either to some family or feudal alliance, or to indicate some territorial rights or pretensions. Very many Badges are allusive, and consequently they are *Rebuses* (see "Rebus," p. 146). Some are taken from the charges of the bearer's Shield, or they have a more or less direct reference to those charges. Some trace of Marshalling or of feudal Difference may constantly be observed in Badges; and even where the motive for the selection of certain devices has not been discovered, it may fairly be assumed that a good heraldic motive still exists, although it has become obscured or been forgotten. It was not uncommon for the same personage or family to use more than one Badge; and, on the other hand, two or more Badges were often borne in combination, to form a single compound device, as in Nos. 235 and 270. The *ragged staff*, in like manner, No. 294, and the *bear*, both of them Badges of the BEAUCHAMPS, Earls of WARWICK, were sometimes united to form a single Badge, and by the successors of that great family the "bear and ragged staff" were generally borne as a single device. (See No. 448, and p. 319.)

Two distinct classes of Badges were in general use in the fourteenth, fifteenth, and sixteenth centuries. Those of the first class, well known as the insignia of certain eminent personages and powerful houses, were borne by all the followers, retainers, dependants, and partisans of those personages and houses: and they were so borne by them, and they were used by their owners for every variety of decorative purpose, because they were *known and understood;* and, consequently, because the presence of these Badges would cause all persons and objects bearing them to be readily and certainly distinguished. By means of these most useful devices a wide and comprehensive range was given to the action and the influence of true Heraldry, without infringing in the slightest degree upon the lofty and almost sacred exclusiveness of the Coat-Armour of a noble or

a gentle house.   In the words which SHAKESPEARE teaches
CLIFFORD to address to WARWICK, "Might I but know thee
by thy household Badge!" it is implied that all the followers
of Warwick were well known by his "household Badge,"
which was displayed by them all, while some other insignia
were worn by the great Earl upon his own person.

Mr. Lower has remarked ("Curiosities of Heraldry,"
p. 145) that "something analogous to the fashion" of em-
broidering the household Badges of their lords "upon the
sleeves or breasts" of the dependants of great families in
the olden times, " is retained in the Crest which adorns the
buttons of our domestic servants." The accomplished
writer might have added that, in thus employing *Crests* to
discharge *Badge*-duties, we are content to indulge a love for
heraldic display without observing becoming heraldic distinctions. Crested livery buttons are heraldic anomalies
under all circumstances—even the head of a house himself,
if he were a Herald, would not display his Crest, as a Crest,
upon buttons to be used exclusively by himself. Crests
are to be borne on helms, or represented as being borne on
helms: Badges are decorative insignia, and fulfil with
consistent significance their own distinct and appropriate
functions.

Badges of the second class were devices that were borne
exclusively by the exalted personages who were pleased to
assume them, often for temporary use only, and generally
with some subtle or latent significance, which had been
studiously rendered difficult to be detected, and dubious in
its application.

These Badges, thus displayed rather to effect disguise or
to excite curiosity than to secure recognition, must be
regarded for the most part as the expressions of heraldic
revelry—as the fantasies and eccentricities of an age, which
loved to combine quaint conceits and symbolical allusions
with the display of gorgeous magnificence.   Accordingly,

Badges of this order are found generally to have been assumed on the occasion of the jousts or Hastiludes, the masques, and other pageants that in feudal times were celebrated with so much of elaborate and brilliant splendour.

The adoption of Badges of this peculiar character is exactly in keeping with the sentiment which prompted men of exalted rank and eminent distinction to appear in public, on occasions of high festivity, bearing the arms of some friend, kinsman, or ally, instead of their own. A mark of especial favour and of peculiar distinction would be conferred, when a Sovereign or a Prince thus would display upon his own person the armory of some honoured subject or comrade. EDWARD III. delighted thus to honour the most distinguished cavaliers of his chivalrous Court. For example, in or about the year 1347, royal Hastiludes were celebrated at Lichfield with great splendour, the jousters consisting of the KING and seventeen Knights, and the Earl of LANCASTER and thirteen Knights. A conspicuous part was taken in these festivities by the King's daughter ISABELLE, afterwards Countess of BEDFORD, and by six Ladies of high rank, with twenty-one other Ladies, who all wore blue dresses and white hoods of the same materials as well as the same colours as the robes of the Knights, together with various masks or vizors. On this occasion, the KING himself over his armour wore a surcoat with the Arms of Sir THOMAS DE BRADESTONE. These Arms in a Roll of EDWARD III. are blazoned as—*Arg., on a canton gu. a rose or* (see *Archæologia*, xxxi., pp. 40 and 118). On another occasion, during Hastiludes at Canterbury, EDWARD III. "is said to have given eight harnesses, worked with the arms of Sir STEPHEN DE COSYNTON (*az., three roses arg.*), to the PRINCE OF WALES, the Earl of LANCASTER, and six other Knights." In the same spirit, RICHARD DE BEAUCHAMP, Earl of WARWICK, at a great festival of arms held at Calais under his presidency, on the first day entered the lists decorated with the arms of his ancestor the Lord TONEY: on the second day, he wore the arms of Hanslap: and, on the third day, "he appeared as the Earl of WARWICK, quartering Beauchamp, Guy, Hanslap, and Toney, on his trappings; his vizor open, and the chaplet on his helm enriched with pearls and precious stones." In such times, Badges of curious device and occult signification could not fail to enjoy a popularity, not the less decided because of the restricted use and exclusive character of the Badges themselves.

EXAMPLES OF BADGES, such as are distinctive, and consequently of the class that I have first described. The Badges of PERCY are a *silver crescent* and a *double manacle*: of HOWARD, a *white lion*: PELHAM, *a buckle*: DOUGLAS, a *red heart*: SCROPE, a *Cornish chough*: CLINTON, a *golden mullet*: TALBOT, a *hound*: BOHUN, a *white swan*: HUNGERFORD, a *sickle*: PEVEREL, a *garb*: STOURTON, a *golden "drag" or sledge*. The various "Knots," described and illustrated in Chapter X., Nos. 219, 235, 263, 270, 274, 304, and 313, are Badges. The *bear and ragged staff* of the BEAUCHAMPS, and, after them, of the NEVILLES and DUDLEYS, I have already noticed. Seals frequently have Badges introduced upon them, in very early times, by themselves, the Badge in each case constituting the device of the Seal (see p. 193). The Secretum or private Seal of ROBERT BRUCE, Earl of CARRICK, the father of the King, appended to the homage-deed extorted by EDWARD I. from the Scottish nobles, is a good example, No. 390: this is another of Mr. Laing's beautiful woodcuts. Badges also constantly appear upon Seals in association with Shields of arms. Thus, a Seal of one of the BERKELEYS, A.D. 1430, has a mermaid on each side of an armorial shield. Two other examples of this kind I have already given: No. 318, the Seal of JOAN DE BARRE, which is charged with the *castle* and *lion* of Castile and Leon, as Badges: and No. 321, the Seal of OLIVER DE BOHUN, charged, about the Shield, with the Bohun *Swan*. On his Seal, No. 391, Sir WALTER DE HUNGERFORD, K.G., Lord of HEYTESBURY and HOMET (the latter a Norman barony), displays his own Badge, the *sickle*, in happy alliance with the *garb* of Peverel (borne by him in right of his wife, CATHERINE, daughter and co-heir of THOMAS PEVEREL), to form his Crest. The Crest, it will be observed, in No. 391, is *a garb between two sickles*. The Shield of

No. 390.
Secretum of Robert Bruce,
Earl of Carrick; A.D. 1296.

No. 391.
Seal of Sir Walter de Hungerford, K.G.,
A.D. 1425.

Hungerford only—*sa. two bars arg., and in chief three plates*, is also placed between *two sickles*. Two banners, denoting important alliances, complete the Heraldry of this remarkable composition: the banner to the dexter, for Heytesbury, bears—*per pale indented gu. and vert., a chevron or ;* and that to the sinister, for Hussy—*barry of six erm. and gu.* Lord HUNGERFORD died in 1449, and was succeeded by his eldest surviving son, Sir ROBERT DE HUNGERFORD. The Seal of this Sir Robert, used by

P

him during the lifetime of his father, precisely the same in its heraldic composition as his father's Seal, is remarkable from having *each of its four sickles differenced with an ermine-spot upon the blade,* to mark Cadency ; and also, with the same motive, it shows that a label of three points was charged upon the Shield, and upon each of the two banners ; No. 392.

Through an alliance with the Hungerfords, *sickles* were borne, as one of their Badges, by the great family of

No. 392.—Seal of Sir Robert de Hungerford : before A.D. 1449.

COURTENAY. They appear, with a *dolphin,* a *tau-cross,* and this same *tau-cross* having *a bell* attached to it, as in No. 393, sculptured on the fine heraldic chimney-piece, the work of Bishop PETER DE COURTENAY (died in 1492), now in the hall of the Episcopal Palace at Exeter.

The BADGES of our early Heraldry are comparatively but little understood. They invite the particular attention of students, both from their own special interest, and the light they are qualified to throw upon the personal history of the

English people, and also from their peculiar applicability for use by ourselves at the present day. Indeed, at this time, when the revival of true Heraldry is in the act of being accomplished with complete success, it appears to be peculiarly desirable that Badges should be·brought into general use. It is not enough for us to revive our old English Heraldry as once in the olden time it flourished in England, and to rest content with such a revival: but we must go on to adapt our revived Heraldry, in its own spirit and in full sympathy with its genuine feeling, to conditions of our age and of the state of things now in existence. And very much may

No. 393.
A Courtenay
Badge, at
Exeter.

be done to effect this by the adoption of Badges, as our favourite and most expressive heraldic insignia, both in connection with Coat-Armour and for independent display. Unlike Crests, which must necessarily be associated with helms and the wearers of helms, and consequently have both a military and a mediæval character, Badges are equally appropriate for use by Ladies, as well as by men of every profession, and they belong alike to every age and period. This has been recognised officially, to the extent that the officers of arms have now reverted to the ancient practice of granting and confirming badges and Standards.

ROYAL BADGES.—I conclude this chapter with a concise list of the more important of the Badges that have been borne by the Sovereigns and Princes of England; and with some general remarks upon the famous Badge of the *Ostrich Feathers*, now considered to be exclusively the Ensign of the PRINCES OF WALES, not as such, but as the heirs-apparent to the Throne.

The *Planta-genista*, or Broom-plant, No. 21, is well known as an English Royal Badge, from the surname derived from it for one of the most remarkable of the Royal Houses that ever have flourished in Europe.

As well known are the *Rose, Thistle,* and *Shamrock,* severally the Badges of the three realms of the United Kingdom of ENGLAND, SCOTLAND, and IRELAND. A *golden Rose stalked proper* was a badge of EDWARD I.: and from it apparently were derived, but by what process it is unknown, the *White Rose* of YORK, the *Red Rose* of LANCASTER, and the *White and Red Rose* of the House of TUDOR.

WILLIAM RUFUS: *A Flower of five foils.*

HENRY I.: *A Flower of eight foils.*

STEPHEN: *A Flower of seven foils: a Sagittarius.*

HENRY II.: *The Planta-genista: an Escarbuncle: a Sword and Olive-Branch.*

RICHARD I.: *A Star of thirteen rays and a Crescent: a Star issuing from a Crescent: a Mailed Arm grasping a broken Lance, with the Motto—" Christo Duce."*

JOHN and HENRY III.: *A Star issuing from a Crescent.*

EDWARD I.: *An heraldic Rose or, stalked ppr.*

EDWARD II.: *A Castle of Castile.*

EDWARD III.: *A Fleur de lys: a Sword: a Falcon: a Gryphon: the Stock of a Tree: Rays issuiug from a Cloud.*

RICHARD II.: *A White Hart lodged: the Stock of a Tree: A White Falcon: the Sun in splendour: the Sun clouded.*

HENRY IV.: *The Cypher SS: a crowned Eagle: an Eagle displayed: a White Swan: A Red Rose: a Columbine Flower: A Fox's Tail: a crowned Panther: the Stock of a Tree: a Crescent.* His QUEEN, JOAN OF NAVARRE: *An Ermine,* or *Gennet.*

HENRY V.: *A Fire-beacon: a White Swan gorged and chained: a chained Antelope.*

HENRY VI.: *Two Ostrich Feathers in Saltire: a chained Antelope: a Panther.*

EDWARD IV.: *A White Rose en Soleil: a White Wolf and White Lion: a White Hart: a Black Dragon and Black Bull: a Falcon and Fetter-lock: the Sun in splendour.*

HENRY VII.: *A Rose of York and Lancaster, a Portcullis and a Fleur de lys, all of them crowned: a Red Dragon: a White Greyhound: a Hawthorn Bush and Crown, with the cypher* H.R.

HENRY VIII.: The same, without the Hawthorn Bush, and with a *White Cock.* His QUEENS: CATHERINE OF ARAGON—*A Rose, Pomegranate, and Sheaf of Arrows,* ANNE BOLEYN—*A Crowned Falcon, holding a Sceptre.* JANE SEYMOUR—*A Phœnix rising from a Castle, between Two Tudor Roses.* CATHERINE PARR—*A Maiden's Head crowned, rising from a large Tudor Rose.*

EDWARD VI.: *A Tudor Rose: the Sun in splendour.*

MARY: *A Tudor Rose impaling a Pomegranate—* also *impaling a Sheaf of Arrows, ensigned with a Crown, and surrounded with rays: a Pomegranate.*

ELIZABETH: *A Tudor Rose* with the motto, "*Rosa sine Spinâ*" (a Rose without a Thorn): *a Crowned Falcon and Sceptre.* She used as her own motto—"*Semper Eadem*" (Always the same).

JAMES I.: *A Thistle: a Thistle and Rose dimidiated and crowned,* No. 308, with the motto—"*Beati Pacifici*" (Blessed are the peacemakers).

CHARLES I., CHARLES II., JAMES II.: The same Badge as JAMES I., without his motto.

ANNE: *A Rose-Branch and a Thistle growing from one branch.*

From this time distinctive personal Badges ceased to be borne by English Sovereigns. But various badges have become stereotyped and now form a constituent part of the Royal Arms, and will be found recited later in Chapter XVIII.

The *Ostrich Feather Badge*. The popular tradition, that the famous Badge of the Ostrich Feathers was won from the blind KING OF BOHEMIA at Cressi by the BLACK PRINCE, and by him afterwards borne as an heraldic trophy, is not supported by any contemporary authority. The earliest writer by whom the tradition itself is recorded is CAMDEN (A.D. 1614), and his statement is confirmed by no known historical evidence of a date earlier than his own work. As Sir N. HARRIS NICHOLAS has shown in a most able paper in the *Archæologia* (vol. xxxi. pp. 350–384), the first time the Feathers are mentioned in any record is in a document, the date of which must have been after 1369, and which contains lists of plate belonging to the King himself, and also to Queen PHILIPPA. It is particularly to be observed, that all the pieces of plate specified in this roll as the personal property of the Queen, if marked with any device at all, are marked with her *own initial*, or with some heraldic insignia that have a direct reference to *herself.* One of these pieces of plate is described as "a large dish for the alms of the Queen, of silver gilt, and enamelled at the bottom with *a black escutcheon with Ostrich Feathers— eym in fund vno scuch nigro cum pennis de ostrich.*" And these "Ostrich Feathers," thus blazoned on a sable field upon the silver alms-dish of Queen PHILIPPA, Sir N. H. Nicholas believed to have been borne by the Queen as a daughter of the House of HAINAULT; and he suggested that these same "Ostrich Feathers" might possibly have been assumed by the Counts of the Province of Hainault from the Comté of Ostrevant, which formed the appanage of their eldest sons.

At the first, either a single Feather was borne, the quill generally transfixing an escroll, as in No. 394, from the monument of Prince ARTHUR TUDOR, in Worcester

Cathedral; or, two Feathers were placed side by side, as
they also appear upon the same monument. In Seals, or
when marshalled with a Shield of Arms, two Feathers are
seen to have been placed after the manner of Supporters,
one on each side of the composition: in such examples the
tips of the Feathers droop severally to the dexter and
sinister: in all the early examples also the Feathers droop
in the same manner, or they incline slightly towards the
spectator. Three Feathers were first grouped together by

No. 395.   No. 394.   No. 396.
At Peterborough Cathedral.   At Worcester Cathedral.   At Peterborough Cathedral.

ARTHUR TUDOR, PRINCE OF WALES, eldest son of HENRY
VII., as in Nos. 395 and 396, from Peterborough
Cathedral; or with an escroll, as in No. 397, from a
miserere in the fine and interesting church at Ludlow. The
plume of three Feathers appears to have been encircled
with a coronet, for the first time, by Prince EDWARD, afterwards EDWARD VI., but who never was PRINCE OF WALES:
No. 398, carved very boldly over the entrance gateway to
the Deanery at Peterborough, is a good early example. In
No. 399 I give a representation of another early plume of
three Ostrich Feathers, as they are carved, with an escroll
in place of a coronet, upon the Chantry of Abbot
RAMRYGE in the Abbey Church at St. Albans: and again,
in No. 400, from the head of a window near the east end of
the choir, on the south side, in Exeter Cathedral, the three

Feathers are charged upon a Shield *per pale azure and gules,* and this Shield is on a roundle.

The Ostrich Feathers were borne, as a Badge with his Shield of Arms, upon one Seal of EDWARD III. himself: they were used, as an heraldic device, about the year 1370,

No. 397.—In Ludlow Church.

No. 398.—The Deanery, Peterborough.

No. 399.—In the Abbey Church of St. Alban.

No. 400.—In Exeter Cathedral.

by PHILIPPA, his Queen: they appear on some, but not on all, the Seals of the BLACK PRINCE, and they are omitted from some of his Seals after the battle of Cressi (A.D. 1346): and they were also borne, generally with some slight difference, marking Cadency, in all probability by all the other sons of EDWARD III.—certainly by JOHN OF GHENT, Duke of LANCASTER, and by THOMAS OF WOODSTOCK, Duke of Gloucester. They were adopted by Richard II., and placed on either side of his crested Helm in the heraldic sculpture of Westminster Hall, as appears in two of these beautiful examples, Nos. 199 and 384: by this Prince the Ostrich Feathers were placed on his first Royal Seal, and they were habitually used for decoration and heraldic display; and they also were formally granted by him, as a mark of especial favour, to be borne as an Augmentation of the highest honour, to his cousin Thomas Mowbray, Duke of Norfolk. The Ostrich Feathers were borne, in like manner, by the succeeding Princes, both Lancastrian and Yorkist: by at least two of the Beauforts: by the Princes of the House of Tudor: and by their successors the Stuarts. Thus, it is certain that the Ostrich Feathers were held to be a *Royal Badge*, from the time of their first appearance in the Heraldry of England about the middle of the fourteenth century; and that in that character they were adopted and borne by the successive Sovereigns, and by the Princes, sometimes also by the Princesses (as in the instance of a Seal of Margaret Beaufort, the mother of Henry VII.), of the Royal Houses, without any other distinction than some slight mark of Cadency, and without the slightest trace of any peculiar association with any one member of the Royal Family. From the time of the accession of the House of Stuart to the Crown of the United Kingdom, however, the coroneted plume of three Ostrich Feathers appears to have been regarded, as it is at this present day, as the special Badge of the Heir to the Throne.

In accordance with the express provision of his will, two armorial Shields are displayed upon the monument of the Black Prince in Canterbury Cathedral, which Shields the Prince himself distinguishes as his Shields "for War" and "for Peace"; the former charged with his quartered arms of France and England differenced with his silver

Label, No. 337 ; and the latter, *sable,* charged with *three Ostrich Feathers argent,* their quills passing through scrolls bearing the Motto, " *Ich Diene,*" No. 401. The same motto is placed over each of the Shields that are charged with the Feathers, as in No. 401 : and over each Shield charged with the quartered arms (there are on each side of the tomb

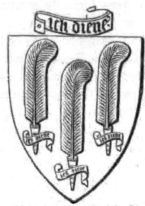

No. 401.—Shield " for Peace " of the Black Prince.

six Shields, three of the Arms, and three of the Feathers, alternately) is the other motto of the Prince, " *Houmout.*" In his will, the BLACK PRINCE also desired that a "*black Pennon with Ostrich Feathers*" should be displayed at his Funeral ; and he further appointed that his Chapel in Canterbury Cathedral should be adorned in various places with his Arms, and " *likewise with our Badge of Ostrich Feathers —noz bages dez plumes d'ostruce.*"

The will of the BLACK PRINCE proves the Feathers to have been a Badge, and not either a Crest or the ensign of a Shield of Arms, since twice he expressly calls them " *our Badge*" : and it also is directly opposed to the traditional warlike origin and military character of the Feathers, as a Badge of the BLACK PRINCE, for it particularly specifies the peaceful significance of this Badge, and distinguishes it from the insignia that were worn and displayed by the Prince when he was equipped for war. The Mottoes " *Ich Diene* " and " *Houmout* " are old German, and they signify, " I serve," and " magnanimous." It has been suggested by Mr. Planché, that " Houmout " is Flemish, and that the three words really form a single Motto, signifying, "Magnanimous, I serve," that is, " I obey the dictates of magnanimity " (*Archæologia*, xxxii. 69).

Upon a very remarkable Seal, used by HENRY IV. a

No. 402.—From the Seal of King Henry IV.

No. 403.—From the Seal of Thomas, Duke of Gloucester.

No. 404. — From the Garter-Plate of John Beaufort, K.G.

short time before his accession, the shield with helm and crest are placed between two tall Feathers, about each of which is entwined *a Garter* charged with his favourite and significant Motto—the word SOVEREYGNE, as in No. 402. His father, Prince JOHN OF GHENT, placed *a chain* upon the quills of his Feathers, as in the very curious boss in the cloisters at Canterbury. The uncle of HENRY IV., THOMAS, Duke of GLOUCESTER, on one of his Seals, differenced his two Feathers with *Garters* (probably of the

Order) displayed along their quills, as in No. 403. And, about A.D. 1440, JOHN BEAUFORT, K.G., Duke of SOMERSET, on his Garter-plate placed two Ostrich Feathers erect, their *quills componée argent and azure,* and fixed in golden escrolls; No. 404. In the Harleian MS. 304, f. 12, it is stated that the Ostrich Feather of silver, the pen thus componée argent and azure, " is the Duke of Somerset's ": also that the " Feather silver, with the pen gold, is the King's: the Ostrich Feather, pen and all silver, is the Prince's: and the Ostrich Feather gold, the pen ermine, is the Duke of Lancaster's."

The Shield charged with three Ostrich Feathers, No. 401, was borne by Prince JOHN OF GHENT; and it appears on the splendid Great Seal of HENRY IV., between the Shields of the· Duchy of CORNWALL and the Earldom of CHESTER. HUMPHREY, Duke of GLOUCESTER, is also recorded to have borne this same Feather Shield.

In the Vaulting of the ceiling over the steps leading to the Hall at Christchurch, Oxford, the Ostrich Plume Badge is carved within a Garter of the Order: and, again, the Badge is represented after the same manner, environed with the Garter, in the beautiful binding of a copy of the Bible which is reputed to have been used by CHARLES I. in his last moments.

The Ostrich Feathers are repeatedly mentioned in early documents; and they are shown to have been constantly used for various decorative purposes, always evidently with an heraldic motive and feeling, by the same Royal personages who blazoned them on their Seals, and displayed them elsewhere as their armorial insignia. A well-known example of a diaper of White Ostrich Feathers on a field per pale argent and vert, is preserved in the stained glass now in the great north window of the transept of Canterbury Cathedral.

CHAPTER XVI

SUPPORTERS

"Standing by the Shield
In silence."—IDYLLS OF THE KING.

A SUPPORTER is a figure, sometimes of an angel, frequently of a human being, but more generally of some animal, bird, or imaginary creature, so placed in connection with a Shield of Arms as to appear to be protecting and supporting it. In English Heraldry a single Supporter is of comparatively rare occurrence, but a number of examples are to be found in the Heraldry of Scotland. In early examples, when two Supporters appear, they are in most cases alike: but, more recently (except in the Heraldry of France), the two figures are generally quite distinct the one from the other, the earlier usage of having the two Supporters alike being less frequent. The modern prevailing practice in England is happily exemplified in the well-known instance of the present Royal Supporters, the Lion and the Unicorn.

Supporters are considered to have been introduced into the Heraldry of England during the reign of EDWARD III.; but they may with greater accuracy be assigned to the middle of the fifteenth century, than to the second half of the fourteenth. As armorial insignia of a very high rank, Supporters are granted in England only by the express command of the Sovereign, except to Peers and Knights Grand Cross and Knights Grand Commanders. In Scotland, where they occur more frequently than in the Heraldry of the South of the Tweed, the "Lord Lyon" has power to grant Supporters. Originally by the Scottish Heralds these accessories of Shields were entitled "Bearers."

Supporters are now granted, on payment of fees, to all Peers of the Realm to descend to the holders of a specified Peerage, and to Knights of the Garter, Thistle, and St. Patrick, and to Knights Grand Cross and Knights Grand Commanders of all other orders of knighthood to be borne for life. Most Nova Scotia Baronets and Chiefs of Scottish Clans have supporters registered with their arms.

Supporters probably owe their origin rather to several concurrent circumstances, than to any one particular circumstance. The mere fact of a Knight carrying his own armorial Shield, or his Esquire bearing it beside him, might suggest the general idea of some *supporting* figure in connection with a representation of that Shield. The act of carrying a Banner of Arms, in like manner, might suggest a representation of a "Supporter" for a Shield of Arms. To early Seals, however, Heraldry is in an especial degree indebted for the development of the idea of Supporters, and for bringing it into a definite form. Again, the prevalent use of Badges in the fourteenth century, and in the fifteenth also, would necessarily exercise a powerful influence in the same direction; and would lead Heralds to associate with Shields of Arms certain other figures which, while in themselves distinct and independent, were closely allied with certain Shields of Arms. The prototypes of true Supporters, indeed, as they appear on Seals, are Badges. In fact, it is often difficult to determine whether specified figures on the Seals of a certain period are heraldic supporters or merely representations of Badges.

An Effigy represented upon a Seal, as in No. 405, the

Seal of DEVORGUILLA CRAWFORD, about A.D. 1290, from LAING'S Volume: or in Nos. 316, 317, would be even more than a suggestion of a Supporter. The same may be said, when some figure, almost certainly a Badge, was introduced into the composition of a Seal, holding or supporting a Shield by its guige, as in No. 203; or when a Shield, or two or more Shields, were charged upon some figure, as in No. 204: both of these examples, indeed, might be regarded as illustrations of the origin or first adoption of single Supporters.

The introduction of angelic figures, which might have the appearance of acting as "Guardian Angels," in their care of Shields of Arms, was in accordance with the feeling of the early days of English Heraldry; and, while it took a part in leading the way to the systematic use of regular Supporters, it served to show the high esteem and honour in which armorial insignia were held by our ancestors of those ages.

No. 405.—Seal of Devorguilla Crawford; about 1290.

In No. 159 I have already shown an example of a sculptured Shield thus supported by Angels, from St. Albans. In the same noble church there are other examples of the same character in stained glass. Angel Supporters, the figures treated in various ways, occur in very many Gothic edifices; particularly, sculptured as corbels, bosses or pateræ, or introduced in panels, and employed for the decoration of open timber roofs, as in Westminster Hall. They appear also on Seals; as on the Seal of HENRY OF LANCASTER, about A.D. 1350, which has the figure of an Angel above the Shield, and a lion on each side of it.

The representation of armorial Banners upon Seals would lead to at least the occasional introduction of some figure to hold, or *support*, the Banner; and here, again, we discern the presence of some of the immediate predecessors of "Supporters," properly so called. In the Seals, Nos. 391, 392, the Banners are not supported, and yet they are indirectly suggestive of giving support to the Shield which is marshalled with them in the same composition. Another Hungerford Seal, that of MARGARET BOTREAUX, widow of the second Baron HUNGERFORD (who died in 1477), in the centre of the composition has a kneeling figure of the noble lady, and on each side a banner of arms is held (*supported*)

No. 406.—Part of Seal of Margaret, Lady Hungerford.

erect, so that the two banners form a kind of canopy over her head, by a lion and a gryphon. In No. 406 I give a part only of this elaborate Seal, sufficient to show how its general composition bears upon the adoption of Supporters. The Monument in Westminster Abbey of Sir LUDOVIC ROBSART, K.G., Lord BOURCHIER, Standard-Bearer to HENRY V. at Agincourt, has two banners sculptured in the stone-work of the canopy, which are placed precisely in the same manner as the banners in No. 406; and, like them, they are held by Badges acting as Supporters. Two well-known seals of the PERCIES are charged with banners, and in each case the banner-staff is held by a single Supporter : one of these figures is a man-at-arms, A.D. 1386 ; the other is a lion, A.D. 1446. At the same period, two lions appear on another Percy Seal. Another, of the same date, has the shield supported by an armed man, without any banner, but having a lance with a long pennon charged with the Crescent badge of PERCY, No. 412, p. 247. Other Percy Seals, again, of the fourteenth century, on either side of the Shield have two lions or two birds.

Numerous examples of great interest illustrate the early introduction of Badges into the composition of Seals, as accessories of Shields. A Seal of Prince JOHN OF GHENT, which has two falcons and padlocks, is one of the most beautiful and suggestive works of its class : in this Seal the two birds are addorsed, and consequently they also have their backs turned towards the central achievement. This position of the figures on early Seals is not uncommon ; but it is an illustration that the use of Badges in the form from which they developed into supporters was an artistic necessity, arising from the form of the spaces to be occupied by the figures upon the Seal. Another most characteristic example of that marshalling of Badges upon Seals, which certainly led the way to true Supporters, is the Seal of Sir MAURICE DE BERKELEY, A.D. 1430, upon which *a mermaid*—the Berkeley badge—is blazoned on each side of the Shield. The two figures are drawn with much skill and elegance. The Shield itself quarters *Berkeley* within a bordure, and a differenced coat of *Bottetourt :* it hangs from a large helm, which, in its turn, is ensigned by as large a *mitre*—the singular Crest of the Berkeleys. The two figures, generally animals, which fill up the spaces to the dexter and sinister of the central achievement on Seals, in the fifteenth century are almost invariably drawn of a comparatively large size ; and, for the most part, they really act as *Supporters to the Crested Helm*, being themselves *supported by*

Q

the Shield. The composition of the Seal of EDMUND DE MORTIMER, Earl of MARCH, A.D. 1400, though now mutilated, exhibits in a most satisfactory manner this very effective arrangement, from which true Supporters to a Shield of Arms might obviously be derived. In this Seal, No. 407, the Shield quarters *Mortimer*, No. 131, and—*or, a cross gu.*, for *Ulster*. The Seal of WM. DE WYNDESOR, No. 382, illustrates with no less happy effect the occasional use

No. 407.—Seal of Earl Edmund de Mortimer :
A.D. 1400.

of birds instead of beasts, as Supporting Badges. Other examples exist in great numbers, and in abundant variety: the two that I add from Mr. Laing's Volume, Nos. 408 and 409, are in every respect most characteristic; they are severally the Seals of ROBERT GRAHAM, of Kinpont, and of Sir WILLIAM LINDSAY, of the Byres.

It is scarcely necessary for me to point out to students that Supporters always have a decided heraldic significance. In supporting a Shield of Arms, they discharge an heraldic duty: but, in themselves, Supporters are armorial symbols of a high rank; and, with peculiar emphasis, they record descent, inheritance, and alliance, and they blazon illustrious deeds.

Supporters should always be represented in an erect position. In whatever direction also they actually may be looking, they always ought to appear to fulfil their own proper office of giving vigilant and deferential *support to the Shield*. It would be well, in our blazoning of supported Achievements, not only for us to regard a becoming position and attitude for Supporters to be matters determined by positive heraldic law, but also that some satisfactory

No. 408.
Seal of Robert Graham, of Kinpont:
A.D. 1433.

No. 409.
Seal of Sir Wm. Lindsay, of the Byres:
A.D. 1390.

arrangement should be made and recognised for general adoption, by which an equally becoming *support* would be provided for "Supporters." An unsatisfactory custom has been either to place the Supporters, whatever they may be, upon some very slight renaissance scroll-work that is neither graceful nor consistent; or, to constrain the Motto scroll to provide a foundation or standing-place for them. In the latter case, an energetic lion, or a massive elephant, and, in a certain class of achievements of comparatively recent date, a mounted trooper, or a stalwart man-of-war's man, probably with a twenty-four pounder at his feet, are made to stand on *the edge of the ribbon* that is inscribed with the Motto. Mr. Laing has enabled me to give an excellent example of

Supporters—two lions standing upon a motto-scroll or ribbon—in No. 410, the Seal of JOHN DRUMMOND, created Earl of MELFORT and Viscount FORTH in the year 1686: the Shield is *Scotland, within a bordure componée;* the Supporters are gorged with collars charged with thistles; and the Crest is the Crest of Scotland issuing from a celestial Crown. As says the Motto of Sir WILLIAM MAHON, " *Moniti, meliora sequamur*"—now that we have been told of it, let us produce something better than this support for our Supporters. Happily the best heraldic artists of the

No. 410.—Seal of John Drummond, Earl of Melfort: A.D. 1686.

moment seem very generally to have reverted to the older and more preferable form.

The Heralds of France still restrict the term "Supporters"—"*Les Supports*"—to animals; whilst to human beings, to figures of angels, and to mythological personages or other figures in human form, when supporting a Shield, they apply the term "*Les Tenants.*" When trees or other inanimate objects are placed beside any armorial shield, and so discharge the duty of Supporters in French achievements, they are distinguished as "*Les Soutiens.*" An old French writer on Heraldry, PALLIOT, however, says that in his time (A.D. 1660), *Tenant* is used in the singular number, and denotes any kind of *single Supporter*, while *Supports* is used when there are *two*.

In the French Heraldry of the present time, a single Tenant or Support is of rare occurrence; and when two Tenants or Supports appear in blazon, they are generally, though not always, alike.

CHAPTER XVII

FLAGS

The Pennon—The Banner—The Standard—The Royal Standard —The Union Jack—Ensigns—Military Standards and Colours —Blazoning—Hoisting and Displaying Flags.

> " Many a beautiful Pennon fixed to a lance,
> And many a Banner displayed."
> —SIEGE OF CARLAVEROCK, A.D. 1300.
> " Prosper our Colours ! "—SHAKESPEARE, *Henry VI.*, *Part* 3.

ADMIRABLY adapted for all purposes of heraldic display, rich in glowing colours, and peculiarly graceful in their free movement in the wind, FLAGS are inseparably associated with spirit-stirring memories, and in all ages and with every people they enjoy an enthusiastic popularity peculiar to themselves.

In the Middle Ages, in England, three distinct classes of heraldic Flags appear to have been in general use, each class having a distinct and well-defined signification.

1. First, the PENNON, small in size, of elongated form, and either pointed or swallow-tailed at the extremity, is charged with the Badge or some other armorial ensign of the owner, and by him displayed upon his own lance, as his personal ensign. The Pennon of Sir JOHN D'ABERNOUN, No. 286, fringed and pointed, A.D. 1277, bears his arms— *Az., a chevron or:* and No. 411, another example of the pointed form of Pennon, is from the Painted Chamber, Westminster, about A.D. 1275. No. 412, a long swallow-tailed Pennon, charged with the Percy crescent Badge, is from the Seal of HENRY DE PERCI, first Earl of NORTHUMBERLAND.

Before the true heraldic era, *Lance-Flags* with various decorative devices, but without any blazonry having a definite signification, were in use: See Nos. 5, 6. The *Pennoncelle* was a modification of the Pennon.

2. Second, the BANNER, square or oblong in form, and of a larger size than the Pennon, bears the entire Coat of Arms of the owner blazoned over its whole surface,

No. 411.
Pennon, from the Painted Chamber.

No. 412.
Pennon of Percy: A.D. 1400.

precisely as the same composition is blazoned upon a Shield: No. 162. The Banner has been described as the ensign of the Sovereign, or of a Prince, a Noble, or a Knight who had been advanced to the higher rank or degree of a "Banneret"; but it would seem almost certain that the display of Arms upon a Banner was never confined to a Banneret. Two Banners are represented in each of the Hungerford Seals, Nos. 391, 392. A small group of oblong Banners, with two pointed Pennons, is represented in No. 413, from the Painted Chamber.

In the olden time, when a Knight had distinguished himself by conspicuous gallantry, it was the custom to mark his meritorious conduct by prompt advancement on the very field of battle. In such a case, the point or points of the good Knight's Pennon were rent off, and thus the small Flag was reduced to the *square* form of the Banner, by which thenceforth he was to be distinguished. FROISSART, in his own graphic manner, has described the ceremonial which attended the first display of the Banner of a newly-created Banneret on the field of battle. Sir JOHN CHANDOS, one of the Knights Founders of the Garter, appeared with his maiden Banner on the field, on the morning of the battle of Naveret, in Castile, April 3rd, 1367 :—"He brought his banner in his hands," says the chronicler, "rolled up" (rolled round the staff), "and said to the PRINCE OF WALES"—it was the BLACK PRINCE,—"'My Lord,

No. 413.—Oblong Banners and Pointed Pennons, from the Painted Chamber.

behold, here is my Banner : I deliver it to you in this way," —still rolled round the staff, that is—"'that it may please you to display it, and that this day I may raise it; for, thank God, I have land and heritage sufficient to support the rank as it ought to be!' Then the Prince and the King"—Don PETRO, King of Castile—"took the Banner, which was of silver with a sharp pile gules, between their hands by the staff, and displayed it, and returned it to him, the Prince saying—'Sir John, behold your Banner; may God grant you may do your duty!' Then Sir JOHN CHANDOS bore his Banner (displayed) to his own Company, and said—'Gentlemen, see here my Banner and yours;

preserve it as your own!'" We see that, like another hero of a later period, the BLACK PRINCE held the maxim—"England expects every man to do his duty."

Quarterings, Marks of Cadency, and Differences (but not impalements) are blazoned on Banners under the very same conditions that they appear on Shields of Arms. For ex-

No. 414.—Seal of Earl John Holland, Admiral of England, &c.; A.D. 1436.

ample, the Banners, as well as the Shield, on the seal of Sir Robert de Hungerford, No. 392, are Differenced with a label for Cadency, and thus are distinguished from the corresponding Banners and Shield on the Seal of Sir Robert's father, No. 391.

Crests, Badges, Supporters, and other external accessories and ornaments of Armorial Shields have no place on Banners, a Banner representing a Shield, and being charged

as a Shield.   In the seventeenth century, however, English
Banners sometimes were charged with Achievements of
Arms, including all the accessories and ornaments of Shields.

In early times Banners appear in use at sea, as well as
on land ; and the same Banners were used both on shore
and afloat.   The *sails* of our early shipping, also, are constantly represented as covered with armorial blazonry, and
they thus were enabled to act as Ship-Flags.   Many curious
and interesting representations of the strange, unwieldy,
unship-shape looking craft that were the ancestors of the
British Navy, are introduced with their *heraldic sails* and
their Banners into the compositions of Seals.   A fine
example of its order is the Seal of JOHN HOLLAND, Earl of
HUNTINGDON, A.D. 1436, " Admiral of England, Ireland,
and Aquitaine," No. 414.   The ship is really a noble-looking
vessel, with her solitary sail blazoned with the Lord
Admiral's Arms—*England, within a bordure of France*,—the
same arms that were borne by Prince JOHN OF ELTHAM,
No. 24.   In this example the crew are not represented :
but in other Seals of early shipping figures are commonly
introduced, and almost always they are drawn of ludicrously
disproportionate size.   This ship does not display any
Banner from a banner-staff, but has a nautical Pennon of
ample size flying at the mast-head : when Banners are
displayed on board ships upon early Seals, they are generally narrow in proportion to their height, a form of Banner
adopted on land as well as at sea, in consequence of the
greater inconvenience attending the display of broad or
really square Banners.   At a later period, however, Ship-
Flags of very large size came into favour.

3. The STANDARD, the third variety of early heraldic
Flags, which first appears about the middle of the fourteenth century, and was in general use by personages of
high rank in the two following centuries, appears to have
been adopted for the special purpose of displaying the

Badge. The Badge was worn on his livery by a servant as retainer, and consequently the Standard by which he mustered in camp was of the livery colours, and bore the Badge, with both of which the retainer was familiar.

This Flag is of ample proportions, and great length; but its size varies with the owner's rank. Next to the Staff was usually to be found the *red cross on a silver field* of St. George. The rest of the field is generally divided per fesse into two tinctures, in most cases the livery colours of the owner, or the prevailing tinctures of his Coat of Arms, which in such cases may almost be assumed to have been his livery. With some principal figure or device occupying

No. 415.—Standard of Sir Henry de Stafford, K.G. : about A.D. 1475.

a prominent position, various Badges are displayed over the whole field, a Motto, which is placed bend-wise, having divided the Standard into compartments. The edges are fringed throughout, and the extremity is sometimes swallow-tailed, and sometimes rounded.

The Standard of Sir Henry de Stafford, K.G., second son of Henry, second Duke of Buckingham (executed in 1483), is represented in No. 415, from a drawing in the Heralds' College. It is charged, first, with *a cross of St. George*: then, on a *field per fesse sable and gules* (the colours of the Duke's livery), *the White Swan* of the De Bohuns, with the *silver Stafford-knot* (No. 304), differenced with *a Crescent gules* for Cadency; the Motto is HVMBLE: ET: LOYAL; and the fringe, of the same colours as the field, is *componée sa. and gu.* In other examples a greater variety of Badges is introduced. The student will not fail to take notice of the systematic display of the ensign of St. George in these Standards, as the national armorial device of England. The use and heraldic display of these standards had practically lapsed, but the College of Arms has now reverted to its ancient practice of recording them in cases of the grant or confirmation of a Badge.

The ROYAL STANDARD (to give it its popular name) is not really a Standard at all, but is the King's Banner of his

No. 416.
The Royal Standard, or Banner.

arms. It stands at the head of our English Flags of the present day, and bears the full blazonry of the Royal Arms of His Majesty THE KING, as they are marshalled on the Royal Shield: No. 416. It is personal to the King, and its use by other people is not permitted. This splendid Flag, so truly heraldic in its character, and charged with Coat-Armour and not with Badges, ought to be styled the ROYAL BANNER. The same Standard is duly differenced with their own Marks of Cadency and their Shields of Pretence for the different members of the Royal Family. For use at sea, whilst the PRINCE OF WALES has his own Flag or Banner of his arms, all other members of the Royal Family use a flag showing the Royal Arms within a bordure ermine. QUEEN MARY and QUEEN ALEXANDRA fly flags of their impaled arms.

The UNION JACK, which is regarded as the national British Flag, as we now display it, is the second of its race. Strictly speaking, it is as much the property of the Sovereign as the Royal Banner, but objection to its use and display is not officially made. The *First Union Jack*, No. 417, was produced in obedience to a Royal Proclamation of JAMES I. in the year 1606. Its object was to provide a single National Flag for both England and Scotland as a single kingdom, which might put an end to certain serious disputes concerning the precedence of their respective Banners of St. George and St. Andrew, Nos. 418, 419, between the natives of England and Scotland—of " South and North Britain." This " Union " Flag combined the blazonry of the two rival ensigns, not marshalling them by quartering after the early heraldic usage, but by reviving a still earlier process, and by blending the cross and the saltire of Nos. 418 and

No. 418.
St. George.

No. 419.
St. Andrew.

No. 417.—The First Union Jack.

419 in a single composition. This was effected, accordingly, by charging the Cross of St. George, with a narrow border or " fimbriation " of white to represent its white field, *upon* the Banner of St. Andrew, the result being the Flag shown in No. 417. On the final " Union " between England and Scotland in 1707, this device was formally declared to be the " Ensign armorial of the United Kingdom of Great Britain."

Upon the first day of January, 1801, the *Second Union Jack*, the " Union Jack " of to-day, No. 420, superseded the Flag of King JAMES and Queen ANNE. The " Union " with Ireland rendered a change necessary in the Union Jack, in order to incorporate with its blazonry the Banner of ST.

PATRICK, No. 421, *arg., a saltire gu.* There seems good reason to believe that the so-called Cross of St. Patrick had little, if indeed any, separate or prior existence. The process that had been adopted before was again brought into action, but now a single compound device had to be formed by the combination of a cross and two saltires, Nos. 418, 419, and 421. As before, in this new Flag the blue field of St. ANDREW forms the field: then the two Saltires, the one white and the other red, are formed into a single compound Saltire counter-changed of the two tinctures alternating, the white having precedence; a narrow edging of

No. 420.
The Second Union Jack.

No. 421.
St. Patrick.

white is next added to each red side of this new figure, to represent the white field of St. Patrick, as the narrow edging of white about the red cross represented the white field of St. GEORGE in No. 418; and, finally, the red cross of St. George fimbriated with white, as in the First Jack, is charged over all. Such is the Second Union Jack, No. 420. In this compound device it will be observed that the *broad diagonal white* members represent the *silver saltire* of St. Andrew, No. 419: that the *red diagonal* members represent the *saltire gules* of St. Patrick, No. 421, and that the *narrow diagonal white* lines are added in order to place this *saltire gules on a field argent:* that the *diagonal red and the broad diagonal white members* represent the two Saltires of St. Andrew and St. Patrick in combination: and that the *fimbriated red cross* in the front of the goodly alliance declares the presence of the symbol of St. George.

Sir HARRIS NICHOLAS has suggested that this flag may have acquired its name of "Jack" ("Union" is obvious enough) from the original author of the First Union Flag, King JAMES, who, in the Heralds' French language, would be styled *Jacques*: and so the Flag would be called "Jacques' Union," which would easily settle down into "Jack's Union," and finally would as easily become "Union Jack." The Second Union Flag is always to be hoisted as it is represented in No. 420, the diagonal white having precedence in the first canton. To reverse the

No. 422.
The Red Ensign.

proper display of the Flag implies distress or danger; or such a procedure (very often, as I am aware, unconsciously adopted, through ignorance of the real meaning of the Flag itself) subjects the Union Jack to degradation.

By a recent warrant Lords Lieutenant fly the Union Jack charged with a sword fesseways.

The ENSIGNS now in use are:—

1. The *Red Ensign*, a plain red Flag cantoning a Union Jack—having a Jack in the dexter chief angle next to the point of suspension: No. 422. This Ensign shares with the Union Jack the honour of being the "Ensign of England" —the Ensign, that is, of the British Empire. When displayed at sea, it now distinguishes all vessels that do not belong to the Royal Navy: but, before the year 1864, it was the distinguishing ensign of the "red squadron of the Navy," and of the "Admirals of the Red"—the Admirals of the highest rank.

2. The *White* or *St. George's Ensign* is the old banner of St. George, No. 418, with a Jack cantoned in the first quarter. It now is the Ensign of the Royal Navy: but, before 1864, it distinguished the "white squadron" of the Navy, and the Admirals—second in rank—of that Squadron.

3. The *Blue Ensign* differs from the Red only in the field being plain blue instead of red. It now is the Ensign of the Naval Reserve: before 1864 it was the Ensign of "Admirals of the Blue," third in rank, and of their Squadron of the Royal Navy.

A Red Ensign is often charged with a Crown, or with some appropriate device, to denote some particular department of the public service.

With the Ensigns may be grouped the *Flag of the Admiralty*, which displays a yellow anchor and cable set fesse-wise on a red field.

The Ensigns are always to be hoisted so as to have the Jack next to the point of suspension, as in No. 422.

MILITARY FLAGS. 1. *Cavalry Standards*, being lineal descendants of the knightly Banners of mediæval chivalry, are small square Flags, the colour of the field the same as the regimental facings; and each Standard bears the Number, Motto, and specific Title of its own Regiment, with whatever heraldic Badge or Device may be associated with it. Upon these Standards also are blazoned the regimental "*Honours*"—such words as WATERLOO, ALMA, LUCKNOW, and others, which briefly and with most emphatic significance declare the services of the corps. The Household Cavalry, the Life Guards and Blues, have all their Standards of Crimson, and they are blazoned with the Royal Insignia and their own "Honours" and Devices.

2. *Infantry Colours.* In the first instance, each Regiment of Infantry had one "Colour": subsequently, two others were added: and, finally, in the reign of Queen ANNE, it was decided that every Infantry Regiment or

Battalion of the Line (the Rifles of the Line excepted, who have no "Colours") should have its own "Pair of Colours." Of this "Pair," one is the "*King's Colour*"—a Union Jack charged with some regimental Devices: the other, the "*Regimental Colour,*" is of the tincture of the facings, on which the "Honours" and "Devices" of the Regiment are charged, and in the dexter chief angle a small Jack is cantoned: in fact, the "Regimental Colour" is the same as the Red or Blue Ensign (No. 422), the Colour of the field varying with the regimental facings, and the field itself being charged with the various Devices.

In their Colours, the Guards reverse the arrangement that obtains with the Regiments of the Line. With them, the *King's Colour* is always crimson, with or without a Jack, but charged with the Royal Cypher and the regimental Devices: the *Regimental Colour* of the Guards is the Union Jack.

3. The *Royal Artillery* have no Colours or Standards.

Military Flags are not now used in actual warfare by British troops.

I conclude this Chapter, which treats briefly of the Heraldry of the most important English Flags, with four still more brief general remarks :—

1. First: by all English people who are disposed to exclaim, making SHAKESPEARE's words their own, "*Prosper our Colours !*" it ought to be understood that their National Flags are endowed with heraldic, that is, with historical significance, recorded after an heraldic fashion.

2. Second: this significance of their Flags ought also to be understood, that it may be appreciated, by all true English people.

3. Third: our Flags ought always to be made and represented correctly.

And 4. Lastly: our Flags, and all other Flags also, ought always to be hoisted and displayed rightly and properly.

R

CHAPTER XVIII

THE ROYAL HERALDRY OF ENGLAND
AND SCOTLAND

Shields of Arms of the Reigning Sovereigns of England ; of Scotland ; of the United Kingdom of Great Britain and Ireland—Crests—Supporters—Mottoes—Crowns—Banners—Armorial Insignia of the late Prince Consort ; of the Prince and Princess of Wales ; of the other Princes and Princesses.

"On his Banner were three Leopards, courant, of fine gold, set on red : fierce were they, haughty and cruel, to signify that, like them, the KING is dreadful to his enemies ; for his bite is slight to none who inflame his anger : and yet, towards such as seek his friendship or submit to his power his kindness is soon rekindled."—ROLL OF CARLAVEROCK.

"With Scotland's Arms, Device and Crest
Embroidered round and round."—MARMION.

How the "three Leopards courant" of the shrewd chronicler of Carlaverock are identical with the "three Lions passant guardant" of the Royal Shield of England I have already shown (see page 84). To the Norman Sovereigns of England, WILLIAM I., WILLIAM II., HENRY I., and STEPHEN (A.D. 1066–1154), the same Shield of Arms has been assigned—*Gu., two lions pass. guard., in pale, or*, No. 22. It must be distinctly understood, however, that there exists no certain authority for these Arms.

In like manner, STEPHEN is also *said* to have borne on a red Shield three golden *Sagittaries*, or Centaurs, with bows and arrows. And, again, HENRY II. is *considered* to have added a third lion to the two on the Shield of his father, a *single golden lion passant guardant on red* being (also considered to be) the armorial ensign of the province of Aquitaine, acquired by HENRY in right of his Consort, ALIANORE.

As early as the reign of HENRY III., a Shield of Arms, No. 23, was assigned to the Anglo-Saxon Kings: another Shield, No. 2, was assigned to EDWARD THE CONFESSOR: and a third Shield, No. 3, to another sainted Anglo-Saxon Prince, EDMUND.

From the appearance of the Second Great Seal of RICHARD I., about A.D. 1195, all uncertainty concerning

No. 22.
Royal Arms, supposed to have been borne before A.D. 1189.

No. 187.
Royal Arms, from A D. 1189 to 1340.

the Royal Arms of England is at an end, and they are borne as follows by the successive English Sovereigns:—

RICHARD I.: JOHN: HENRY III.: EDWARD I.: EDWARD II.: and EDWARD III., till the thirteenth year of his reign, A.D. 1340:—*Gu., three lions passant guardant in pale or,*—No. 187.

EDWARD III., from the thirteenth year of his reign, when he claimed to be King of France as well as of England, and so styled himself: RICHARD II.: and HENRY IV., till about the fifth year of his reign:—*France Ancient and England quarterly,*—No. 252.

RICHARD II. sometimes bore the Arms of the CONFESSOR, No. 2, with his own, on a separate shield, as at Westminster Hall; and sometimes he impaled the Con-

fessor's Arms with his own quartered Shield, the arms of
the Confessor having the precedence.

HENRY IV. from about 1405: HENRY V.: HENRY VI.:
EDWARD IV.: EDWARD V.: RICHARD III.: HENRY VII.:

No. 252.—Royal Arms from A.D. 1340   No. 253.—Royal Arms from about
to about 1405.   A.D. 1405 to 1603.

HENRY VIII.: EDWARD VI.: MARY: and ELIZABETH, to
A.D. 1603:—*France Modern and England Quarterly*, No.
253.

The Royal Shield of SCOTLAND, No. 138, first appears
upon the Seal of ALEXANDER II. about A.D. 1235; and, as

Mr. Seton well observes, the origin
of its bearings "is veiled by the mists
of Antiquity." The same Shield,
without any modification or change,
was borne by all the Sovereigns of
Scotland.

JAMES I.: CHARLES I.: CHARLES
II.: JAMES II.: WILLIAM III. and
MARY: and ANNE, till May 1, 1707:
Quarterly: 1 and 4, *Grand Quarters,
France Modern and England* (No.

No. 138.—Royal Arms of
Scotland.

253): 2, *Grand Quarter, Scotland* (No. 138): 3, *Grand
Quarter—Az., a harp or, stringed arg., for Ireland:* No. 423.

WILLIAM III., as an elected Sovereign, charged his
paternal shield of NASSAU, No. 424—*Az., billettée, a lion*

rampt. or,—in pretence upon the Royal Shield : also, during the life of his Consort, till Dec. 28, 1694, he bore the *Stuart* shield with *Nassau* in pretence on the dexter half of

No. 423.—Royal Arms of the Stuart Sovereigns.

his Shield, and thus impaled in the sinster half of his Shield the same Stuart arms, as in the Diagram, No. 425, to denote their joint Sovereignty : the Shield represented in

No. 425.—Diagram of Shield of William III. and Mary. No. 424. Arms of Nassau. No. 426.—Diagram of Shield of William III alone.

this Diagram, No. 425, bears the whole of No. 423 on its dexter half, with No. 424 in pretence; and on its sinister half it also bears the whole of No. 423. When he reigned

alone, WILLIAM III. bore his own dexter half of the impaled Shield alone, as in the Diagram, No. 426: the
Shield represented in this Diagram being the dexter half
of No. 425.

Queen ANNE, from May 1, 1707, till 1714, bore the Royal
Arms marshalled as in the Diagram, No. 427 :—1 and 2,
England impaling *Scotland ;* 3, *France Modern* (No. 253);
4, *Ireland* (the Harp, as in the third quarter of No. 423).

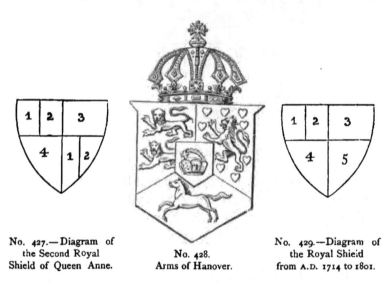

No. 427.—Diagram of
the Second Royal
Shield of Queen Anne.

No. 428.
Arms of Hanover.

No. 429.—Diagram of
the Royal Shield
from A.D. 1714 to 1801.

The Arms of HANOVER, on the accession of GEORGE I.,
August 1, 1714, were added to the Shield of the United
Kingdom. This was accomplished by removing the
charges (*England and Scotland impaled*) from the fourth
quarter of the Shield, No. 427, and charging that quarter
with the arms of *Hanover* as they appear on the Shield, No.
428 :—*Per pale and per chevron,* 1, *Gu., two lions passant
guardant or,* for *Brunswick :* 2, *Or, Semée of hearts, a lion
rampt. az.,* for *Lunenburgh :* 3, *Gu., a horse courant arg.,* for
Westphalia : 4, *Over all, on an inescutcheon gules, the golden
crown of Charlemagne.* This marshalling is shown in the

Diagram, No. 429, which represents a Shield bearing,—
1 and 2, *England* impaling *Scotland;* 3, *France Modern;*
4, *Ireland;* 5, *Hanover* (as in No. 428, without the
Crown).

On January 1, 1801, the Fleurs de Lys of France
were removed from the Royal Shield of Great Britain,
which then was marshalled as in the diagram, No. 430,
quarterly, 1 *and* 4, *England;* 2, *Scotland;* 3, *Ireland;*
5, *Hanover*—the shield of Hanover being ensigned with
the *Electoral Bonnet*, No. 240, till 1816, but, after
Hanover became a kingdom, with a *Royal Crown* in place
of the Electoral Bonnet from 1816 till
1837, as it appears in No. 428.

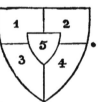

GEORGE I.: GEORGE II.: GEORGE
III., till Jan. 1, 1801 :—The arms indicated in the diagram, No. 429.

GEORGE III., till 1816 :—The arms
indicated in the diagram, No. 430, the
inescutcheon ensigned with an electoral
bonnet.

No. 430.—Diagram of
the Royal Shield
from A.D. 1801 to
1837.

GEORGE III., after 1816: GEORGE
IV.: WILLIAM IV. :—The same arms as No. 430, but the
inescutcheon ensigned with a Royal Crown.

QUEEN VICTORIA, KING EDWARD VII., and KING
GEORGE V.:—The same as No. 430, but without the
inescutcheon, the four quarters being marshalled as on
the Royal Standard, No. 416.

ROYAL CRESTS.

For ENGLAND:—*A golden lion statant guardant, imperially crowned;* assumed by EDWARD III., and by him
borne on his Helm standing upon a Cap of Estate; retained
from his time, and now borne standing on an Imperial
Crown. No. 431.

For Scotland :—First Crest. *A lion statant guardant gu.*, assumed by Robert II., about A.D. 1385 ; retained, and with some modifications used by his successors, till about A.D. 1550. Second Crest. *On an Imperial Crown, a lion sejant affronté erect gu. ; imperially crowned, holding in the dexter paw a sword, and in the sinister paw a sceptre, both erect and ppr.* ; with the motto— IN : DEFENSE ; assumed by James V. ; borne by Mary, and shown in her signet-ring, No. 432, about 1564 ; retained, and now in use.

No. 431.—Royal
Crest of England.

ROYAL SUPPORTERS.

For England. Of uncertain authority before Henry VI., who bore *two white antelopes :* also, *a lion and a panther,* or *antelope.*

Edward IV. :—*A lion or,* or *argent, and a bull sable :* or, *two lions argent :* or, *a lion and a hart argent.*

Richard III. :—*A lion or and a boar arg.:* or, *two boars arg.*

Henry VII. :—*A dragon gu., and a greyhound arg. :* or, *two greyhounds arg. :* or, *a lion or and a dragon gu.*

Henry VIII. :—*A lion or and a dragon gu.:* or, *a dragon gu., and either a bull sable, a greyhound argent, or a cock arg.*

Edward VI. :—*A lion or, and a dragon gu.*

Mary and Elizabeth :—*A lion or, and a greyhound arg.,* or *a dragon gu.*

For Scotland.—First Supporters :—*Two lions rampt. guard.* ; first seen on a Seal of James I., A.D. 1429. Second Supporters : *Two silver unicorns, crowned with imperial and gorged with open crowns and chained or ;*

assumed by JAMES IV., and retained in use. On the signet of Queen MARY STUART, No. 432: for this beautiful cut once more I am indebted to Mr. Laing.

For the UNITED KINGDOM. Dexter Supporter: *A lion rampt. guard., royally crowned, or.* Sinister Supporter: *A*

No. 432.—The Signet of Queen Mary Stuart, considerably enlarged.

unicorn rampt. arg., armed, crined and gorged with a coronet composed of crosses pattée and fleurs de lis, and chained or. Assumed by JAMES I. of Great Britain: retained, and still in use.

ROYAL MOTTOES.

The ancient English war-cry — DIEU . ET . MON . DROIT!—"*God and my Right!*" assumed as a regular Motto by HENRY VI., has been retained in use since his time.

Queens ELIZABETH and ANNE also used—SEMPER . EADEM—"*Always the Same.*" JAMES I. used—BEATI . PACIFICI—"*Blessed are the Peace-makers.*"

Mottoes of Scotland: NEMO . ME . IMPUNE . LA-CESSIT—"*No man with impunity attacks me:*" and, above the Crest—IN . DEFENSE. The former is really the Motto of the Order of the Thistle.

THE CROWN

Till the time of HENRY IV., the Crown, the symbol of the Sovereignty of England, was a golden circlet richly jewelled, and heightened with conventional *strawberry-leaves*: fine examples are represented in the effigies of HENRY III., JOHN, and EDWARD II.

HENRY IV., as shown by his splendid effigy at Canterbury, introduced *fleurs de lys*, alternating with the leaves.

From the time of HENRY V., the circlet has been heightened by *crosses pattées* and *fleurs de lys* alternating, four of each, and without any leaves. HENRY V. also first *arched the circlet with jewelled bands*, which at their inter-

No. 234.
Crown of H.M., The King.

section he surmounted with a *mound and cross.*

The arched Crown of HENRY V. has four half-arches,—that is, it is arched over twice: HENRY VI. and CHARLES I. arched their crown three times: all the other Sovereigns have had two complete arches only, and the Crown still retains these two arches intersecting at right angles, as in No. 234.

At different periods, while the design of the Crown has remained unchanged, the contour of the arches, and the artistic treatment of the ornamentation have undergone various modifications.

The ROYAL BANNERS, or STANDARDS, are charged with the bearings of the Royal Shield of Arms for the time being.

The Armorial Insignia of H.R.H. the late PRINCE CONSORT. The SHIELD was—*Quarterly,* 1 *and* 4,—*The Royal Arms of the late Queen*, as in No. 416, but differenced with *a silver label of three points charged on the central point with a cross of St. George: 2 and* 3,—*Saxony*, No. 225. This Shield was encircled with the Garter of the Order, and ensigned with the Prince's own Coronet, shown in No. 441.

The CREST was the *Royal Crest of England*, No. 431, the lion having the same *label* that differences the Shield adjusted about his neck as a collar, and being crowned with the coronet, *vide* Fig. 441, in place of the Imperial Crown.

The SUPPORTERS were those of the Royal Arms, *the golden lion and silver unicorn*, both of them differenced with the same *label*, and the lion crowned with the same coronet.

The MOTTO.— TREU . UND . FEST —" True and Faithful." To the dexter of this Achievement, the complete Royal Achievement of QUEEN VICTORIA.

The Arms of KING EDWARD VII. were and those of KING GEORGE V. are practically the same as those of QUEEN VICTORIA. As PRINCES OF WALES, these Arms were differenced by a plain *label* of three points argent, and an inescutcheon of SAXONY was superimposed. In each case upon accession to the throne, the inescutcheon of Saxony was removed, and consequently there has been no change whatsoever in the Royal Arms, those of KING EDWARD and KING GEORGE being the same as those of QUEEN VICTORIA, save, of course, the necessary change in the Royal Cyphers— the full blazon of the Royal Arms for the present reign being :—

ARMS.—*Quarterly*, 1 *and* 4, *gules, three lions passant guardant in pale or* (ENGLAND); 2, *or, a lion rampant within a double tressure flory and counterflory gules* (SCOTLAND); 3, *azure, a harp or, stringed argent* (IRELAND).

HELMET—*of gold, affronté and with grylles.*

MANTLING, *cloth of gold lined with ermine.*

CRESTS *upon the Imperial Crown, a lion statant guardant, crowned or* (ENGLAND).

Upon the Crown of Scotland, a lion sejant erect affronté

gules ; crowned or, holding in the dexter paw a sword, and in the sinister a sceptre, both proper (SCOTLAND).

On a Wreath, *or and azure, a tower triple-towered of the first, from the portal a hart springing argent, attired and unguled gold* (IRELAND).

SUPPORTERS (dexter), *a lion guardant or, crowned as the crest;* (sinister), *a unicorn argent, armed, crined and unguled or, gorged with a coronet composed of crosses patée and fleurs de lis, a chain affixed thereto, passing between the forelegs and reflexed over the back of the last.*

BADGES.—

1. *The Red and White Rose, united and crowned* (ENGLAND).
2. *The Thistle, crowned* (SCOTLAND).
3. *A Harp or, stringed argent, crowned* (IRELAND).
4. *A Trefoil slipped vert, crowned* (IRELAND).
5. *The Rose, Thistle and Shamrock united on one stem and crowned* (UNITED KINGDOM).
6. *A Shield, crowned and bearing the device of the Union Jack* (UNITED KINGDOM).
7. *Upon a mount vert, a dragon passant with wings elevated gules* (WALES). *N.B.*—This badge is not crowned.

MOTTO.—DIEU . ET . MON . DROIT in the compartment below the Shield, with the Union, Rose, Shamrock, and Thistle engrafted on the same stem.

The Shield is encircled by the Garter of that Order.

The Arms of H.M. QUEEN ALEXANDRA, early in the reign of KING EDWARD, were declared by Royal Warrant. Within the Garter are impaled (dexter) the Arms of KING EDWARD VII. and (sinister) the undifferenced Arms of DENMARK as under :—

The ROYAL ARMS OF DENMARK. The Shield divided into four quarters by the national *white cross*, having a *border of red* to represent the red field of the Danish Ensign.

First Quarter:—DENMARK—*Or, semée of hearts gu., three lions pass. guard. in pale az.* Second Quarter:—SLESWICK —*Or, two lions pass. in pale az.* Third Quarter:—*Per fesse, in chief,* SWEDEN—*Az., three crowns or ; in base,* ICELAND— *Gu., a stock-fish arg., crowned or ; impaling,* for FAROE ISLANDS—*Az., a buck pass. arg. ;* and, for GREENLAND—a *polar bear rampt. arg.* Fourth Quarter:—*Per fesse, in chief,* for JUTLAND—*Or, ten hearts, four, three, two, one, gu., and in chief a lion pass. az. ; in base,* for VANDALIA—*Gu., a wyvern, its tail nowed and wings expanded, or.*

On an Inescutcheon, quarterly: First, for HOLSTEIN— *Gu., an inescutcheon per fesse arg. and of the first, in every point thereof a nail in triangle, between as many holly-leaves, all ppr.* Second, for STORMERK—*Gu., a swan arg., gorged with a coronet or.* Third, for DITZMERS—*Az., an armed knight ppr., brandishing his sword, his charger arg.* Fourth, for LAUENBURGH—*Gu., a horse's head couped arg.*

Over all, in pretence upon a second Inescutcheon, OLDENBURGH—*Or, two bars gu. ;* impaling—*Az., a cross patée fitchée or,* for DALMENHURST.

The above-mentioned warrant for Her Majesty declares the arms to be surmounted by the Royal Crown, and supported (dexter) by a lion guardant, and imperially crowned or, and (sinister) by a savage wreathed about the temples and loins with oak and supporting in his exterior hand a club all proper.

The Arms of H.M. QUEEN MARY, as declared by Royal Warrant, are :—Within the Garter ensigned with the Royal Crown the Arms of the United Kingdom of Great Britain and Ireland impaling quarterly (for Cambridge) the Royal Arms as borne by GEORGE III. differenced by a label of three points arg., the centre point charged with the St. George's Cross, and each of the other points with two hearts in pale gu., 2nd and 3rd (for Teck) or, three stags' attires fesseways in pale, the point of each attire to the sinister sa., impaling or, three lions passant in pale sa., langued gu., the dexter fore paws of the last, over all an inescutcheon paly bendy sinister sa. and or. *Supporters* (dexter) a lion guardant or, crowned with the Royal Crown ppr.; (sinister) a stag ppr.

H.R.H. the PRINCE OF WALES bears a Shield— *Quarterly*, 1 *and* 4, ENGLAND; 2, SCOTLAND; 3, IRELAND, differenced by a plain *label of three points argent*. In pretence over these Arms he bears an Inescutcheon of the Arms of WALES, viz. quarterly or and gu., four lions passant guardant counter-changed, the Inescutcheon sur-mounted by the Coronet of the Heir-Apparent. His Crest is the Crest of England, and his Supporters are also the same, but the Crest and each of the Supporters are differ-enced by a similar *label*, and for the Imperial Crown in the Crest and dexter supporter the coronet of the Prince of WALES is substituted. The Badges of the Prince of WALES are two:—viz. 1, *A plume of three ostrich feathers arg., quilled or, enfiled by a coronet composed of crosses patée and fleurs de lys*, with the MOTTO, "ICH DIEN": 2, *on a mount vert, a dragon passant with wings elevated gu., differ-enced with a label of three points arg.* Below the SHIELD the MOTTO "ICH DIEN" is repeated, and the Shield is surrounded by the Garter.

The other PRINCES and PRINCESSES, younger children of the late QUEEN VICTORIA, all bore the Royal Arms of the Sovereign, the Princes on *Shields*, the Princesses on *Lozenges*. All their Royal Highnesses bore the Royal *Supporters;* all have a Shield of *Saxony*, in pretence on their own Shield or Lozenge; all ensign their Shield or Lozenge with their own Coronet, No. 290; and the Princes bear the Royal *Crest.* In every case, the dexter Supporter is crowned and the sinister Supporter is gorged, and the Crest stands upon and is ensigned with the same Coronet which appears above the Shield as their particular coronet of rank: all the Shields,

Lozenges, Crests, and Supporters, are differenced with a *silver label of three points, the labels being differenced* as follows :—

H.R.H. the late Duke of EDINBURGH, &c. :—*On the central point a red cross; on each of the other two points a red anchor* (when the Duke succeeded to the throne of Saxe-Coburg and Gotha, a radical change in his Arms was made). H.R.H. the Duke of CONNAUGHT :—*Red cross, and two blue fleurs de lys.* H.R.H. the late Duke of ALBANY:— *Red cross, and two red hearts.* H.I.M. the late GERMAN EMPRESS, PRINCESS ROYAL OF ENGLAND, on the central point of her *label* had a *red rose*, and on each of the other two points a *red cross.* H.R.H. the late Princess ALICE OF HESSE had on her *label* a *red rose*, between two *ermine spots.* H.R.H. the Princess HELENA, Princess CHRISTIAN, has on her *label* a *red cross* between two *red roses.* H.R.H. the Princess LOUISE (Duchess of ARGYLL) :—*Red rose, and two red cantons.* H.R.H. the Princess BEATRICE :—*Red heart, and two red roses.*

The Warrants for the three daughters of King EDWARD were issued in the lifetime of Queen VICTORIA when they were grandchildren of the Sovereign, and no change has since been made. Consequently the *labels* are of *five points* instead of *three.* The Charges upon the label of H.R.H. the Duchess of FIFE (Princess ROYAL OF ENGLAND) are: *Three red crosses, and two thistles slipped alternately.* H.R.H. Princess VICTORIA has a *label* of *five points argent*, charged with *three roses* and *two crosses gules;* and H.M. the Queen of NORWAY a similar *label*, charged with *three hearts* and *two crosses gules.*

The *label* of H.R.H. the first Duke of CAMBRIDGE was silver, of three points, and the points differenced with *a red cross* in the centre, and on each of the two side points *two red hearts in pale.* The second and late Duke bore the same *label* as his father, and below it a second *label* of three

points *gules*. The *label* of H.R.H. the first Duke of CUMBER-
LAND (son of King GEORGE III.) was of silver, and of *three
points* charged with a *fleur de lys* between *two crosses gules*.
The second Duke bore an additional *label* of *three points
gules*, the *centre point* charged with the *white horse of
Hanover*. These Dukes bore the Royal Arms as used
in the reign of GEORGE III. and not as altered for Queen
VICTORIA, differencing the accessories as well as the Shield
with their *labels*.

In 1904 a warrant was issued for H.R.H. Prince
ARTHUR OF CONNAUGHT. The label was of five points
charged with three red crosses and two blue fleurs de lys
alternately. The coronet assigned to him was of crosses
patée and strawberry leaves alternately.

An interesting warrant was issued for the Princess
VICTORIA EUGENIE OF BATTENBERG, now Queen of SPAIN,
in view of her then approaching marriage. This assigned to
her the arms of her father within a bordure of England, and
each of the supporters had a banner of the Royal Arms of
the United Kingdom placed in his paws.

Even more interesting was the warrant issued in 1913
to H.H. Princess ALEXANDRA, Duchess of FIFE. This
assigned to her upon a lozenge the Royal Arms, differenced
by the same label as that of her mother the Princess Royal,
and upon an inescutcheon the quarterly coat of Duff, the
inescutcheon being surmounted by the coronet of a Duchess
of the United Kingdom, and the lozenge itself being surmounted by the coronet of a Princess of the rank of Highness. The dexter supporter is the Royal Lion of England
crowned with the last-mentioned coronet and charged with
the label as in the arms. The sinister supporter is a savage
taken from the supporters of the late Duke of Fife.

CHAPTER XIX

ORDERS OF KNIGHTHOOD AND INSIGNIA OF HONOUR

Feudal Knighthood—Orders of Knighthood: Knights of St. John; Knights Templars; The Order of the Garter; of the Thistle; of St. Patrick; of the Bath; of St. Michael and St. George; of The Star of India—Order of Merit—Royal Victorian Order—Imperial Service Order—The Victoria Cross—The Albert Medal—Naval and Military Medals—Foreign Insignia bestowed on British Subjects.

"The same King would make an Order of KNIGHTS of himself and his Sons, and of the bravest of his land."—FROISSART.

"I will say as I have said,—
Thou art a noble KNIGHT."—LORD OF THE ISLES.

KNIGHTHOOD, as that term is generally understood in its comprehensive acceptation, has been well defined to be "a distinction of rank amongst freemen, depending not upon birth or property, but simply upon the admission of the person so distinguished, by the girding of a sword or other similar solemnity, into an order of men having by law or usage certain social or political privileges," and also a certain appropriate title. It is evident, therefore, from this definition that Knighthood implies the existence of these two conditions: the one, that the man to be admitted to the rank of Knighthood should possess such qualifications as may entitle him to that distinction; and the other, that Knighthood should be conferred by a personage endowed with a competent power and authority.

In feudal times the qualifications for Knighthood were military exploits of a distinguished character, and eminent services, of whatever kind, rendered to the King and the realm : also, the holding a certain property in land (in the time of EDWARD I., land then of the yearly value of £20, or upwards), whether directly from the King, or under some Noble, by the feudal tenure of personal military service to be rendered under certain established conditions ; but it has been disputed whether there was any necessary connection between Knighthood, as such, and the Knight Service of Feudal Tenure.   During the first two centuries after the Conquest, Knighthood was conferred by the great Barons and by the Spiritual Peers, as well as by the King himself, or by his appointed representative : but, after the accession of HENRY III., the prevailing rule appears to have been that in England no persons should be created Knights except by the King, or the Prince Royal acting for his Father, or by the King's General-in-Chief, or other personal representative.

The knightly rank, as it gave an increase of dignity, implied also the maintenance of a becoming state, and the discharge of certain civil duties : and, more particularly, all Knights were required to make such a provision for rendering military service as was held to be consistent with their position and their property ; and it was expected from them that they should take a dignified part in the chivalrous exercises and celebrations of their times.   It followed, that feudal Knighthood was a distinction which, if not conferred for the sake of honour, became obligatory ; and fines, accordingly, were imposed upon men qualified for Knighthood who, notwithstanding, were found not to be Knights. In the course of time, as the rigour of the feudal system abated, the numbers of the military tenants of small tenures greatly increased : and, since many of these persons had no inclination for the profession of arms, they gladly accepted the alternative of paying a fine, which enabled them to evade an honour unsuited as well to their means as to their personal tastes and their peaceful avocations. A fruitful source of revenue thus was secured for the Crown, while the military character of Knighthood was maintained, and at the same time a new and important class of the community gradually became established.

The Knights of Norman England, who at first were soldiers of the highest order, derived their designation from their warlike predecessors of Anglo-Saxon times, the word "*cniht,*" in the late Anglo-Saxon tongue, signifying a military attendant. When they had established themselves in the position and in the possession of the lands of the Anglo-Saxons, the Anglo-Norman Knights retained their own original title. The Latin equivalent for that title of "Knight" is "*Miles,*" and the Norman-French is "*Chevalier.*"

These Knights may be grouped in two classes. The first class contains all persons who had been admitted into the comprehensive Order of Chivalry—who were Knights by reason of their common Knighthood. The second class is formed of Knights who, in addition to their Knightly rank, were members of some special and distinct Fraternity, Companionship, or Order of Knighthood. Every Society of this kind has always possessed Laws, Institutions, Titles, and Insignia peculiar to itself.

The peculiar character and object of the Crusades led to the formation of two Orders of *Priest-Knights*—Orders not belonging to any particular nation, but numbering amongst their members men of all nations. These are the Orders of the KNIGHTS OF ST. JOHN OF JERUSALEM, or HOSPITALLERS, and of the KNIGHTS TEMPLARS.

The HOSPITALLERS, instituted about A.D. 1092, were introduced into England about 1100. In the year 1310 they were established at Rhodes, and in 1530 at Malta, under their forty-third Grand Master, PHILIPPE DE VILLIERS DE L'ISLE-ADAM. Their device is a *silver cross of eight points*, No. 107, charged upon a *black field*, or worn upon a black surcoat or mantle. The Order was finally suppressed in England in 1559.

The TEMPLARS, instituted about A.D. 1118, were introduced into England about 1140. In the year 1309 they were suppressed, and in 1312 their Order was finally abolished. They wore *a Cross* of the same form as No. 107, but of a *red colour upon a white field*. This red cross they charged upon a white banner: and they bore another banner, No. 13, of *black and white*, entitled "*Beau Seant.*" The same words, "*Beau Seant !*" were their war-cry. The Badges of the Templars were the *Agnus Dei*—the Holy Lamb, holding a red-cross banner; and a device representing two Knights mounted on a single horse, intended to denote the original poverty of the Order.[1]

THE ORDER OF THE GARTER, a military Fraternity under the special patronage of "ST. GEORGE, the good Knight," was instituted at Windsor by King EDWARD III. in, or about, the year 1350—very probably in the summer of 1348, but the exact time is not positively known. It may safely be assumed, that the occasion which led to the institution of this most noble and renowned Order, was a Tournament or Hastilude of unusual importance held at his Castle of Windsor by EDWARD III. at the most brilliant period of his reign: and it is highly probable that the Order suggested itself to the mind of the King, as a natural result of his own chivalrous revival of a knightly "Round Table," such as flourished in the days of King Arthur. How much of historical fact there may be in the popular legend, which professes to derive from a certain romantic incident the

---

[1] The Arms of the Inner Temple of the present day are—*Azure, a pegasus* (or winged horse) *argent*, or sometimes *or*. This Coat is derived from the early Badge, *the two horsemen* having been mistaken in later times for *wings*. The Arms of the Middle Temple are—*Argent, on a cross gules*, the Agnus Dei.

Title certainly borne by King EDWARD's Order from the
time of its original institution, it is not possible to determine: but the legend itself is not in any way inconsistent
with the spirit of those times; nor would the Knights
Founders of the Garter regard their Order as the less
honourable, because its Title might remind them of the

No. 433.—Insignia of the Order of the Garter.

happy gallantry, with which the casual misadventure of a
noble Lady had been turned to so good an account by a
most princely Monarch. The Statutes of the Order have
been continually modified and altered, and the original
military character of the Institution has long ceased to
exist: still, no changes in the Order of the Garter have
affected the pre-eminence of its dignity and reputation.
Illustrious now as ever, and foremost in rank and honour in

our own country, the GARTER is second to no knightly Order in the world.

The MOST NOBLE ORDER OF THE GARTER consists of the SOVEREIGN and Twenty-five KNIGHTS COMPANIONS, of whom the PRINCE OF WALES always is one. By a Statute of the year 1805, the Order includes such lineal descendants of GEORGE III. as may be elected : and still more recent statutes have provided for the admission of foreign Sovereigns, and also of certain " Extra Knights," who are elected " Companions " as vacancies occur.

The OFFICERS of the Order are—The *Prelate*, the Bishop of Winchester : the *Chancellor*, the Bishop of Oxford : the *Registrar*, the Dean of Windsor : the *Herald*, Garter King of Arms : and, the *Usher of the Black Rod*.

Knights of the Garter place the initials " K.G." after their names ; and these letters take precedence of all other titles, those of Royalty alone excepted.

The Stalls of the Knights are in the choir of St. George's Chapel, Windsor Castle, where their Garter-plates are fixed, and their Banners are displayed.

The INSIGNIA of the Order of the Garter are—The *Garter* itself, of a light blue originally, now of a dark blue, with border, buckle, and pendant of gold. On it, in golden letters, the *Motto*—HONI . SOIT . QVI . MAL . Y . PENSE—" Dishonour to him who thinks ill of it ; " and not, as it is commonly rendered, " Evil to him that evil thinks."

The Badge of the Order is circular, and formed of a buckled Garter enclosing a Shield of St. George, the whole blazoned in the proper tinctures : it is worn on the left shoulder of the blue velvet Mantle. When irradiated with eight rays of silver or diamonds, a device resembling the Badge in every respect, except that the cross of St. George is enclosed within the Garter without being charged on a Shield, forms the *Star* of the Order.

The *Collar*, of gold enamelled, is formed of twelve buckled Garters, each encircling a Tudor Rose, and as many knots of intertwined cords.   Attached· to this Collar is the *George*—a mounted figure of the Saint in the act of trampling down the dragon and piercing him with his lance. The Collar and George were added to the Insignia by HENRY VII.

The *Lesser George*, or *Jewel*, added by HENRY VIII., has the same device placed on an enamelled field, and forming a jewel generally oval in form; it is encircled by a buckled Garter of the Order, and represented in No. 434. It was this Lesser George that CHARLES I., immediately before he suffered, delivered to Archbishop JUXON, with the word, "Remember." As a matter of course, the figure of ST. GEORGE ought always to be represented as a Knight, armed and equipped as one of the Christian chivalry of the Middle Ages—not as a pagan horseman of antiquity, and more particularly not in the guise of such a nude champion as appears on some of our modern coins.   The

No. 434.—The Lesser George, of the Garter.

Lesser George, often incorrectly called the Badge, at first was sometimes worn from a gold chain, and sometimes from a *black Ribbon*.   The Colour of the ribbon was changed to *sky-blue* by Queen ELIZABETH ; and it has since been again changed to the *dark blue* of the broad Ribbon now worn.   This *Ribbon* of the Order crosses the figure of the wearer, passing over the left shoulder, and the Lesser George hangs from it under the right arm.

Since the time of CHARLES II. it has been customary

for the nearest representatives of a deceased K.G. to return his Insignia to the Sovereign.

Each Officer of the Order, except the Usher, has his own proper Badge.

THE ORDER OF THE THISTLE, OF SCOTLAND, styled "Most Noble and Most Ancient," and indicated by the

No. 450.—Insignia of the Order of the Thistle.

Initials "K.T.," was originally instituted long before the accession of a Scottish Sovereign to the Crown of England; but it is now governed by statutes framed by JAMES II. of Great Britain, ANNE, and GEORGE IV.

The Order consists of the SOVEREIGN and sixteen KNIGHTS. Its OFFICERS are—The *Dean ; the Lord Lyon King of Arms ;* and the *Gentleman Usher of the Green Rod.*

The INSIGNIA are—The *Badge* of gold enamelled, being

a figure of St. Andrew standing upon a mount holding his silver Saltire and surrounded by rays in the form of a glory. This Badge is worn from the *Collar* of the Order, formed of sixteen Thistles alternating with as many bunches of rue-sprigs; or, from a broad *dark green Ribbon*, which crosses the left shoulder. There are fine examples of these Insignia sculptured upon the Monument of MARY, Queen

No. 435.—Jewel of the Thistle.   No. 436.—Badge of St. Patrick.

of Scots, in Westminster Abbey. The jewel is shown in Fig. 435.

The *Star* of this Order, of silver or diamonds, is in the form of a St. Andrew's Saltire, having its four limbs alternating with the four points of a lozenge: in the centre, surrounded by the Motto (NEMO ME IMPUNE LACESSIT), is a Thistle proper.

The Most Illustrious ORDER OF ST. PATRICK, OF IRELAND, indicated by the Initials, " K.P.", and instituted in 1783 by GEORGE III., consists of the SOVEREIGN, the GRAND MASTER, and twenty-two KNIGHTS. The OFFICERS are the Grand Master, the *Chancellor*, the *Secretary*, *Ulster King of Arms* and *Registrar*, two

Heralds, and one *Pursuivant*, the *Genealogist*, and the *Usher of the Black Rod*.

The INSIGNIA are—The *Badge* or *Jewel*, of gold enamelled, and oval in form.   It has a Shamrock (or Trefoil slipped) having on each leaf a Royal Crown, charged on the Saltire of St. Patrick, the field being surrounded by

No. 451.—Insignia of the Order of St. Patrick.

the *Motto*—QVIS . SEPARABIT . ("Who will sever?") MDCCLXXXIII., on a blue band, which in its turn is encircled with a wreath of Shamrocks on gold. This Badge, No. 436, is worn from the *Collar*, composed of Roses and Harps, alternating with each other and with knotted cords, a Crown surmounting a Harp being in the centre; or, the Badge is worn from a broad *sky-blue Ribbon*, crossing the right shoulder.

The *Star* resembles the Badge, except that its centre is circular instead of oval; and that it has eight rays of silver or diamonds, in place of the wreath of Shamrocks.

The Most Honourable ORDER OF THE BATH is an early Institution which, after having long been in abeyance, has been revived and remodelled, and has received fresh statutes in the years 1725, 1815, 1847, and 1859.

The Order, now numbering about a thousand members, consists of several distinct Groups or Classes, which include, with the SOVEREIGN, the Royal Princes, and

No. 452.— Collar and Military Badge.
Insignia of the Order of the Bath.

some few distinguished Foreigners, Officers of our own Navy and Army, and also Diplomatic and Civil Servants of the Crown.

The Three "Classes" of the Order alike include members of the Three Services, and each class is divided into two divisions, viz. Military and Civil.

The "First Class," of KNIGHTS GRAND CROSS OF THE BATH—G.C.B.—has 55 Military and 27 Civil Knights.

The "Second Class" numbers (with power to increase these numbers) 145 Military and 108 Civil KNIGHTS COMMANDERS OF THE BATH—K.C.B.

The "Third Class," not of Knights, but of COMPANIONS OF THE BATH—C.B.—has 705 Military and 298 Civil Members, who take rank between Knights and Esquires.

The Military INSIGNIA are—The BADGE, a complicated combination of devices, characteristic of the debased period which produced it. It is represented in No. 437.

No. 437.—Badge of the Bath (Military Division).

The Cross is white; the circle with the Motto, red; and the small scroll in base, blue; all the rest being enamelled "proper." This Badge is worn by the G.C.B. attached to a *Collar*, formed of nine Crowns and eight clusters of the Rose, Thistle, and Shamrock issuing from a Sceptre, alternating with seventeen Knots enamelled argent: or, this Badge is suspended by the G.C.B. from a broad *red Ribbon*, crossing the left shoulder. By the K.C.B. the Badge is worn from a narrower red Ribbon about the

453.—Star of Knight Grand Cross (Civil).

454.—Star of Knight Commander (Military).

neck, or a still narrower at the button-hole. Also, by the C.B. it is attached to a narrow red Ribbon at the button-hole.

The *Star* of the G.C.B. is similar to the Badge without The Cross and the lions, surrounded by silver rays having a lozenge-shaped outline. The *Star* of the K.C.B., which is in the form of a Maltese Cross, omits the Cross of the Badge. The C.B. have no Star.

The Diplomatic and Civil INSIGNIA are—The *Badge*, No. 438, worn with the same distinctions as the Naval and Military Badge; but the C.B. Badge is of smaller size than the Badges of the two higher Classes.

The *Star* of the G.C.B. has eight silver rays encircling their Badge in a circular form. The Star of the K.C.B. is the same as that of the Naval and

No. 438
Badge of the Bath
(Civil Division).

Military K.C.B., omitting the laurel-wreath and the small scroll and motto.

The *Motto* of the Order—TRIA . JUNCTA . IN . UNO

—"Three united in one," refers to the Union of the three Realms of England, Scotland, and Ireland, in the Order.

The *Stalls* of the Knights of the Bath, before the Order was divided into classes, and those of their Esquires, are in Henry the Seventh's Chapel, Westminster Abbey; but no installation has taken place since 1815, when the Order was reorganised, and no new plates or banners have been set up.

THE ORDER OF MERIT (O.M.) instituted in the year 1902, although it gives to its members neither style nor

No. 455.—Order of Merit.

precedence, ranks next to the Order of the Bath, and is divided into two classes, Military and Civil. The only INSIGNIA are the Badge and the Ribbon parti-coloured of *red* and *blue*. The Badge is *a cross pateé of four arms*, the outline of the cross being circular. The cross is of *blue enamel* and superimposed thereupon a smaller cross of the same design of *red*. The centre is *blue*, bearing the words, "FOR MERIT," in gold letters within a laurel wreath. The cross is surmounted by the Royal Crown. The reverse of the Badge shows the Royal and Imperial Cypher. To the Badge *two swords saltirewise* in the angles of the cross are added in the case of members of the Military Division.

The Most Exalted ORDER OF THE STAR OF INDIA, instituted by Queen Victoria in 1861, to render especial honour to high merit and loyalty in the Indian Empire, was enlarged on the 24th of May 1866, and ordained to consist of the SOVEREIGN, a GRAND MASTER, and 291

No. 456.—Collar and Insignia of the Exalted Order of the Star of India.

Ordinary COMPANIONS or MEMBERS; together with such extra and Honorary Members as the Sovereign at any time may be pleased to appoint.

The VICEROY AND GOVERNOR-GENERAL OF INDIA for the time being is always the GRAND MASTER. The Ordinary Members are divided into Three Classes:—The "First Class" comprises 36 KNIGHTS GRAND COM-

MANDERS: G.C.S.I. In the "Second Class" there are 85 KNIGHTS COMMANDERS: K.S.I. And, the "Third Class" numbers 170 COMPANIONS: C.S.I.

The INSIGNIA are—The *Badge*, No 439, formed of diamonds, having the Motto on a field of light blue enamel, and the bust of the late Queen executed as an onyx cameo. This Badge is attached by a mullet to the *Collar*, composed of heraldic roses and lotus flowers alternating with palm-

No. 439.—Badge of the Star of India.

branches, a crown being in the Centre: or, the Badge is worn from a *Ribbon of pale blue with white borders* crossing the left shoulder. The *Star*, of diamonds, has a mullet upon an irradiated field in its centre, within the *Motto*— HEAVEN'S . LIGHT . OUR . GUIDE, the whole being environed with wavy rays having a circular outline.

The Most Distinguished ORDER OF ST. MICHAEL AND ST. GEORGE, originally instituted in 1818 for use in Malta and the Ionian Islands, has been extended and enlarged in 1868, 1877, and 1902, and now is awarded for Colonial and for Foreign Services. It consists of 100 KNIGHTS GRAND CROSS (G.C.M.G.), 300 KNIGHTS COMMANDERS (K.C.M.G.), and 600 COMPANIONS (C.M.G.), in addition to Honorary Members. The numbers are not adhered

No. 457.—Star and Collar of the Order of St. Michael and St. George.

to. The *Star* is of seven long rays, smaller rays intervening. This is charged with the Cross of St. George, and in the centre is a representation of St. Michael encountering Satan within a blue circle, bearing the Motto of the Order, "AUSPICIUM MELIORIS ÆVI."

The *Collar* is composed alternately of lions of England, Maltese Crosses, and Cyphers, S.M. and S.G. In the centre is the Crown *over two winged lions passant guardant, each holding a book and seven arrows.*

T

The *Badge* is a gold cross of fourteen points of white enamel, and has in the centre, within the Motto of the Order (on the one side), St. Michael encountering Satan (and on the other side), St. George and the Dragon. The Badge is surmounted by the Crown.

The Most Eminent ORDER OF THE INDIAN EMPIRE, instituted in 1878 and subsequently enlarged, is the second

No. 458.—Eminent Order of the Indian Empire.

Indian Order, and consists of three classes, KNIGHTS GRAND COMMANDERS (G.C.I.E.), KNIGHTS COMMANDERS (K.C.I.E.), and COMPANIONS (C.I.E.).

The *Star* is of five rays of silver, alternated with as many rays of gold. In the centre, within a purple circle, inscribed with the Motto, "IMPERATRICIS AUSPICIIS," and surmounted by the Crown, is an effigy of Queen VICTORIA.

The *Collar* is composed of elephants, lotus-flowers, peacocks in their pride, and Indian roses, all connected by gold chains.

The *Badge* is a red enamelled rose, in the centre of which is the effigy within the Motto as on the Star.

No. 459.
The Badge.

The ROYAL VICTORIAN ORDER was instituted in 1896 as the personal Order of the British Sovereign, and is divided into five classes—KNIGHTS GRAND CROSS (G.C.V.O.), KNIGHTS COMMANDERS (K.C.V.O.), COM-

No. 460.—G.C.V.O. Star.

No. 461.—K.C.V.O. Star.

No. 462.—G.C.V.O. Badge.

No. 463.—K.C.V.O. Badge.

MANDERS (C.V.O.), and Members of the Fourth and Fifth Classes (both M.V.O.).

The *Star* is of eight points, and of chipped silver, having in the centre a representation of the Badge.

The BADGE is a white Maltese Cross. It has an oval enamelled centre of crimson with the monogram V.R.I., within a blue enamelled circle, carrying the Motto of the Order "VICTORIA," the circle surmounted by the Crown. There is no collar for the order, but the King occasionally bestows, as an extreme mark of favour, "The Royal Victorian Chain," a decoration not governed by express Statute.

The DISTINGUISHED SERVICE ORDER is a Military Decoration instituted in 1886, but which does not carry

No. 464.
Distinguished Service Order.

No. 465.
Imperial Service Order.

the style of Knighthood. The *Badge* is a gold cross enamelled white and of a circular outline. In the centre (on the one side) is the Crown on a red enamel ground within a wreath of laurel, (and on the other side) the Royal Cypher takes the place of the Crown.

The IMPERIAL SERVICE ORDER, a purely Civil Decoration instituted in 1902, is confined to the Administrative Services of the Empire. The *Badge* is an eight-rayed star bearing (on one side) the Royal Cypher and (on the other side) "For faithful service," surrounded by a wreath of laurel and surmounted by the Crown.

The VICTORIA CROSS, of bronze, was instituted by her late Majesty Queen VICTORIA in 1856, to render honour to "conspicuous bravery" in actual conflict, by sea or land.

No. 440.—The Victoria Cross.   No. 441.—The Albert Medal.

This Cross, No. 440, is worn on the left breast, attached to a *blue* ribbon for the Navy, and to a *red* ribbon for the Army. A Bar is attached to the ribbon for every additional such act of bravery as would have won the Cross.

The ALBERT MEDAL, No. 441, which was instituted also by Queen VICTORIA, dates from March 13, 1866, and is to distinguish those who save, or who at the peril of their own lives endeavour to save, life or perform other meritorious

acts of bravery. The Coronet is that of H.R.H. the late
PRINCE CONSORT; and the Monogram consists of the
Initials V. A., with an anchor. This Medal is executed
in Silver and Bronze for two classes of recipients. The
anchor in the Badge is omitted when awarded for land
services.

Other Decorations are " The Royal Order of Victoria
and Albert " (of four classes) and the Imperial Order of
the Crown of India (of one class), both confined to ladies,
the Kaisar-i-Hind Medal, the Volunteer Officers' Decoration, the Territorial Decoration, the Edward Medal, the
King's Police Medal, the Royal Red Cross, and the Order
of Mercy; whilst the Order of the Hospital of St. John of
Jerusalem in England receives official recognition.

CHAPTER XX

PRECEDENCE. GENEALOGIES

"ORDERS and DEGREES
Jar not with Liberty, but well consist."
—*Paradise Lost*, Book V.

"The use of ARMS was closely connected with the Study of GENEALOGY."
—DALLAWAY, *Science of Heraldry* (A.D. 1793).

WHEN JAMES I. succeeded to the Crown of England while he was actually the King regnant of Scotland, and accordingly became Sovereign of the two Realms, he found it necessary to produce a "Union Flag" for the whole of Great Britain, in consequence of the serious disputes for Precedence that arose between the natives of South and North Britain. Before the time of the peace-loving son of MARY STUART, a Sovereign of another mould, HENRY VIII., had felt the necessity of framing and establishing some definite system of Precedence amongst the various degrees, orders, and ranks of his subjects: and, in 1539, a statute to that effect was enacted. Other statutes afterwards were added; and, from time to time, Royal Letters Patent on the same subject have been issued; and thus the Precedence now recognised and in use amongst us has been established.

The General Scale of Precedence follows, but there are Special scales for use in (*a*) Scotland, (*b*) Ireland, (*c*) India, (*d*) Canada, (*e*) Colonies, (*f*) Army and Navy, (*g*) Diplomatic Service.

THE GENERAL ORDER OF PRECEDENCE.

The SOVEREIGN.

The Prince of Wales.
The Younger Sons of the Sovereign.
The Grandsons of the Sovereign
The Brothers of the Sovereign.
The Uncles of the Sovereign
The Nephews of the Sovereign.

The Archbishop of Canterbury.
The Lord Chancellor.
The Archbishop of York.
The Premier.
The Lord High Treasurer.
The Lord President of the Council.
The Lord Privy Seal.

> The following GREAT OFFICERS OF STATE *precede all Peers of their own Degree*—that is, if Dukes, they precede all other Dukes; if Earls, all other Earls; &c. :—

The Lord Great Chamberlain.
The Lord High Constable.
The Earl Marshal.
The Lord High Admiral.
The Lord Steward of the Royal Household.
The Lord Chamberlain of the Royal Household.
The Master of the Horse.

> The Peers of each Degree take Precedence in their own Degree, according to their Patents of Creation.

Dukes (*a*) of England, (*b*) of Scotland, (*c*) of Great Britain, (*d*) of Ireland, (*e*) of the United Kingdom and, if created since the Union, of Ireland.
Marquesses (*vide* Dukes).

> Eldest Sons of Dukes.

Earls (*vide* Dukes).
    Eldest Sons of Marquesses.
    Younger Sons of Dukes.
Viscounts (*vide* Dukes).
    Eldest Sons of Earls.
    Younger Sons of Marquesses.
Bishops of (*a*) London, (*b*) Durham, and (*c*) Winchester.
Bishops, according to Seniority of Consecration.
Barons (*vide* Dukes).
The Speaker of the House of Commons.
Commissioners of Great Seal.
The (*a*) Treasurer and the (*b*) Comptroller of the Royal
    Household.
Vice-Chamberlain of the Household.
The Secretaries of State, when not Peers.
    Eldest Sons of Viscounts.
    Younger Sons of Earls.
    Eldest Sons of Barons.
Knights of the Garter, Thistle, and St. Patrick, not being
    Peers.
Privy Councillors.
The Chancellor of the Exchequer.
The Chancellor of the Duchy of Lancaster.
The Lord Chief Justice.
The Master of the Rolls.
Lord Justices of Appeal and Pres. of Probate Court.
Judges of High Court.
    Younger Sons of Viscounts.
    Younger Sons of Barons.
    Sons of Lords of Appeal in Ordinary (Life Peers).
Baronets.
Knights Grand Cross of the Bath.
Knights Grand Commanders of the Star of India.
Knights Grand Cross of St. Michael and St. George.
Knights Grand Commanders of Indian Empire.

Knights Grand Cross of Victorian Order.

Knights Commanders of the various Orders (in the same order of progression).

Knights Bachelors.

Commanders of Victorian Order.

County Court Judges.

Serjeants-at-Law.

Masters in Lunacy.

Companions of the various Orders.

Members of Fourth Class of Victorian Order.

Companions of Distinguished Service Order.

> Eldest Sons of the Younger Sons of Peers.
>
> Eldest Sons of Baronets.
>
> Eldest Sons of Knights.

Members of Fifth Class of Victorian Order.

> Baronets' Younger Sons.
>
> Knights' Younger Sons.

Esquires:—Including the Eldest Sons of the Sons of Viscounts and Barons, the eldest Sons of all the younger Sons of Peers, and their eldest Sons in perpetual Succession : the younger Sons of Baronets : the Sons of Knights, the eldest Son of the eldest Son of a Knight in perpetual Succession : persons holding the King's Commission, or who may be styled "Esquire" by the King in any Official Document.

Gentlemen.

THE PRECEDENCE OF WOMEN

is determined, before marriage, by the Rank and Dignity, but not by the Office, of their Father.

All the unmarried Sisters in any family have the same Degree, which is the Degree that their eldest Brother holds (or would hold) amongst men. Thus :—Of the Sons of an Earl the *eldest* alone has an honorary Title of Nobility and is styled "My Lord," while *all* the Daughters of an Earl have a similar honorary Title, and are styled "My Lady."

By Marriage Women share the Dignities and Precedence of their Husbands : but, the strictly Official Dignity of a Husband is not imparted to a wife (except in India), in the case of the Archbishops and Bishops or holders of other offices.

The Dignities which Ladies have by Birth or by right of Inheritance, are not imparted by Marriage to their Husbands : nor does Marriage with an inferior in Dignity in any way affect the Precedence that a Lady may enjoy by Birth, Inheritance, or Creation—both her own Precedence and that of her Husband remain as before their Marriage, unless the Husband be a Peer.

In the ROYAL FAMILY the following Precedence takes effect :—

The Queen.
The Queen Dowager.
The Princess of Wales.
The Daughters of the Sovereign.
The Wives of the Younger Sons of the Sovereign.
The Granddaughters of the Sovereign.
The Wives of the Grandsons of the Sovereign.

The Sovereign's Sisters.
Wives of the Sovereign's Brothers.
The Sovereign's Aunts.
Wives of the Sovereign's Uncles.
The Sovereign's Nieces.
Wives of the Sovereign's Nephews (Brothers' and Sisters' Daughters)
Granddaughters of the Sovereign not bearing the style of Royal Highness.

To whatever Precedence she may be entitled by Birth, the Wife of a Peer always takes her rank, and therefore takes her actual Precedence, from her Husband.

The Widow of a Peer, so long as she remains a Widow, retains the rank she enjoyed whilst married : but, should she contract a second Marriage, her Precedence then is determined either by the rank of her second Husband, or by the rank that was her own by Birth and which she enjoyed before her first Marriage.

The Wife of the Eldest Son of any degree precedes all her Husband's Sisters, and also all other Ladies having the same degree of rank with them. Thus :—the Wife of the

Eldest Son of an Earl takes Precedence of *all* Daughters of Earls.   In actual practice, however, by a principle of Precedence that is accepted and adopted in all families of the same degree amongst themselves, the Sisters in every case have their place immediately after the Wife of their own Eldest Brother.

GENEALOGIES.

GENEALOGIES, the Records of the Descents and Alliances of Families, are necessarily associated with the Armorial Ensigns borne by those Families, and by the several Members and Branches of them.   Still, it does not apparently follow, in the same manner, as a matter of necessity, that the study and investigation of Genealogies should be interesting and even attractive, because interest and attractiveness are inseparable from Heraldry.   And yet, I do not hesitate to claim for genealogical researches the favourable regard of students of Armory, on the very ground of the interest which they are certain to feel in such researches; and also in confident reliance on that inherent power of attraction, inseparable from the subject itself, that will not fail both to win their favourable regard, and to lead them on from one inquiry to another.

The very act of tracing up some eminent and illustrious personage, from generation to generation of his forefathers, noting down the alliances that have interwoven one thread of a brilliant line with others not less lustrous; or, the reverse of this process, the following the lineage of some worthy of the olden time onward down the stream, observing both the tributaries that flow into the main channel and the streamlets that issue from it—all this, when once it has been systematically undertaken, leads the student through the most picturesque regions of historical romance.

The popular idea of Genealogy may be, that it consists

in placing in a formal order of arrangement a series of dry
names, connected with dates that (if it be possible) are even
more dry. It is not uncommon to dispose of many things
precisely in the same way, when an opinion is formed without even the slightest attempt to judge of a question by its
true merits—it is so easy to decline the trouble and to
avoid the effort attendant on inquiry and investigation, and
so pleasant to become the possessor of an "opinion" and
"views," without any outlay in acquiring them. A Map
has no value in the estimation of those who ignore Geo-
graphy: the claims of Archæology are disregarded by all
who are content to remain in ignorance even of what it
implies: and History itself becomes and continues to be a
dead letter, so long as an acquaintance is formed only with
the exterior of its volumes. And, in like manner, Genealogy appears under a very different aspect to those who
know it only by name, and to lovers of Biography and
History who are familiar with its lucid and yet ever suggestive guidance. Without written Genealogies, who can
clearly understand the political and historical position of
the rival Princes of the red and white Roses; or of HENRY
VII. and the "last of the Plantagenets"; or of Queens
ELIZABETH TUDOR, MARY STUART, and JANE GREY? Or
who, without similar aid, will follow out the fortunes of the
Houses of BEAUCHAMP and NEVILLE and DUDLEY, and
connect them with the existing noble lord of Warwick
Castle; or, when reading of the DE CLARES, the BOHUNS,
or the PERCIES, will see at a glance the connection between
"STRONGBOW" and the "red Earl GILBERT," or will
understand the significance of the white swan Badge of the
STAFFORDS, or will read at sight the quartered Shield of
the Duke of NORTHUMBERLAND, of to-day, and will discern
the line that connects the living Earl PERCY with the
"HOTSPUR" whose fame was two centuries old when
SHAKESPEARE wrote of him? And further, who, that is

unable to accomplish such things as these, can appreciate
History, can enjoy it and apply its lessons aright?

In arranging a Genealogy the utmost conciseness is essential, all details being left for full description elsewhere. All
the members of the same family are placed side by side, on
the same level, in their order of seniority; and all are connected by lines with one another and with their parents.
Successive generations also, throughout all the branches of
any family, or in allied families, have their places on the
same levels; and the connecting and distinguishing lines
are continued throughout. Examples of Genealogies treated
in the most scientific and yet simple manner, easy to be
understood, and perfect as models for students, may be
obtained in any Part of the *Herald and Genealogist,*
formerly edited by the late Mr. J. G. NICHOLS, F.S.A.,
Parliament Street, Westminster. I refer to this excellent
Periodical, because it is not possible for me here in the
space at my disposal to set forth a really useful example of
a Genealogy: and, I must add, because it is most desirable
that students of Heraldry should form such an acquaintance
with Mr. Nichols, as may be acquired through his works.
Miscellanea Genealogica et Heraldica, now edited by Mr. W.
B. BANNERMAN, is another Periodical, which ought to be in
the hands of all Genealogists.

In Genealogies, this mark = denotes alliance by marriage,
and it is placed between the names of a husband and wife:
and the lines that proceed from this mark, thus,=

point out their issue. The initials S.P. (of the Latin words
Sine Prole, "without issue") show where a line or a branch
ceases. Other abbreviations and signs in general use will
suggest their own signification.

As I began this Chapter with quotations, so with a
quotation I conclude it. "There are some persons," writes
Mr. LOWER, in his "Curiosities of Heraldry" (p. 292), "who

cannot discriminate between the taste for pedigree" (or genealogy) "and the pride of ancestry. Now these two feelings, though they often combine in one individual, have no necessary connection with each other. Man is said to be a hunting animal. Some hunt foxes; others for fame or fortune. Others hunt in the intellectual field; some for the arcana of Nature and of mind; some for the roots of words, or the origin of things. I am fond of hunting out a pedigree." And, gentle reader, when you have joined the chase genealogical, I promise you, so also will you be.

CHAPTER XXI

*The College of Arms—The Lyon Office of Scotland—Grants of Arms—
Tax on " Armorial Bearings," and on " Arms Found "*

"They were conspicuous for judgment, experience, learning, and
elegance; they gained honour wherever they were employed."
—NOBLE, *History of the College of Arms.*

"What is your Crest and Motto?—Send name and county to ——'s
Heraldic Office. For plain Sketch, 3s. 6d. In heraldic colours, 6s."
—*Morning Newspapers.*

I. THE HERALDS OF ENGLAND, who before had been attached
to the Household either of the Sovereign or of some
Personage of exalted rank, were incorporated as a Fraternity
by RICHARD III., a Prince whose historical reputation is by
no means in harmony with that early act of his reign, which
has done such good service to English History — the
Foundation and Establishment of the COLLEGE OF ARMS,
or, as it is commonly called, the HERALDS' COLLEGE.

The Letters Patent, issued for this purpose by RICHARD
III., bear date March the 2nd, 1483, the first year of his
reign. Very important privileges and immunities, with
high powers and authority, were granted to the incorporated
Heralds: and the "right fair and stately house," called
"Pulteney's Inn," situate in the metropolitan parish of All
Saints, was assigned to them as their permanent official
residence. The Charter granted to the Heralds by the last
Plantagenet Sovereign was confirmed by his successors.

The buildings of the College were destroyed by the
great fire of 1666; but all the records and documents
fortunately escaped, having been removed to Whitehall;

and the edifice was subsequently rebuilt, chiefly at the cost of the Heralds themselves, where it now stands between St. Paul's Cathedral and the Thames. There, in the College of Arms, are still carefully preserved all that the early Heralds recorded and transmitted to our times. There, not the least valuable of the contents of the College, an unique Library is in the keeping of Guardians, who understand its true uses, as they appreciate its preciousness. And there also the Headquarters of English Heraldry are as duly established, as those of the British Army are at the Horse Guards in Whitehall.

The great change that has come upon London since the Heralds rebuilt their official home, has already caused some structural alteration in the building, and has resulted in the College of Arms now appearing out of place in its original position in the City. Other changes, which follow in such rapid succession in that busy neighbourhood, render it by no means improbable that the site of their College may be required for some great "City improvement"; and so the Heralds may be constrained to establish themselves in the more congenial regions of the metropolitan "far west." This, as I am disposed to consider, is one of those consummations that are devoutly to be desired.

The times have been in which Heraldry could not number amongst its true friends the official Heralds of the College of Arms: but, happily, a very different, and in many most important respects a thoroughly satisfactory condition of things now obtains at the College. So far as the Heralds are concerned, as a body of learned, accomplished, and courteous gentlemen, Heraldry now is admirably represented amongst us, and faithfully supported. What still is deficient in the existing constitution of the College of Arms, as a National Institution, is adaptation to existing circumstances, sentiments, and requirements. It is but a truism to assert that, as a National Institution, the

U

College of Arms does not fill its proper position : and, to all who are familiar with the facts of the case, it is equally obvious that this is simply because the College does not vindicate its indisputable title to that position which really is its own.

Heraldry is decidedly popular. This popularity also is assuming a more practical, and at the same time a more enduring form, through gradually becoming the result of a correct appreciation of the true character of Heraldry, and of its intrinsic value. At a time in which people are beginning to feel and to admit that they *ought to know* something about Heraldry, the College of Arms *ought to take the lead* in making Heraldry still better understood, still more justly appreciated, still more popular. The time, also, is indeed come in which it is the bounden duty of the College of Arms to impress upon the community at large, that *the sole source and fountain-head of authority in all matters armorial, under the Sovereign, centres in itself.* This is to be accomplished by the same process, and only by the same process, by which the College of Arms may win for itself thorough popularity and universal confidence. If the College requires fresh or increased powers, application to that effect should be made to the Legislature. The Heraldry of Scotland has been dealt with by Parliament : and it would be equally easy to obtain such a statute as would enable English Heraldry to do justice to itself, while fulfilling its own proper duties.

Without abating or compromising in the slightest degree its own dignity or the dignity of Heraldry, the College of Arms requires to be transmuted from an exclusive into a popular Institution. It requires, not indeed to have its object and aim and system of action changed, but to have them expanded, and expanded so widely as to comprehend all the heraldic requirements of the age. This is a subject of too urgent importance not to be noticed here; but still, it is not possible to do more than to notice it in very general terms.

Upon one specific point, however, a few plain words may be spoken without hesitation, and may be left by themselves without comment. The Fees and Charges of all kinds for granting, matriculating, confirming, and recording the rightful possession of armorial Insignia must be arranged upon a perfectly fresh system, with such provisions and modifications as may adapt them to every variety of circumstance and of requirement. This is a question which can be regarded only from one point of view by every true lover of Heraldry, and consequently by every true friend of the College of Arms.

II. The National Heraldic body in Scotland, entitled the LYON OFFICE, is under the presidency of the *Lyon King of Arms*. The Chief of the Scottish official Heralds from May 1796 to a recent period had been a Peer of that realm; and the duties of the office, accordingly, had been discharged for seventy years by a *Lyon Depute*. But, on the death of the Earl of KINNOUL, in February 1866, it was determined to remodel in some respects the arrangements of the Lyon Office; and Mr. GEORGE BURNETT, who had long been "Lyon Depute," was appointed by Her Majesty to be "Lyon King." He has been succeeded by Sir J. BALFOUR PAUL. The Arms of the Lyon Office I have already given, No. 265.

The action of the Scottish Lyon King of Arms, and of the Institution over which he presides, after having degenerated from the worthy standard of earlier days, has revived under far happier conditions, and with prospects that are eminently gratifying. It may be fairly expected, indeed, that the most salutary results will be produced by the very decided "tendency" that for some time has existed, "to cultivate the rules and principles of that earlier age, to which"—writes Mr. Seton—"we are indebted for a system of Scottish Heraldry, whose purity certainly has not been surpassed in any other corner of Christendom." These words occur in a highly interesting memoir of the Lyon Office, in the fourth chapter of the work entitled "The Law and Practice of Heraldry in Scotland," an able and admirable volume, published in 1863 in Edinburgh, which shows the growing popularity of a true Heraldry north of the Tweed, and proves that in the author, Mr. SETON, Scottish Heraldry possesses an advocate no less powerful than zealous and judicious.

III. Arms and Armorial Insignia are granted *only* through the College of Arms in England, and through the Lyon Office in Scotland, in both realms with the direct sanction of the CROWN expressed in England by the Earl Marshal. In Ireland all Grants are made by Ulster King of Arms with the same sanction.

It is to be observed and kept in remembrance that the *sole right* to Arms is a Grant from the College or the Crown, or Inheritance by lineal descent from an ancestor to whom a Grant was made or in whom a right to bear Arms has been officially recognised and registered by the Crown.

All "Grants" and "Confirmations of Arms" (Confirmations, that is, of the Claims of certain individuals to bear certain Arms, by some uncertain right and title duly set forth and approved and thereafter legalised by the Crown) are formally and regularly recorded, with a full blazon of the insignia, at the College or Offices of Arms.

It is very greatly to be desired that, in addition to this time-honoured usage of the Heralds in making these records, some simple plan could be adopted for the periodical registration at the College of Arms of all armorial insignia that are borne by right. Almost equally desirable, also, it would be to make a corresponding registration, as far as might be possible, of whatever insignia are borne *without* any right. The contents of both registers would form unquestionably useful publications of a periodical character. In connection with any such project as I have just suggested, it appears to me that good service might be rendered to the cause of true Heraldry amongst us, if *Badges and Mottoes* (without any other insignia whatever) were formally granted by the College, under certain conditions, and at the cost of a small Fee.[1]

In new Grants of Arms, as in so many formal documents, something of the early form of Expression, with some traces of its piquant quaintness, are still retained. Very quaint indeed, and very extravagant also, is the style that was generally adopted by the Heralds of the sixteenth and seventeenth centuries, and yet characteristic of both the men and their times. As an example of one of these old documents, an example of no common interest in itself, I now give the Grant of Arms to JOHN SHAKESPERE, the Poet's father, in the year 1596. Two draft copies of the original Grant are preserved in the College of Arms; the following transcript is printed from the later of the two copies, the earlier having been used to supply any word or passage that now is wanting in the other. The insertions thus obtained are printed in brackets.

GRANT OF ARMS TO JOHN SHAKESPERE, A.D. 1596.

To ALL and singuler Noble and Gentelmen of what estate [or] degree bearing arms to whom these presentes shall come, William Dethick alias Garter principall King of Armes sendethe greetinges. Know yee that, whereas by the authoritie and auncyent pryveleges perteyning to my office from the Quenes most excellent Ma^te and by her highnesse most noble and victorious progenitors, I am to take generall notice and record and to make declaration and testemonie for all causes of arms and matters of Gentrie thoroughe out all her Majestes Kingdoms, Domynions, Principalites, Isles, and Provinces, To th' end

---

[1] I leave this sentence as it has hitherto stood in the book. Badges are now granted and recorded, but a prior right to arms is required —A. C. F.-D. 1908.

that, as manie gentelmen, by theyre auncyent names of familles, kyndredes and descentes, have and enjoye certeyne enseignes and cotes of arms, So it is verie expedient in all ages that some men for theyr valeant factes, magnanimite, vertu, dignites, and desertes, may use and beare suche tokens of honour and worthinesse, whereby theyre name and good fame may be the better knowen and divulged, and theyre children and posterite in all vertu (to the service of theyre Prynce and Contrie) encouraged. Wherefore being solicited and by credible report informed that John Shakespeare of Stratford uppon Avon in the counte of Warwik, whose parentes and late antecessors[1] were for theyre faithefull and va[leant service advaunced and rewarded by the most prudent] prince King Henry the Seventh of [famous memorie, sythence which tyme they have continewed at] those partes, being of good reputacion [and credit; and that the] said John hathe maryed [Mary, daughter and one of the heyrs of Robert Arden, of Wilmcote, in the said] counte, esquire.[2] In consideration whereof, and for the encouragement of his posterite, to whom such Blazon [or Atchevement] by the auncyent custome of the lawes of armes maie descend, I the said Garter King of Armes have assigned, graunted and by these presentes confirmed this shield or cote of arms, viz. Gould, on a bend sables a speare of the first, steeled argent; and for his crest or cognizance a falcon, his winges displayed, argent, standing on a wrethe of his coullors, supporting a speare gould, steeled as aforesaid, sett upon a helmett with mantelles and tasselles as hath ben accustomed and dothe more playnely appeare depicted on this margent. Signefieng hereby, and by the authorite of my office aforesaid ratifieng, that it shalbe lawfull for the sayd John Shakespeare gent. and for his cheldren, yssue and posterite (at all tymes and places convenient) to bear and make demonstracion of the said Blazon or Atchevement uppon theyre Shieldes, Targets, Escucheons, Cotes of arms, Pennons, Guydons, Ringes, Edefices, Buyldinges, Utensiles, Lyveries, Tombes or Monumentes, or otherwise, for all lawfull warrlyke factes or civile use and exercises, according to the lawes of armes, without let or interruption of any other person or persons for use or bearing the same. In witnesse and perpetuall remembrance hereof I have hereunto subscribed my name, and fastened the seale of my office endorzed with the signett of my armes, At the Office of Armes, London, the xx. daye of October, the xxxviij. yeare of the reigne of our Soveraigne Lady Elizabeth, by the grace of God Quene of England, France, and Ireland, Defender of the Faythe, etc. 1596.

---

[1] *Above the word* antecessors *is written* Grandfather.
[2] Gent. *was first written, and it is altered to* esquire.

Like other documents of its class, in this Grant the language is framed after certain regular forms; so that it is to be read without that exact observance of particular expressions, which is rightly bestowed upon legal and historical records. The interest inseparable from this Grant is enhanced in no slight degree by the strong probability that John Shakespere made his application to the College of Arms by the advice and in consequence of the request of his son. Had the worthy Garter been able to divine the "dignities and desertes" of the son, he might possibly have employed formal language of a still more complimentary character, when drawing up a Grant of Arms for the father.

A much more curious specimen of the heraldic style and form of expression (and also of the spelling) of the earlier days of the Queen ELIZABETH era, is a Grant of Augmentation and Crest, by LAWRENCE DALTON, Norroy King of Arms, to JOHN BENNETT, of Newcastle-on-Tyne, Gentleman, A.D. 1560. The Preamble to this Grant, which is printed in full in *Miscellanea Genealogica et Heraldica* (p. 48), is thus written :—

To All and Singuler as well nobles and gentles as kings herauldes and officers of Armes as others wch thes presentes shall see Reade or heare Lawrence Dalton Esquire Al's Norrey Kinge of Armes of thest and west p'tyet of Englande fro the Ryver of trent northwarde Sendythe Due and humble comendacons and greatinge fforasmuche as awncyentlye fro the begynnynge and not w^thowt great Delyberacon Equitie and Reason hyt hathe byn by the moste noble and famous princes Constytutyd and ordeynyd that men of wysdom knoledge vertue and of noble lyefe and Coorage haue byn notoryowslye commendyd to the Woorlde wth Sonndrye monumentes and Remembrances wth tokens of honnor for A testamonye of theyre good Desertes As Amonge the Romayns ye Erecc'on of Statues and Images wth tytles and Appellac'ons of honnour And of more latre Dayes wth the moste p'te of nac'ons bearinge of Signes and tokens in Shyldes callyd Armes wch be the Demonstrac'ons and Evidences of noblenes vertue and woorthynes that to eu'ry man according to theyre Desertes be Dyu'slye Dystrybutyd   Wherby such signes and tokens of the woorthye and cooragyous might appeare before the cowarde vnwoorthye and Ignorant Even so yt ys yet obs'vyd that suche wch have merytyd or donne com'endable s'vice to theyre prince or countrye or by theyre woorthye and Lawdable lyefe Do Daylye encrease in vertue wysdom and knowledge shulde not be forgoten and so put in oblyvyon but rewardyd wth som token of honnor for the same the Rather to move and styrre other to the Imytac'on of lyke noblenes vertue and woorthynes ffor wch purpose hyt was not therefor w^thowt great provydence ordeynyd and yet ys that there Shulde be officers and herauldes of Armes to whose office hyt shulde be appropryate to kepe in Regestre tharmes pedegrees and Descentes of nobles and gentles wth theyre woorthye and valyant actes and to have power and awethorytye to allowe and Ratefye vnto the woorthye Som awgmentac'on token or Remembrance of noblenes for theyre seyde woorthynes   And now beinge Desyryd ——

And so forth, worthy Mr. Norroy having forgotten such "signes and tokens" as stops, while carefully showing what style and form it is *not* desirable for us to adopt, however excellent may be his system of building up honourable insignia upon a foundation of nobleness, virtue, and worthiness.

I add one other early document of another kind, which is an excellent model for present use by the Heralds of our own days, the orthography having by them been duly corrected.

EXAMPLE OF A CONFIRMATION OR RECORD OF ARMS :— Theis are the anncient Armes and Creast, belonging to the name and famely of LEECHFORDE in the County of Surrey, descended from the LEECHFORDS in Buckinghamsheire.   Which at the request of S^R RICHARD LEECHFORDE of Shelwood in the County of Surrey Knight, I WILL'M SEGAR Garter, Principall King of Armes have blasoned, and sett forth in coullors, according as they are here depicted in the margent. Viz." (here follows a written blazon). . . . .   "Testifying hereby the saide armoryes to belong vnto the saide S^R RICHARD LEECHFORD and to his yssue, to vse, beare, and shewe forth at all tymes, and in all places, at their free lib'ty and pleasure.   In Witnes wherof. . . . .

&c. &c., with Seal and Signature, and the Date 3rd of JAMES I.

I presume that an argument in support of the aboli-
tion of all Taxation of "Armorial Bearings," on the plea
of the utter absurdity of a tax upon an honourable distinction, would be met with the reply that "Armorial
Bearings" are taxed purely as "luxuries," and without the
slightest reference to their intrinsic character. If the
validity of this plea must be admitted, still this tax might
be levied with what may be styled a becoming heraldic
discrimination.

For example :—Arms distinguished by " Augmentations
of Honour" might be altogether exempted; a higher rate
might be fixed in the case of Arms that are ensigned with
Coronets, and that display Supporters. Arms borne by
unquestionable right, and which are duly recorded at the
College, might be rated at a comparatively low charge,
certainly not to exceed five shillings a year. On the other
hand, all Arms or armorial insignia borne with a very
questionable right, or without even the pretence of any
right whatever, might be subjected to the ordinary tax for
"Armorial Bearings" of their class multiplied (according
to circumstances) by four, six, or ten.

The tax estimated by the aid of the multiplication-table,
that has just been suggested, would extend, under a special
schedule possessing a high multiplying power, to any self-
constituted "Establishment" or "Office," which, powerless
to "grant" Arms, undertakes—in consideration of a very
trifling fee—to "find," and either to "sketch" or to "colour"
them. Exceedingly simple is the process, by means of
which this undertaking is accomplished. It consists in
consulting a printed Armory; and, when the desired
"Arms" have been "found" in its well-stored columns,
they then at once are assigned to the applicant, in conformity with the comprehensive and beautifully simple
theory, that all persons having the same surname and who
also live (or were born) in the same county are equally

entitled to bear the same Arms. Probably it does not occur to the patrons of advertising Heraldry-dealers, that upon precisely the same principle every person who has the same "name and county" with any officer who may be "found" in the Navy or the Army List, might assert a right to whatever rank and title such an officer may enjoy by virtue of his commission.

The almost universal desire to possess some kind of armorial insignia, implies a corresponding recognition of the necessity to obtain them from some Institution or Personage, supposed to be competent and authorised both to determine what they should be, and to impart a right to accept and to assume and bear them. It rests with the Heralds of the College of Arms to take the initiative in a course of action, which would direct all aspirants for heraldic distinctions, as a matter of course, to their own doors. The Heralds, who really are Heralds, and who alone are real Heralds, may rely on the support of Public Opinion. If a fictitious Heraldry is not only prevalent, but in some sense actually in the ascendant, it is not because the counterfeit is preferred to the genuine, but because it is unconsciously mistaken for it. In very many instances, indeed, a determination to obtain "Arms" is coupled with an ignorance of Heraldry so complete, as to ignore the existence of any such thing as a Heraldry that is fictitious.

A popular College of Arms, without any serious difficulty, might establish its own authority with all classes of the community; and, at the same time, it would not fail to impress upon the public mind the very decided difference that exists between the heraldic and the non-heraldic acceptation of the expression—"*an escutcheon of pretence.*" Much real good would certainly result from the rude shock that would be given to many a complacent display of armorial insignia, by showing the proud blazonry to be *abated* with the baton sinister of heraldic untruth and unwarrantable assumption.   And better still it would be to show to all who possess, or who desire to possess and to bear "Arms," that the "Pride of Heraldry" is a worthy and a noble pride, because it is the Pride of Truth and Right.

CHAPTER XXII

"The Spandrels over the Wall-arcading are exquisitely beautiful. . . . Those in the western arm contained Shields of a large number of the great men of the day . . . the few which remain are nobly executed."— GLEANINGS FROM WESTMINSTER ABBEY, by G. G. Scott, R.A.: 2nd Edition, p. 33.

I. THE HERALDRY OF THE COINAGE, in addition to the Shields of Arms of successive Sovereigns, exemplifies the changes that have taken place in the form and adornment of the Crown, and it also is rich in various Badges and Devices having an historical significance.

In Coins the Royal Shield is sometimes quartered by a cross charged upon it, as in the silver penny of EDWARD VI. A mediæval ship, having a sail covered with heraldic blazonry, appears on the *Noble*—a coin worthy of its name. A figure of the King in armour (not particularly well proportioned to the size of the vessel), his sword in one hand, and his Shield of arms in the other, is also represented in these fine examples of mediæval numismatic art. A ship without any sail, but in its stead charged with the Royal Shield heightened by a Cross, forms the reverse of another excellent coin, the *Angel*, the obverse bearing a figure of ST. MICHAEL with his lance thrusting down the dragon. The Angel of EDWARD IV. on either side of the Cross has the initial E and the white rose of York; and the legend is— PER : CRVCEM : TV̄A : SALVA : NOS : XTE : REDEMPT : ("By thy Cross save us, O Redeemer

Christ!"). A Crowned Rose, with a Royal Cypher, is another favourite device; as in the Shilling of HENRY VIII., with the legend—POSVI : DEV̄ : ADIVTOREM : MEVM :(" I have placed God (before me as) my helper ").

Such are a few examples of the early Heraldry of English Coins. More recently, and particularly in our own Coinage, Heraldry and Art have declined together, so that feeble designs, but too commonly executed with lamentable consistency, are associated with heraldic inaccuracies which continue uncorrected to this day—witness the *tressure of Scotland* often incorrectly blazoned on the Royal Shield; and poor BRITANNIA, in her old position, sitting forlorn on the copper and bronze coinage, as if conscious of being constrained to display on her oval Shield an obsolete blazonry, that placed the reign of Queen VICTORIA in the eighteenth century![1]

II. To what has been already said on the value of heraldic SEALS I desire here to add a few words, in the hope of inducing all students of Heraldry to study them with the most diligent care.

Casts of fine impressions are not difficult to obtain. Almost every accessible fine Seal has been copied by Mr. Ready, of the British Museum, who supplies admirable casts at a very moderate cost. The Scottish Seals of the late Mr. H. Laing, of Edinburgh, were purchased on his decease by the authorities of the British Museum. The most satisfactory casts are made in gutta-percha, which may be gilt by simply rubbing a gold powder with a soft brush upon them, after slightly warming their surfaces. Moulds for reproducing casts or impressions may be made in gutta-percha; and from

[1] The specimens of the existing Coinage of Europe, displayed at the Universal Exposition, at Paris, showed that if the art of the English Mint is now at a low ebb, the prevailing standard of numismatic art is not a single degree higher, the coins of France alone being in many respects an honourable exception to the general rule.

these moulds casts, also in gutta-percha, may be obtained. The process is very simple: the gutta-percha, softened by immersion in hot water, is pressed upon an impression in relief, until a perfect intaglio is formed. When this mould is cold and hard, it will stamp an impression upon gutta-percha softened in the same manner.

I add to the examples of fine heraldic Seals that I have already given, the richly traceried Seal bearing the armorial Shield of JOHN, Lord BARDOLF, of Wormegay in Norfolk,

No. 442.—Seal of Lord Bardolf.

about A.D. 1350; No. 442. This most beautiful Seal, which in the original in diameter is only one and one-sixth inches, has been somewhat enlarged in the engraving, in order to show the design more plainly. The arms of BARDOLF are —*Az., three cinquefoils or.*

The liberality and kindness of Mr. Laing enable me to associate with the Seal of Lord BARDOLF a small group of additional examples of Scottish Seals: two of them are good illustrations as well of English as of Scottish Heraldry, and they exemplify the usage of introducing Gothic traceries into the composition of Seals with Shields of Arms: in both these examples, however, the leading outlines only of the traceries remain, and the rich cusping (which is so perfect in the Seal of Lord BARDOLF) is lost. No. 443, the Seal of WILLIAM MURE, A.D. 1397, has a Shield bearing—*Arg., on a fesse az. three mullets of the field.*

No 443.—Seal of William Mure.   No. 444.—Seal of Thomas Monypeny.

No. 444, the Seal of THOMAS MONYPENY, A.D. 1415, has the Shield *couchée* charged with *Az., a chevron between three crosses crosslets fitchée issuing from as many crescents arg.:* the Crest, on a helm, is a bird, probably a popinjay or parrot. The Seal of RICHARD STUART, No. 445, probably about 1350, may be compared with No. 414, p. 249: in the smaller and earlier example, the solitary individual who represents the crew may be assumed to be Richard Stuart himself; his vessel displays

No. 445.—Seal of Richard Stuart.

two banners which are evidently affected by contrary currents of air, and a pennon.

The noble Seal, No. 446 (*see* Frontispiece), engraved from a most perfect impression recently discovered appended to a document in the guardianship of the Dean and Chapter of Westminster, represents its illustrious owner, THOMAS DE BEAUCHAMP, K.G., third Earl of WARWICK, in armour, with his shield and jupon charged with the armorial insignia of Beauchamp (*gu., a fesse between six crosses crosslets or*), and with the same insignia repeated upon the bardings of the charger upon which the Earl is mounted. The engraving of the Seal itself appears on the Frontispiece to this Volume: and the

No. 447.—Counter-Seal of Earl Thomas de Beauchamp: A.D. 1344.

Counter-Seal, one of the most beautiful and most perfect examples in existence of the early seal-engraver's art, is here represented in No. 447. The Shield displayed on this Counter-Seal is charged only with the Arms of the NEW-BURGHS (*chequée or and az., a chevron erm.*), from whom the Earldom of Warwick passed by inheritance to the House of

Beauchamp. The inscription is commenced on the Seal, No. 446, and continued on the Counter-Seal, No. 447, and is as follows:—S: THOE: COMITIS: WARRWYCHIE: ANNO : REGNI : REGIS : E : T'CII : POST : CŌ-QVESTV̄: ANGLIE: SEPTIO: DECIO: ET: REGNI: SVI : FRANCIE : QVARTO—"The Seal of Thomas, Earl of Warwick, in the seventeenth year of the reign of King Edward III. (of that name) after the Conquest of England, and the fourth of his reign over France." Thus, the date of the execution of this fine Seal is the year 1344. The Earl himself died in 1369.

A second Beauchamp Seal is also represented in the Frontispiece. This is the Seal of RICHARD DE BEAUCHAMP, K.G., fifth Earl of WARWICK, who died in the year 1439. The Heraldry in this example is particularly interesting. The Shield, charged with *Newburgh* and *Beauchamp* quarterly, is couchée from the helm of the Earl which is ensigned with his coronet and crest; and on either side is *a bear with a ragged staff*, the famous Badges of the BEAU-CHAMPS: No. 448 (*see* Frontispiece). The Inscription is —SIGILL : RIC : DE : BELLO : CAMPO : COMIT : WARWICII—"The Seal of Richard de Beauchamp, Earl of Warwick" (see pages 223 and 224).

III. In GOTHIC ARCHITECTURE Heraldry is always a consistent, beautiful, and most effective accessory. Indeed, so thoroughly is the spirit of Heraldry in harmony with the great Architecture which grew up in the Middle Ages, that Heraldry must be considered rather as an element of its nature than as an allied Art. Gothic Architecture is essentially heraldic; and hence, as well as from its elastic nature and its equally consistent and happy applicability to every use and requirement, it is peculiarly appropriate as our own national style.

From the earliest years of its existence as a definite Science, Heraldry is found to be most intimately associated with the Gothic Architecture of England: and happy it

X

was for the early Heralds, that in their days the English
Gothic was at work in the full strength of its first maturity.
And this alliance was never interrupted, or permitted to
decline from its original cordiality. As long as the Gothic
flourished, Heraldry held its own place in Architecture.
And in the finest works that exist amongst us, relics of the
grand Gothic Ages of English Architecture, Heraldry is ever
present to adorn them with its graphic records. In the
spandrels of arcades, in panels, upon bosses in vaulting, in
stained glass, in encaustic floor-tiles, and indeed in almost
every position in which such ornamentation could be
admissible, the early Herald is found to have been the
fellow-worker with the early Gothic architect. Gothic
Architecture, accordingly, has preserved for us very noble
collections and specimens of the most valuable illustrations
of our national Heraldry. Canterbury and York Cathedrals,
and the Abbey Churches of Westminster and St. Alban's,
with the Chapel of King's College, Cambridge, are
especially rich in heraldic treasures: and Westminster Hall
and the northern Castles of Alnwick and Warkworth may be
specified as noble examples of secular Architecture, which
retain their heraldic enrichments.

IV. Gothic MONUMENTS, and in common with them
their successors of the Renaissance era, abound in every
variety of armorial blazonry. And fine examples of
heraldic Monuments are no less abundant, than are the
Shields and other insignia that appear on particular
memorials. The principles which directed the selection of
Shields to be introduced into the composition of early
Monuments are worthy of careful consideration: and the
same remark is no less applicable in the case of Architecture.
I must be content to specify a very small group of heraldic
Monuments of especial interest and value. In Westminster
Abbey: the Monuments of Queens ALIANORE of Castile,
PHILIPPA of Hainault, ELIZABETH TUDOR, and MARY
STUART; the Monuments of King EDWARD III. and King

HENRY VII.; and those of ALIANORE DE BOHUN, Duchess
of GLOUCESTER, the Countess of LENNOX, the Countess
of DERBY, the two DE VALENCES, Earls of Pembroke,
EDMUND, Earl of Lancaster, Lord BOURCHIER, and Sir
GILES DAUBENEY, K.G.   In Canterbury Cathedral: the
Monuments of the BLACK PRINCE, and of HENRY IV. and
JOANNA of Navarre.   In Salisbury Cathedral: the Monu-
ment of Earl WILLIAM LONGESPÉE.   In St. Alban's Abbey
Church: the Monuments of HUMPHREY, Duke of GLOU-
CESTER, and of the Abbots WHEATHAMSTEDE and RAMRYGE.
Also, other fine Monuments in the Churches at Elsyng in
Norfolk, Ewelme and Northleigh in Oxfordshire, King's
Langley in Hertfordshire, and Cobham in Kent; in Beverley
Minster, and in the Beauchamp Chapel at Warwick.

V. In the ILLUMINATIONS of the Middle Ages Heraldry
has a place of honour: and in the revival of that early
Art, which is held in such high estimation at the present
day, Heraldry ought to occupy a position of corresponding
prominence.   This implies in the Illuminators of to-day
some knowledge of Heraldry, and at least some degree of
familiarity with good early examples.   I venture to suggest,
therefore, to students of Illumination the study both of the
Herald's Art and his Science, as no unimportant part of
their preparation for the practice of the Art of Illumination on the principle of the sagacious maxim of a great
modern painter, quoted by Mr. RUSKIN in his "Seven
Lamps of Architecture"—"Know what you have to do,
and *then* do it."

VI. In the ornamentation of early ENCAUSTIC or INLAID
PAVEMENT TILES, Shields of Arms and various heraldic
devices frequently occur: and in many examples the Shields
of Arms are arranged with much skill and in excellent taste,
to form decorative compositions in combination with foliage
and traceries.   Numerous heraldic Tiles of a very interesting
character remain in the Cathedrals of Worcester, Gloucester,
and Exeter; and in the Churches of Great Malvern, King's

Langley, the Abbey Church of St. Alban, and many others. The student will observe that the devices upon these Tiles are frequently *reversed*, evidently the result of the neglect to reverse the designs upon the original dies or stamps.

VII. Heraldic blazonry was highly esteemed in the Middle Ages as a becoming decoration for PERSONAL COS-TUME. The Knights wore their *Coats of Arms,* and they carried and used their *Shields of Arms,* and their armorial insignia were displayed upon their weapons and upon the various accessories of their personal equipment. The Ladies adapted this usage to their own Costume, and they also wore *Mantles and Dresses of Arms;* and many of their personal ornaments were strictly heraldic. Without even suggesting now to our Ladies any revival of heraldic costume, properly so called—such as dresses, mantles, or shawls emblazoned with the bearings of armorial shields—I certainly do desire to see Heraldry exercising a powerful influence in all designs for personal ornaments, the works of the goldsmith and the jeweller more especially. Badges also may supply the motive for designing many patterns that are to adorn fabrics used for costume: and, in like manner also, the designs woven into carpets, curtains, and various other fabrics may be derived with the greatest advantage from the same source. The loom is employed in blazoning heraldic insignia in white damask: why should it not work, under judicious and cautious guidance, in silk and velvet, in satin and every woollen fabric? [1]

It must be understood, however, that heraldic orna-ments and devices, unless they be of such a character that they are universally applicable, must have a reference to the wearer, or they degenerate at once into heraldic parodies.

[1] I have lately seen a design for the embroidery of a dress for a young lady of the Clan CAMPBELL; its characteristic features are the Scottish Thistle and the Myrtle, the latter the Badge of the Campbells. I may express my approval of the motive of this design: others, as I have reason to believe, have approved the treatment of it.

Personal ornaments, costume, furniture, if heraldic, must display devices that have a significance as well as a beauty : such costume and ornaments must be,. not " becoming " only to the wearer, but (in the heraldic acceptation of that term) " belonging " also.   And so in every instance.

For purposes of universal decoration and adornment, Heraldry is no less applicable now than when EDWARD III. or HENRY IV. reigned in England.   Happily, a taste for furniture and all the appliances of every-day life in the Gothic style is gradually becoming prevalent ; and this is inseparable from the use of Heraldry for the purposes of ornamentation.   I presume that the fallacy of regarding the Gothic style of Art as exclusively ecclesiastical in its associations and uses, or as no less necessarily inseparable from mediæval sentiments and general usages, is beginning to give way to more correct views, as the true nature of the Gothic and its original universal employment are ·better understood.   I consider it to be unnecessary for me, therefore, to enter here, in support of my own sentiments, into any detailed explanations to show that the revival of a Style of Art which flourished in bygone ages, and with it the revival of Heraldry as it was invented and grew into its early dignity and popularity, are in no way or degree whatever connected with an implied return to the mode of life of four, five, or six centuries ago.   We have used Roman and even what we intended to be Greek Architecture in nineteenth-century England ; we are still in the habitual use of Roman and Greek designs for every variety of decoration ; and of late we have added Egyptian and Scandinavian works of Art to the deservedly prized collections of models, that we have formed for the express purpose of imitating them : and yet we do not consider that we thus in any way bind ourselves to adopt Roman, or Greek, or Egyptian, or Scandinavian costumes or customs ; nor in our use of the Arts of Antiquity do we perceive any demonstration of retrogression in ourselves.

It is the same with Mediæval Heraldry and Gothic Art
We may apply to our own times, our own uses, our own
delight, what the old Heralds and the Gothic Artists have
taught us, without even dreaming of wearing armour or re-
establishing the feudal system. True Heraldry (for it is
with Heraldry that I am now more especially concerned)
is a Science, and it also is an Art, for all time—for our
times, and for future times, as well as for the times that are
past. If we understand and ap-
preciate it, we shall not fail to use
and to apply it aright.

No. 449.
Seal of Sir WALTER SCOTT, of
Branxholm and Kirkurd: A.D.
1529. (Laing.)

From the initial-letter of my
first Chapter I suspended the
Shield borne by that Sir WALTER
SCOTT, of Abbotsford, whose name
will ever be a household word with
every lover of what is chivalrous
and knightly. Here I place the
Seal, No. 449, of an earlier Sir
WALTER SCOTT, of Branxholm
and Kirkurd—a Knight of another branch of the same
distinguished House, who differenced the Shield of Scott
so as to bear—*Or, on a bend azure a mullet and two
crescents gold.*

CHAPTER XXIII

PEERAGE DIGNITIES

The Dignity of Earl—Of Baron—The Parliament of 1295—Landed Qualifications—Creation of the Title Duke of Cornwall—The Title of Marquis—The Premier Baron of England—The Peerage of Scotland—Scottish remainders—Daughter Inherits in her own right—Determination of an Abeyance—The Right to Create Peers of Ireland—Rights and Privileges of a Peeress—The Daughters of Peers—Anomalies of the English Scale of Precedence.

ALTHOUGH the name of the dignity of Earl is derived from a Saxon word, the dignity itself, like all others, is more Norman than Saxon in its character. At the period of the Conquest, and whilst the Norman dynasty was on the throne, there were a number of people who bore this title. At that time and for long afterwards, certainly well into the Plantagenet period, an Earl within his earldom was little short of a petty sovereign. Issues of justice and many other rights of regality were in his hands, and he occupied a position very much akin to a viceroy for the King, seeing that what he did he did in his own name and as Earl, or "comes," of the County. The High-Sheriff was the "vice-comes." Some of the earldoms had more extensive rights of regality than others, some were actual palatinates, and all earldoms originally were honours in fee heritable by the heir-general. Earldoms had a territorial nature, and the Earl took his "third penny" in the issues of the Courts in his earldom.

The only other dignity at that period was that of Baron, and just as the Earls of to-day have little in common save dignity and title with the Earls of the past, so the Barons originally were very unlike the latest creations of modern Prime Ministers in the name of the King. At the Norman Conquest, and for long afterwards, the Barons, an indeterminate number, were those who held their land in barony.

It is a matter of much uncertainty at what date Parliament came into being. The word goes back to a much earlier period, and is used concerning a variety of meetings which are now generally regarded as meetings of different Councils and not of Parliament, but historians are agreed that whether or not any earlier meetings can be properly described as Parliaments, the Parliament of 1295 was properly and fully constituted in all its elements. To this Parliament all those who were personally summoned by the King in their own names and were not nominated or elected by other people are Peers, and of these Peers those who are not described as Earls are Barons. It should, however, be noted that Bishops and Abbots were summoned by right of the offices they held, and there are certain other officials who were summoned also because of their offices and could be distinguished from the Barons and Earls. There is no shadow of doubt that the reason for the summoning of the Barons was the fact that they were great subjects and important because of their ownership of land. It was landowners who had to provide the military services for the country, and Parliament was chiefly concerned, not in law-making, but in authorising and consulting as to military expeditions, or in providing the subsidies necessary for these expeditions, and the other services of the Crown. In addition to this Peers exercised some of the judicial functions of the Crown. But law-making was done by the King and his Council until a later period. The landed qualifications which justified the summoning of a man to Parliament as a Baron usually descended to his heir and similarly justified the summoning of that heir ; and in that way, but without any intention to that end, the right of summons and the right of peerage became hereditary. Originally it had been arbitrary and at the discretion of the Crown. It was not until the reign of Edward IV. that the hereditary peerage character of a barony was fully recognised, and with that recognition came the divorce of the territorial idea from the right of peerage. Like ancient earldoms, ancient baronies were honours in fee heritable by the heirs general. Save that William the Conqueror was Sovereign Lord of the Duchy of Normandy and as such Duke, the dignity of duke did not exist in England until 1337, when Edward the Black Prince was created Duke of Cornwall with remainder to his heirs the eldest sons of the Kings of England. That was the creation of the title now enjoyed by the Prince of Wales, but this Duchy of Cornwall and the Duchy of Lancaster are really Duchies as distinguished from the Dukedoms enjoyed by other people having the designation of Duke.

The title of Marquis dates from 1386, when Richard II. created Robert de Vere Marquis of Dublin ; and the title of Viscount from 1440, when the Viscounty of Beaumont was created. The first Barony by Letters Patent was created in 1387, but the oldest surviving barony by patent now in existence dates from 1448, when Sir John Stourton was created Baron and Lord Stourton of Stourton, co. Wilts. The present Lord Mowbray, Segrave and Stourton, who has inherited the barony of Stourton, also claims, as Lord Mowbray, to be the premier baron of England although the barony of Mowbray is placed on the roll of precedence after the baronies of Le Despenser and De Ros. Although earldoms were granted by charters from the earliest period, because, attached to the earldom, were also material rights which needed to be conveyed, patents did not come into use for baronies until it was desired to limit the succession of the peerage to the heirs male of the body of the grantee, which is a limitation and a less heirship than is comprised in the enjoyment of an honour in fee simple. Privilege of peerage with all it entails has been a slow growth of accretion; and save for place and precedence and the right of any peer or peeress to be tried in the House of Lords, and the now limited and threatened right of peers to legislate, little of privilege of peerage remains.

The peerage of Scotland is very similar to that of England, and, before the Union, the principal difference between the two countries was the persistency with which the Scottish peerage remained attached to the land. Until a late date a patent creating a Scottish peerage erected certain lands into a barony or earldom as the case might be, and entailed those lands with the dignity. The difference arising from this form of procedure was more than counterbalanced by the recognised and constantly-adopted procedure of resigning a Scottish inheritance into the hands of the Crown, and then obtaining what is known as a "Novodamus," with either the same or different limitations.

The many Scottish remainders, which are quite unknown to English peerage law, are all a consequence of this territorial nature of a Scottish peerage. One of the chief differences at the present time between an English and a Scottish peerage is to be found in those which are heritable by females. Unless governed by special remainder contained in the instrument of creation, a Scottish peerage, which in the event of failure of a male heir devolves upon a female heir, differs from an English one in its manner of descent. In Scotland the elder daughter inherits as of right, standing in the line of heirship next after her youngest brother and before any uncle or a younger sister. On the other hand, such an inheritance is only known by virtue of a special remainder in England. All Baronies by writ are Baronies in fee in England, and heritable by the heir general, which means that they can if necessary devolve upon females. If the only child of a peer having such a peerage be a daughter she inherits in her own right, but if his issue is two daughters, then the peerage falls into abeyance between them, because under the law of England there is no seniority amongst daughters, and as both of them cannot enjoy one single peerage, neither of them has it, and it remains in abeyance until the Crown interferes or until by the natural course of events one line becomes extinguished by the extinction of all issue of the one daughter, when the peerage then at once devolves upon the heir of the other. Sometimes an abeyance will last several hundred years, sometimes it may end with the lapse of one or two; but at any time during the continuance of an abeyance the Crown may, at its entire pleasure, signify that any co-heir shall enjoy the peerage. This is what is termed the determination of an abeyance, and this is effected by the issue of a writ of summons to Parliament if the co-heir be a male or by the issue of letters patent in the case of a lady. The co-heir in whose favour the abeyance is determined then at once enjoys the peerage with the same designation and precedence as those who have held it hitherto, and his or her heir succeeds in due course.

Although there is one judgment to the contrary, it is now pretty universally admitted that there is no such thing as an Irish Barony by writ. With the union of England and Scotland, no further peerages of either country were created, and subsequent peerages were either of Great Britain or of Ireland; and it has been already judicially decided by the House of Lords that the power to create a Scottish peerage does not now exist in the Crown. There is no similar judgment in relation to a peerage of England, but the fact is that no attempt has since been made to create one, and though the point up to the present time still has to be decided, it is certainly a matter for argument whether or not such a right remains. Since the union of Great Britain with Ireland no further peerages of Great Britain or of England have been created, but the right to create peers of Ireland was specifically retained under certain conditions and has been constantly taken advantage of. Other peerages since created have, however, been of the United Kingdom. Whether or not we shall ever have peerages of the Empire remains a matter for the future.

Since the latter part of the seventeenth century it has been the custom for peers and peeresses in their own right to sign simply by the designation of their peerage. The peeress by marriage prefixes her Christian name or initials to her husband's title. It is statute law in Scotland, but not in England, that no person may sign his surname without prefixing a Christian name or initials. A peeress by marriage who is also a peeress in her own right signs first her husband's title, adding her own afterwards; for instance, the signature of the Countess of Yarborough is Marcia Yarborough, Fauconberg and Conyers. One cannot call to mind in recent times any instances in which the peeress in her own right has married a peer of lower rank than her own, and until such a case occurs it is difficult to forecast what the signature should be. A peeress by marriage after re-marriage loses all privilege of peerage and precedence, and all right which she acquired by marriage, but as a matter of courtesy she usually retains her peerage designation if her subsequent marriage is to a commoner.

The daughter of a peer if married to another peer takes the precedence of her husband and relinquishes her own, but she retains it if she marries a commoner; and one of the anomalies of the English scale of precedence is to be found in the following circumstances. If the two elder daughters of a Duke were to marry an Earl and a Baron respectively, whilst the youngest daughter were to run away with the footman, she would, nevertheless, rank as the daughter of a Duke above her sisters ranking as wives of an Earl and a Baron.

INDEX

335

Printed by BALLANTYNE, HANSON & Co.
at Paul's Work, Edinburgh

Ingram Content Group UK Ltd.
Milton Keynes UK
UKHW022301070623
423069UK00005B/175